THE S. MARK TAPER FOUNDATION

IMPRINT IN JEWISH STUDIES

BY THIS ENDOWMENT

THE S. MARK TAPER FOUNDATION SUPPORTS

THE APPRECIATION AND UNDERSTANDING

OF THE RICHNESS AND DIVERSITY OF

JEWISH LIFE AND CULTURE

The publisher gratefully acknowledges the
generous contribution to this book provided by
the following organizations and individuals:

DAVID B. GOLD FOUNDATION

LUCIUS N. LITTAUER FOUNDATION

JOSEPH LOW

SKIRBALL FOUNDATION

S. MARK TAPER FOUNDATION

When a Jew Dies

When a Jew Dies

The Ethnography of a Bereaved Son

Samuel C. Heilman

UNIVERSITY OF CALIFORNIA PRESS

Berkeley   Los Angeles   London

University of California Press
Berkeley and Los Angeles, California

University of California Press, Ltd.
London, England

Library of Congress Cataloging-in-Publication Data

Heilman, Samuel C.
    When a Jew dies : the ethnography of a bereaved son /
Samuel C. Heilman.
        p.   cm. — (An S. Mark Taper Foundation imprint
in Jewish studies)
    Includes index.
    ISBN 0-520-21965-1 (cloth : alk. paper)
    1. Jewish mourning customs.   2. Bereavement—Social
aspects.   3. Bereavement—Religious aspects—Judaism.
I. Title.   II. Series.

BM712.H45 2001
296.4'45—dc21
                                                    00-053210

Printed in the United States of America

09   08   07   06   05   04   03   02   01

10   9   8   7   6   5   4   3   2   1

The paper used in this publication meets the minimum
requirements of American National Standard for
Information Sciences—Permanence of Paper for
Printed Library Materials, ANSI Z39.48 1992 (R1997)
(Permanence of Paper).

In memory of my father, Henry Heilman,
who in this and each day is with me,
and for my mother, Lucia Heilman, who has faced death
repeatedly and emerged with her faith in life intact

Contents

Introduction

The author's every exploration of death and continuity must both
include and extend beyond himself.

Robert J. Lifton, *The Broken Connection*

"Who is the man who lives, and shall not see death?" the Psalmist asks (89:49).
As an American, I have lived almost my entire life in a culture that answers that
death cannot be looked at with a steady eye, a culture in which the denial of
death and a desire to keep it from view are part of the basic outlook.[1] I had a
hard time, however, fully sharing in that denial, for death seemed a silent partner in my family's existence, barely hidden, relentlessly shadowing me and all
those about whom I cared. This feeling was, I think, a legacy of my being born
in Germany, just after the end of the Second World War, the only child of concentration camp survivors, almost all of whose relatives perished before I was
born. While my birth and our emigration to America nearly four years later
signaled, for my parents, a readiness to live again, their repeated tales of the
horror that had consumed their families and nearly devoured their own lives
made it clear to me that death was my forebear and hovered nearby. Throughout my growing pains as an only child, I always wondered whether death
might suddenly return to claim my family and me. Inside I harbored the inchoate conviction: "Anything that you have, you can lose, anything you are
attached to, you can be separated from, anything you love can be taken away
from you."[2] So while as a child of Shoah survivors, I knew death was quite
real; as an American I tried to turn my eye away from it. My parents' tales
notwithstanding, I repressed my apprehensions about imminent death and ca-
tastrophe and learned to arm myself with the natural optimism of American
youth, or at least its tacit assumption that life was indestructible.[3]

The America I inhabited hid the dead and dying and even entertained the

possibility that death could be cheated.[4] In the years during which I came of
age, even grieving for the dead was discouraged.[5] Those were the days when
"cryonics," the deep-freezing of human bodies at death for preservation and
possible revival in the future, entered our vocabulary and thinking.[6] Like most
of the youth of my day, I inhabited in the 1960s and 1970s what some sociologists of the time called "the cult of immediacy," trying to live in the moment
and pushing the burdens of death away.[7] Along with my generation, I sought
to adopt as my own the American notion that "life is a boundless experience,"
and that "there is indeed time; more is yet to come than has already gone by."[8]

It was not always easy. The legacy of my family's past, with its echoes of
death, and my youthful American fantasies of boundless opportunity and immortality struggled simultaneously and sometimes uneasily within me. While
I was young, the force of life seemed stronger—although never invincible. But
"thoughts of death pile up to an astonishing degree," Carl Jung once observed,
"as the years increase."[9] By the time I reached my forties, "the secret hour of
life's midday," my anxieties about death were shouting even more loudly than
when I had first encountered them in my youth.[10] The undeniable realities of
mortality made themselves felt as people I had known began to die.

This time, however, instead of turning away, I decided to face my anxieties
and chose as my vehicle service as a volunteer on the local Chevra Kaddisha,
the Jewish burial society. Although my public service was ostensibly performed
as an extension of my strong personal attachments to Jewish tradition and the
Jewish community in which I made my life, my motives were rooted even
more in my personal demon of death. In the work of the Chevra, the death I
had avoided would be laid before me, and I would have to encounter and presumably overcome precisely what I found most terrifying.

The Chevra Kaddisha, this once-exclusive domain, limited to those who
were the pillars of Jewish society, had by my day become a far more modest
assemblage of those few willing to carry out the ritual tasks of preparing for
burial the bodies of those who hewed to Jewish tradition. As I learned the rituals and became familiar with the customary practices of the local burial society, I hoped this personal confrontation with mortality, with the physical reality of cadavers, which I had to wash and dress in traditional shrouds, would
help me finally exorcise the anxieties of an unknown, hidden, insidious death.
In the psychologized posttherapeutic world in which I lived, I believed that at
last to look directly at one's fears would lead beyond them. In some sense, I
also imagined that by serving on the Chevra Kaddisha, I would be allowed "to
enter the palace of death, to dwell there for a while, and then," most important for me, "to exit."[11]

In fact, my experience in the local burial society did take away some of the

anxiety of the unknown and mitigated at least some of my apprehensions, although, as one old-timer in the Chevra once put it, "you never get completely
inured to the sight of the dead." At the same time, my sociological and anthropological imagination was fired up by the experience, as I began to think
about how to depict and comprehend the extraordinary process by which the
living transformed the dead and tamed death in a ceremony—steeped in mystery, religion, and mysticism—that Judaism called *tahara,* purification. As I
had before in my life, I turned to my intellectual disciplines to explore Jewish
behavior and to make it more comprehendible. Learning about the activities
of the Chevra, I was struck at how all that we did reflected the continuing
community shared by the living with the dead and how we seemed to use tradition to cleanse death of its malevolence. Some might say that this intellectual
and disciplinary focus was simply another way for me to avoid looking directly
at the reality of death and hence defuse the anxiety of my situation. I do not
deny the possibility. In any event, I laminated my service to the community
with my training as an ethnographer and began to take notes based on my experiences. To be sure, at first I did not get much beyond the limited circumstances of my local, suburban New York burial society. More extensive field-
work would come later. In the meantime, I believed I was also handling my
concerns with death.

When, however, in March 1996, after a long illness and a series of crushing
strokes, my father died, I discovered the limits of my preparation. Now, in a
way altogether new to me, death entered the innermost circles of my existence. "The death of one we have known and loved brings to the living a sense
of loss which can run as deep as any emotion we are capable of experiencing." [12] As I held onto my mother and wife, staring through tear-soaked eyes
into the abyss of my father's open grave, watching my sons shovel earth into it,
I—like so many before me—at last confronted death not as some stranger lurk-
ing in the shadows or the object of an anthropologist's curiosity. Death became
my father.

I was by no means alone in this personal and timeless discovery. Around me,
my entire generation was now increasingly staring into the graves of their parents, witnessing deaths in the family. Suddenly, we baby boomers, used to being the incarnation of America's youth culture, found the poet's timeless question to be our own: "O strong and long-liv'd death, how cam'st thou in?" [13]
When we were honest with ourselves, moreover, we realized as well that we
were not just wondering about our parents but acknowledging that our turn
was coming next. Time grew increasingly scarce; more had gone than was left,
and neither fantasies of youthful boundlessness nor hopes of immortality could
sustain us or cloud our vision.

As I stumbled through the death of my father and the mourning that followed, reading through the plethora of books that accompanied the experiences of my bereavement, I found them wanting. I needed something that could
tell me not just what was supposed to happen or what the Jewish tradition that
framed my existence required (there were plenty of books for that). I did not
want something purely prescriptive or thinly descriptive. Rather, I sought a
text that could help me see past the many instructions of what is to be done to
discover the underlying meaning of the practices that surrounded Jewish death
and its aftermath, an account informed by both the perspectives of my discipline and a knowledge of Judaism. I wanted a book that not only described but
also explained the cultural meaning behind the Jewish practices and traditions,
that showed me what was particular and what was universal about the Jewish
experiences of death, bereavement, mourning, and their aftermath. I wanted
something that explored the implications of the Jewish traditions of death. Not
finding such a volume, I resolved to write one myself. This is the result.

First, however, a few words about what this book is not. These pages offer no
ultimate answers for the question that haunts all who have suffered a loss:
"Why has this happened to those I care about and not someone else?" Nor
does it answer the question that lies underneath: "Why *me*—why should I
have to be alone, why should I have to suffer, why should my life be out of
kilter—and not someone else?"[14]
    While presenting many of the customs and traditions pertaining to a Jew's
death, this book does not aim to prescribe what Jews *should* do. I leave such
questions and answers to rabbis or preachers. Instead, I have tried to address
questions that a social anthropologist and one in touch with the tradition, as I
am, is equipped answer: How do those who are bereaved act? What does the
community, which must deal with the dead and death, do? What does all of
this mean?[15] As a social anthropologist I seek my answers in the domains of my
discipline and those allied with it, and I try to uncover the deep structure and
something of the collective unconscious of Judaism and Jewish culture that still
have the capacity to animate these practices. As an ethnographer I try to provide an insider's thick description of how this occurs.
    This book crosses back and forth over the boundary between the academic
and the religious, the particular and the general, the observer and the observant. I have tried to provide the book with a double structure, reflecting my
role as social scientist and ethnographer as well as my role as bereaved son and
observant Jew. This is not unprecedented. Ethnography is not simply a neutral description but one in which the ethnographer is the instrument through

which the reality is reconstructed. It requires a series of intense, often emotion-laden, interactions through which an observer learns about the life and meaning of behavior in order to describe it for others, and hence it is also inevitably reflexive.[16] Put another way, one might say that biography is a component part of ethnography. The fact that I am an observant Jew and a recently bereaved son undoubtedly plays a part in what I have chosen to observe, what I have been able to see, and the way I have chosen to write about it. To pretend otherwise is futile. I thus have used my own life story as a bereaved son as the basis of my ethnography, turning my gaze on my experiences, both subjective and objective, and trying to locate and present them in a framework of meaning that others might understand. In the process, I have turned my feelings and life history outward.

That I am personally a religiously observant Jew and an observer of Jewish behavior is both a strength and a weakness. As a practitioner of much that I describe, I am basing my knowledge not simply on a limited period of focused observation—as is the case in most ethnography. Rather, my understanding is intersubjective, the product of a lifetime of engagement buttressed by a period of concentrated observation and reflection.

In large measure I concentrate on long-held traditions and customs. I do so because I wonder, along with the anthropologist Sir James G. Frazer, whether "we of this generation read the riddle" of death better than those who in the past offered answers that we may smile at as "childish and absurd."[17] I do so as well as a response to the sociologist Jane Littlewood's trenchant observation that there is a growing feeling among many contemporary individuals "that the rituals of the past must be helpful to people who have been bereaved but it remains undemonstrated exactly how such rituals might be rehabilitated in order to fit contemporary, complex and secular societies," such as the ones most Jews inhabit today.[18] In all I have written, I have tried to provide an answer that is different from the one offered by those who speak purely in the language of faith and consolation.

I do this because, in the felicitous phrasing of Clifford Geertz, "where there once was faith, there are now reasons," and today's Jews (not altogether unlike the modern Muslims whom Geertz observed) seem to prefer knowing the reasons behind what their religious tradition requires. The explanations that emerge from the interpretive approach of social anthropology can provide more than just revealing insights; often they offer something for those who need understanding and cannot find it in the language of faith. Although not necessarily the case, understanding can both elucidate and rehabilitate the tradition for such Jews. Even those who are guided by faith have something to gain from this perspective, for it enables them to discover what is involved in their religion, to reach a level of religious conviction where they are "holding religious views rather than being held by them."[19]

Because I am both an observant native and an anthropological observer, I realize that I must be completely honest about what my work here can accomplish. As an observant Jew and as one who has used his own experiences as the basis of this ethnography, I explain, describe, and inevitably also rehabilitate the Jewish traditions related to death and mourning. One cannot make the opaque clear without consequence. A window lit up in the darkness may offer a means for outsiders to see inside, but it may also become a display case that makes even the prosaic seem far more charming. Thus, while my book aims to sociologically and anthropologically analyze Jewish custom and tradition following death, it also, in some small way, may cross over into the domains of religion if it simultaneously makes custom and tradition more transparent and attractive for contemporary Jews.

Some may argue that even a small step across that line is too much. Precisely because I am a committed and practicing Jew, they will argue, this will lead inevitably to a collateral pietism that will infect my ethnography. I have endeavored to avoid this infection, but my honesty as a reflexive ethnographer requires me to demonstrate that when I act and describe myself as a bereaved Jewish son, I remain religiously obligated by the strictures of Jewish custom and tradition. My experience is not meant to be a model *for* the Jewish experience of death, only a model *of* it. I have tried not to relinquish the perspective and language of social science, but sometimes my Judaism undoubtedly uses an altogether different vocabulary, and it is for the readers to choose which one speaks most clearly to them. Perhaps in the matter of death, we must all speak more than one language.

Some will see this last sentence as having gone too far, as seeking not just to inform but also to stimulate practice, as turning thick description into a pretext for prescription. But I am only admitting something that has long been one of the unspoken facts of my profession. If accounts of traditional practices among various native minorities—be they Navajo, Maori, or any other such culture that has been subject to assimilation by a dominant (sometimes colonial) way of life—show these cultures to be filled with complexity and contemporary meaning and thereby also serve as an inducement for its natives, who have been exposed to these accounts, to rehabilitate that culture and practice its traditional customs, as many such accounts have done, does that invalidate the ethnography? If the ethnographer is a member of the minority group, does that make a difference? There can be no doubt that anthropological and sociological studies of a variety of cultures not only have explained peoples to themselves but also have enhanced many of these cultures in the eyes of their members.[20] Ethnography is a process fraught with manipulation.[21] That many authors of such accounts did not admit this as an object of their efforts does not alter the fact that their descriptions moved natives to look at themselves and their culture in ways that changed both.

I have tried to use my own closeness to Jewish tradition to go beyond the limits of what might otherwise be a thin description of Jewish death. I believe that, particularly in a subject as charged as death, the peril of too much self-effacement is no less than the risk of putting oneself too much into the picture. In order that my account not remain anchored in the realm of memoir and piety, I have surrounded my personal account with the analysis and structure of my social science discipline. When I write as a social anthropological interpreter of those customs and traditions, I try to be critical and get beyond the feeling of my own religious commitments. The result is two voices, which I hope complement each other, but which at times necessarily appear to go in opposite directions. To alert the reader to these different voices and perspectives, and to keep the personal voice from overwhelming the ethnographic, I have used the device of boxes. Inside the boxes, I am the bereaved Jewish son, the subject, the one who acts according to the imperatives of religious obligation, but also trying to describe my experiences with the language of reflexive ethnography. Outside, I try to retain the distance of the interpretive social anthropologist, offering a structure and framework that help explain what happens when a Jew dies. I enlist these two voices, in spite of the risk that one will drown out the other in the reader's ear, because I believe in the informing power of both insider and outsider perspectives.

Notwithstanding these ambitious goals, I have not provided, nor was it my aim to render, a comprehensive or exhaustive review of all practices and customs. There are many contemporary manuals and Jewish codebooks that fulfill that task. Nor do I claim to articulate a unified Jewish tradition; the Jewish people are too multiethnic and complex for such a notion. Nevertheless, it has been said that although all people die, in each culture people die in their own way. Hence an understanding of the way death is handled by a culture is also a means of understanding that culture, and particularly its core values.[22] I believe there are elements of a "Jewish way" in death and its aftermath.

To be sure, when I write that "this is what happens when a Jew dies" or refer to what "Jews do," many readers may be tempted to object that they are not, nor do they know, those Jews to whom I am apparently referring. My response is that the Jews about whom I write are what Max Weber called *ideal types,* personifications distilled and emerging from the customs and traditions that they shaped and that shaped them. Like the ancient Greeks, whose character and culture we can decipher from the dramas they have left us, so are these Jews revealed in their customs and traditions associated with death. I believe that the practices I have detailed here do define a general Jewish outlook and ethos. And insofar as people make use of Jewish traditions and customs, or engage in practices that have become absorbed by Jewish tradition, they share in this Jewish character and culture.

Although I have tried to fill the pages that follow with enough general description to apply to what may happen when any Jew dies, as an ethnographer who learns by the particular details, I hold fast to the following principle: "No ascent to truth without descent to cases."[23] As other ethnographers before me, I have tried "to find in the little what eludes us in the large, to stumble upon general truths while sorting through special cases."[24] Accordingly, most of what follows draws from particular encounters with death I have observed and those most popular Jewish codebooks and guides I have consulted. While I make some references to Sephardic practices as well as other ethnic examples, the cases from which most of my insights are gleaned are for the most part contemporary Ashkenazic, focused on American and Israeli illustrations.[25]

Although the manifest concern of these pages is Jews and what follows upon their death, much that I shall say is not necessarily unique to Jews. Readers will quickly discover that there are universal human aspects of death that are easily seen in the features of its Jewish incarnation. But that should come as no surprise; after all, the Jews are full-fledged citizens of the human community, in death no less than in life. Their death and its aftermath do not occur in a cultural vacuum. On the contrary, as a people that has endured centuries of minority existence and wandering, Jews have absorbed much from the peoples and faiths surrounding them (to which they have also contributed). Yet even where the elements of Jewish practice reverberate with distinct echoes of outside influences, they have commonly been translated into a particularly Jewish idiom.[26] Even when what I describe as Jewish is universal or at least shared with other groups, my vision is presented through the prism of the particular, and my language reflects that. Thus, for example, if I write that for Jews the encounter with death is transformative, or that in the immediate aftermath of death a Jew's thoughts turn to whom among the living must be informed, I do not mean to say that it is so *only* for Jews. But I do wish to show how this is expressed in the Jewish experience as outlined by particular Jewish traditions and customs.

While it remains the case that, in times of stress, the tradition can offer a structure and meaning that provide support, of course, not all Jews who die make use of the images and metaphors of Judaism, its traditions and time-honored customs or rituals. Increasingly Jews who have a religious sensibility or who are "spiritually inclined" have been drawn into the shifting secularist sands of modernity or attracted to the beckoning practices of the host non-Jewish cultures among whom they find themselves, particularly in the West, especially in America. What happens when these Jews die or suffer a loss? How do Jews whose "machinery of faith" has begun to wear out or whose knowledge of or attachment to traditions has faltered respond to death?[27] I cannot say for certain, and I leave that situation for another to describe and analyze.

Nevertheless, I suspect that Clifford Geertz got it right when, speaking about Islam, Judaism's sister religion, he suggested what happens to the spiritually inclined when they live in a society where traditions begin to falter. According to Geertz,

> They lose their sensibility. Or they channel it into ideological fervor. Or they adopt an imported creed. Or they turn worriedly in upon themselves. Or they cling even more intensely to the faltering traditions. Or they may try to rework those traditions into more effective forms. Or they split themselves in half, living spiritually in the past and physically in the present. Or they try to express their religiousness in secular activities. And a few simply fail to notice their world is moving or, noticing, just collapse.[28]

No single volume can describe what happens when all these sorts of Jews die or grieve. Instead, what this book seeks to do is to provide an informed portrait of what happens when certain Jews attached to Jewish practices die, while trying to understand and reveal the cultural and social meaning of their customs and received traditions. Some readers may be curious to examine the efficacy of some of the practices, to forge new links with the authority of the past. My advice for them is borrowed from one of my own teachers, Philip Rieff: "Perform them, in order to see what lives." [29]

A word about organization. After a brief consideration of the moment when Jews hover between life and death, when they inhabit the role that the rabbis of the Talmud called *gosess,* I move on to the arrival of death, *petira,* trace the transitional period of *aninut,* when the bereaved are first informed of their loss but the dead have not yet been laid to rest, then turn to the preparation of the body for its end, in particular exploring the nature and meaning of *tahara,* the so-called transitional ritual of purification. These pages then assay the substance of the *leveiya,* Jewish funeral, the early seven-day period of mourning, or shivah, and the following periods of *shloshim* (thirty days) and the nearly twelve months during which Kaddish, the memorial prayer, is recited. Finally, I conclude with a consideration of *yahrzeit,* the yearly commemoration of death and bereavement, as well as *Yizkor,* the prayer for the dead that, in line with tradition, is recited in the synagogue four times per year. I have used these indigenous terms to stress that it is the Jewish experience with death that I want to document and explore.

To a degree, these terms also hint at the rhythm that lies beneath the Jewish experience with death. They demonstrate that however much death has thrown life into disequilibrium, the Jewish response is to bring that life back to some equilibrium in a precisely timed series of steps, during which the dead are sent on their way and the living are reintegrated into the group and the world they inhabit. For those who have lost a parent, this is expected to take a year, for all other bereavements, a month. There are benchmarks along the way that help both the bereaved and the community to know where they should be in their journey, where others who have gone through mourning before them have been. In that time, the healing and the transformations will be marked by rituals and customs and will be shaped by relationships. In the pages that follow I will try to outline and analyze this process. What I have presented here is not intended as a procrustean bed into which the practices are to be forced, but as an analytic construction in which they may be illuminated.

Almost thirty years ago, while I was still a young graduate student, I was first exposed to the illuminating ideas of Robert Hertz in his essay "A Contribution to the Study of the Collective Representation of Death" and Sigmund Freud in his "Thoughts for the Times on War and Death."[30] I remember how striking I found their insights and how I marveled at their capacity to look at death with the clear and unsentimental eye of anthropology and psychoanalysis. Hertz's explanation of how death and bereavement could be discovered to be not just personal matters but resonant with collective concerns and desires to surmount mortality was for me not only an intellectual revelation but also an uncanny source of comfort. Freud's assertion that all of us "were prepared to maintain that death was the necessary outcome of life . . . natural, undeniable and unavoidable," but that "in reality," we all "were accustomed to behave as if it were otherwise," and "displayed an unmistakable tendency to 'shelve' death," even "to hush it up," seemed to describe precisely my own attitude.[31] His explanation of how human attitudes toward death—from the most primitive to the contemporary—were contradictory; acknowledging it as "the annihilation of life" and at the same time denying it "as ineffectual to that end" seemed to me to capture the essential truth.[32] While I suspect that both men were exposed in their lifetimes to the Jewish tradition and its treatment of death and bereavement—Hertz through his rabbinic family roots and Freud through his own and his wife's traditionally inclined Jewish families—neither writer had applied his penetrating ideas specifically to what happens when *a Jew* dies.

Now, as I took the matter of Jewish death off the shelf and began considering it, I realized that my work would become my own meditation upon and application of these ideas to the case of the Jews. Thus, in great measure, these pages must also be understood as my own modest effort to look at the Jews through the perspectives that I gained so many years ago from my reading of Hertz and Freud, to bring them back to the Jewish situation. Had they taken their experiences encountering death as Jews, had they not simply allowed those experiences to insinuate themselves subtly into their theorizing but instead actively turned their attention to what happens when a Jew dies, then perhaps what follows in these pages would be at least a part of what they would have concluded.

I wish to thank a number of people for their help and advice with earlier versions of these pages. I include here Haym Soloveitchik, not only for giving me the confidence that I could write this book but also for his meticulous reading, his friendship, and his willingness to help me correct mistakes that would display my great ignorance in various matters touched upon here. I owe special gratitude as well to Henry Abramovitch for the many hours he spent sensitizing me to the anthropological and psychological elements of death and helping me to turn my weaknesses into strengths; to Arthur Green for trying to wean my writing and thinking from the prescriptive tendencies of my piety; to Martin Jaffee for providing me with his generous understanding and perspective that enabled me to discover what I really want to do; and to Michael Rosenak for helping me to admit who I am and to reveal my religious roots in my writing. Dean Savage, a fellow teacher at Queens College, has once again offered me the keen insights of an outsider. Philip Rieff has helped me avoid intellectual sloppiness and solipsism. I received help as well from Nathan Katz, Alana Cooper, Alan Mittleman, Steven Siporin, Bert Stern, Ben Birnbaum, Dennis Gura, Naomi Fatouros, Simcha Raphael, Jeremy Wieder, and Nissan Rubin. I have not always accepted all the advice they have offered, but I have undoubtedly learned much from it.

My wife, Ellin, as always, has been my first critical reader and my most constant, life-affirming guardian angel. I owe her more than I can put into words. My late father, Henry Heilman, whose life and death so deeply moved me and taught me what I could never learn on my own, is in my everlasting memory and prayers. From beyond the grave, he has taught me that death cannot end a relationship.

For encouraging me to write this book when it was just a passing idea and making me write it, I thank Doug Abrams. For seeing it through to the end, I thank my editor, Reed Malcolm, at the University of California Press. For the striking painting that graces the cover, I thank Max Ferguson. I also wish to thank the Research Foundation of the City University of New York for financial support during the research necessary for this book.

This book has been more than an intellectual labor, a chance to explore a subject that taxed my anthropological, ethnographic, and analytic skills. It has no less assisted me in a personal journey to confront and somehow tame the anxieties of death that I have already described. "*Si vis vitam, para mortem,*" Freud concluded. "If you would endure life, be prepared for death."[33] With my work complete, I hope I have contributed to that preparation for death, with which we all will someday have the most intimate of meetings.

Gosess and Petira
Near Death and the End of Life

Death, so poetic because it touches on the immortal, so mysterious because of its silence, had a thousand ways of making its presence known.　　　　　　Chateaubriand, *Le Génie du Christianisme*

Flesh and blood: here today, gone tomorrow.
　　　　　　Jerusalem Talmud, *Sanhedrin* 6

Flesh and blood: here today, tomorrow in the grave.
　　　　　　Babylonian Talmud, *Berachot* 28b

He was unable to speak, so those who were with him recited the *Shema* on his behalf when they saw death was no longer to be denied. And then they sat in silence, tremulous and yet strangely tranquil, until at last they heard the soft gurgle in his throat and saw that his chest no longer rose and fell. They waited a bit to be certain that he had drawn his last breath. Anticipating the end, they had reviewed with the rabbi some of the customs and laws regarding what to do when death came. Now that it had, someone went to fetch a candle and placed it on the shelf above his head. They kindled it, and amid quiet weeping, someone recited the timeless words from the book of Job (1:21): "The Lord has given and the Lord has taken away, blessed be the name of the Lord." Then all repeated the blessing with which Jews meet death: "Blessed art thou O God, the true judge."

The next honor—for an honor it seemed to all present—went to his grandson, who had rushed to be here with him at the end. The young man laid his hands on his grandfather's eyelids and with trembling fingertips gently closed them. Meanwhile someone went to phone the rabbi, and the rabbi in turn contacted the head of the burial society, who came over quickly and guided them through a number of local customs.

First, the man from the burial society explained, although Jewish tradition does not favor leaving the dead unburied any longer than is necessary, these first moments after death should not be rushed. The *mayt*, the dead one—the speaker no longer referred to the man by his name—should be allowed to remain where he died for at least twenty minutes, to allow his soul fully to depart (or, I suppose, to see if he was truly dead). Since about that much time had already passed, the man from the burial society moved to the next step in the Judaic choreography of death.

Raising a window, he asked if there were any open containers of water in the house. If so, he would empty them, for the same liquid that could purify—the aqua vita—was now defiled by having absorbed the death in the house. Now others had arrived who would assist in all that followed: removing the dead man's clothes, which he would no longer need, all the while protecting his modesty by covering him completely with a plain white sheet. Next, grasping the sheet, they lowered the lifeless body it held to the floor, treating it with the same care and respect, even tenderness, that they would have given had the man still been alive. It was as if his body, still warm, could feel pain.

On the ground, the deceased was laid with his arms straightened and feet toward the open door. "A person's feet are kind to him," the rabbis explained. "Whence he must go when he dies, there they shall lead him."[1] It was almost as if they expected this journey to the beyond to be a walk.

Had this taken place in Jerusalem, the holiest of Jewish cities, the bottom sheet would be carefully removed so that the dead man's naked back would rest directly on the floor. A small stone would then be placed under his head to raise it slightly above the level of the floor. This custom of baring the back so that it touched the stone floor and a stone under the head was particular to Jerusalem, where, as the Psalmist wrote, "your servants hold her stones dear" (102:15).

Here, however, in the Jewish Diaspora of America, a few shafts of straw that the men of the burial society had brought were placed on the ground, and the dead man was placed atop a sheet laid diagonally over them while his head rested on a pillow.

As they placed him on the floor, they asked him by name for forgiveness. He was now not the *mayt;* he was once more a person with a particular identity. Then they closed his mouth, for he did not answer.

The candle was now taken down from the shelf and placed on the floor near his head. As they did this, the men recited the verse from the prophet Isaiah, "O house of Jacob, come, and let us walk in the light of the Lord" (2:5). Then, while they waited for the hearse from the funeral home to come and take the body to where the rest of the burial preparations would occur, the words of the Twenty-third Psalm, "Yea though I walk through the valley of death, I shall fear no evil for thou art with me," which they recited as well, echoed in the broken silence.

The imminence of death—called *gosess* in Hebrew—is the penultimate scene in the natural drama that we call life. *Petira* (death), however, must come in its own time. Therefore, according to Jewish law, one need not force the dying, the *gosess,* to put this moment off—thus, for example, the medieval *Sefer Hasidim* urged one not to compel a *gosess* to eat if he or she could not swallow.[2] No less should one bring on or mark the moment of death prematurely—even with such apparently innocuous acts as closing the dying person's eyes or removing a pillow from beneath his or her head. Even allowing the dying to see preparations for the corpse, to see the shrouds, the special garment in which the cadaver is traditionally garbed, was prohibited, lest the sight itself so raise the anxieties of the *gosess* as to bring on death sooner. "Anyone who in any way hastens the death of those in their final moments," the author of *Gesher HaChayim* (The Bridge of Life), one of the classic guides to the rituals of death and mourning, concluded, "has spilled blood, and the consequences for such an act are no less than for one who has murdered a person who is completely healthy."[3]

Yet if the living may not retard or hasten death's appointment with life, Jews nevertheless are enjoined by the tradition that when they see its outline clearly, when the "angel of death" approaches and will not be denied, they may assist the dying in the recitation of a variety of preparatory prayers, most famously the *vidui.* While *vidui* is commonly translated as "confessional," this brief set piece is an ambiguous plea. Its text (which has both a short and a long form and various versions that go back as far as the late Gaonic period [ninth century] of Jewish history) acknowledges an all-powerful God who is "able to heal"; it asks for recovery, yet it also asks that one's death be "an atonement for all the mistakes, sins and rebellions" of a lifetime.[4] In traditional Sephardic custom, some try to include a statement by which one seeks closure and asks to be released from all as yet unfulfilled vows and promises made during life. This confessional, however, neither recalls specific vows nor adumbrates particular sins—as if either could be recollected. There is no need to bring them to consciousness, to arouse the apprehensions of one who is about to die. Indeed, in the effort not to rush death even by engendering such trepidation, the rabbis urged anyone assisting the dying in this recitation to preface it by telling the *gosess:* "Most of those who confessed did not die, and many who did not confess died. Many who are walking the streets recite the confession, and in reward for confessing you will live."[5] Yet, for all these assurances, the whispered *vidui* is indeed the prologue to death, the penultimate prayer of life.

As the *gosess* takes the last breath, it should be with the recitation of the *Shema*, that credal call of Jewish faith. This final cri de coeur was for the rabbis who mandated it as a reenactment of the scene that, according to the Midrash, occurred at the deathbed of the patriarch Jacob, also known as "Israel." As he was about to breathe his last, his children assured him: "*Shema Yisrael, adonai eloheinu adnai echad*" (Hear O Israel, the Lord our God, the Lord is One). This assurance to their dying father that as a community they would maintain his and his fathers' faith in the one and only God allowed him to die in peace. Forever after, Jews were expected to die with this same credo on their lips and to share that same sense of peace, to assert their identity as one of the children of Israel. Others saw these expressions as a kind of mental cleansing and spiritual purification that would protect the heart and soul from the malevolence of death. Whatever their design, these practices were implicitly to provide a map for extreme situations, a way to handle the unique moment of death, an escape from anxiety about the unknown. They answered the question: Here is death, what shall be done?

For Jewish tradition, this singular moment has profound religious significance not just for the dying themselves. According to at least one commentator, those fortunate enough to witness the coming of death should treat it as a supremely holy occasion. In anticipation, they not only should help the dying one to prepare but also, if there is time, should prepare themselves by immersion in a purifying ritual bath, a *mikveh*.[6] As they witness the actual moment of the passing of a life, first of all they should help the one whose soul is departing; but they should no less turn their thoughts to accounting for their own lives, for the death holds a mirror to life in which all those present can reflect on themselves. It is, as Freud declared, what gives birth to "reflection," and "the starting point of all speculation."[7]

As they behold the coming of another's death, some are enjoined by the tradition to whisper the words of the Psalmist:

> A Psalm of ascent: I will lift up my eyes to the mountains, from whence my help does come. My help comes from the Lord, who made heaven and earth. He will not suffer even your foot to be moved; he who watches you will not slumber. Behold, he who watches Israel shall neither slumber nor sleep. The Lord is your guardian; the Lord is your shade, at your right hand. The sun shall not strike you by day, nor the moon by night. The Lord shall preserve you from all evil; he shall preserve your soul. The Lord shall preserve your going out and your coming in from this time forth, and for evermore. (Psalm 121)

In Jewish tradition, the imminence of any death is thus a reminder of our mortality, who we are, and of the human dependence on the one "who made heaven and earth." Yet it also becomes an occasion for asserting that we, the living, having recognized this, also have a capacity to participate in what is happening and prepare ourselves for it without being thrown into oblivion. As a life ebbs, we who still live want to do something, even when we realize that we are in the main observers rather than masters of what is occurring. We dare not be completely powerless in the face of death. Even the apparently malignant can be transformed into an occasion for singing psalms, affirming divine justice, and prayerful reflection. The profanity of death may be made holy; its ominousness mediated. Here begins, even before the last breath is drawn, the Jewish desire to transform death into its opposite.

If the moment of the death demonstrates the limits of human involvement, our ultimate failure to prevent mortality, much of death's aftermath is driven by a repeated display of how much we the living can still do, how life is not vanquished, how we can eliminate death's sting and still take charge. We do this by extending and shaping the nature of the departure, as well as by controlling the actions and reactions of those from whom the dead have departed. Here is an iteration of what Freud called the "remarkable attitude" that "took death seriously, recognized it as the termination of life," but also "denied death, reduced it to nothingness."[8]

Much of the initial attention is paid to the treatment of the corpse and, by implication, to the disembodied spirit of the newly dead. For Jewish tradition, this involves in the main easing and definitively separating spirit from body, allowing the former to rise up like ether and start its journey to what the mystics saw as its source. The body returns to the dust of the earth, the spirit to eternity.

"Everything seeks to return to its sources," writes the author of the *Ma'avar Yabbok,* the seventeenth-century codebook from Mantua that served for generations as the standard work on Jewish practices associated with death and popularized mystical and kabbalistically influenced mortuary ritual. "Hence the supernal parts—the soul, spirit and breath—yearn to ascend, while the lower parts—the limbs and body—seek to descend, for dust they are and to dust shall they return."[9]

The living must enable this parting of the ways; hence, in a room where a Jew has died, they are enjoined to open the windows so that the spirit may escape the corporeal world, and they are to place the body on the floor so that it, too, may begin its journey back to the earth. Through these actions the living help direct or ease the passage of the dead and move on from their own helplessness.

It is of course not always possible to be present at the moment of death; indeed, in contemporary life, such deathbed scenes are the exception rather than the rule. Separated by distance and circumstance from those whose life's end touched us, we may find ourselves feeling even more powerless in the face of another's death. Yet here, too, the desire to do something displays itself, and we look for some words with which to confront the presence of death.

The phone call from my mother startled me. Although my father had been failing since his last stroke, hanging precariously onto consciousness, spending more and more hours of the day asleep, or at least with his eyes closed and mouth silent, in a state of being we the living could barely penetrate, he was still at home. Yet we knew he would not get better, and we saw that the light in his eyes was dimming. He could barely swallow food, slept most of the day, and only with enormous difficulty managed to communicate even with a wan smile or a faint kiss. We knew he had tired of the struggle and had wanted to end his days in the body that once had given him joy but now had become his prison and torture chamber. But no one could know when that time would be, and, for the moment, we contented ourselves that he was there, even if he sat barely awake in his armchair most of the time. With the help of a live-in caretaker, my mother, who stayed by his side continually, had managed to keep him in familiar surroundings, the shelter of their life together. But now my mother was on the line, late in the afternoon during a freak March ice storm that had frozen the Northeast with a last blast of winter.

"I think your father is dying," she said, her voice shaking. "What should I do?"

What should all of us do? What could we do? We knew that our instincts to call for medical help, which we had done only a few weeks before when my father seemed to have been at death's doorway, would lead to a fate he had narrowly missed then. Just as he had been about to be connected to a respirator on which he would have ended his days in a hospital, he miraculously regained his breathing and consciousness. Sent home the next day, he avoided this ignominious end and had returned to the place in which, we were sure, he wanted to close his life. Having once been saved from the bondage of a hospital death, he should surely be spared another mistake from which there would be a very slow exodus. He needed to be free to die now.

"Hold his hand," I said, "Tell him that you love him, say the *Shema*, and I'll call the doctor." The doctor arrived and confirmed what we knew he would: father had died. My son, Uri, arrived shortly afterward. And then came the men from the Chevra Kaddisha, the Jewish burial society, who set him on the floor, lit the candle, opened the window, and then took the body away to prepare it for its final journey.

"This world is but an inn," said the Talmud (*Moed Katan* 9b), "and the world to come, home."

When at last death comes, we want it to be a "good death."[10] People may, however, differ about the essentials of a good death. Moreover, the particular definition of what constitutes a good or a bad death has changed over time. "What today we call the good death, the beautiful death," the historian Phillipe Ariès tells us, "corresponds exactly to what used to be the accursed death: the *mors repentina et improvisa*, the death that gives no warning. 'He died tonight in his sleep: He just didn't wake up. It was the best possible way to die.'"[11] This is a death that does not involve prolonged suffering.[12] In addition to being relatively painless, in modern Western culture good deaths these days include those in which the person is able to die at home — or at the very least not left alone in the impersonal and artificial surroundings of a hospital. A good death in our times is likewise one in which the ultimate breath is taken at the end of a long life and in the comforting presence of those to whom one has been closest and who will be most grieved by the loss. Whatever constitutes a good death, the desire by both the dying and the bereaved to have it punctuate earthly existence remains powerful. Often the first element of consolation — for both the dying and the bereaved — is gaining the conviction that the death will be or was a good one.

In Jewish tradition, a good death requires something more. This something more includes elements of the spiritual, mystical, ritual, and cultural — all of which may be enlisted to suggest that the death, however disturbing, was not profane. Thus a good Jewish death is one that happened at a spiritually auspicious time. A death on Tuesday, for example, is good, since that was the day of creation in which Scripture reports that God twice said the word *good*.[13] Or a death on the eve of Sabbath is one that would allow the soul of the deceased mystically to unite with the special heavenly character of the day of rest, to experience immediately upon demise the supernal repose of Sabbath. A death during the Days of Awe, when the spiritual accounts for the year are closed and a new page of life is turned by the Divine Judge, would be considered propitious, for it indicates a kind of perfect completion of life, as does a death on one's birthday. The permutations of what constitutes a good time to die are, of course, as varied as the religious imagination, but all seek to offer the comfort that the death was spiritually good.

Of course, there are also good deaths that are the result of martyrdom and heroism, deaths that are the supreme price for life. At one time these were the deaths that were embraced by those who chose to die rather than perform a sacrilege—what the tradition called dying for *kiddush hashem,* a death that sanctified God's name. Such good deaths also included those offered on behalf of someone else, most notably the Jewish people. The one who dies so that others might live has died a good death.

Yet Judaism, while valuing the martyr and the hero, never intended such deaths, however good they might be, as an ideal. Even the heroic martyrdom of the famous sage Rabbi Akiva is presented in the Talmud and commentaries as a good death not because it provided Akiva an opportunity to be a martyr but because it allowed him to complete his lifelong wish to fulfill all the divine commandments spelled out in the *Shema* credo. At last, Akiva explains as he dies at the hands of the Roman oppressors, he has had the experience of "loving God with all my soul."[14]

For traditional Jews, a good death would be one that occurred with all the attendant rituals of dying, which put a liturgical punctuation to life. A death that puts life into sacred order, with the recitation of a series of benevolent or hopeful verses from Scripture or the *vidui*—that would be good. To so die in the company of those whom one loves, to mix the sacred and the personal, that, too, would be good. The sure knowledge that the bereaved will be able to properly tend to the remains and mourn according to the time-honored customs also makes a death a good one.[15]

In the broader cultural domain, although there is room for the hero, the fallen soldier who has died for the homeland,[16] in general Jews have not longed for such glorious deaths but have preferred to die at the end of a long life. What constituted a long life was, of course, a matter of much discussion. To some the Scripture was the only guide. Hence, one had lived a long life if one had, like the patriarch Abraham, died "aged and contented," which the medieval exegete Nachmanides interpreted as meaning that one was fully content with what each day had brought him and retained no desire that the future should bring something new.[17] Others, drawing on the biblical account of Joseph, whose death is described as coming after he had seen three generations of descendants who "were raised on his knees" (as the classic Jewish exegetes interpreted the text), have suggested that having had a living connection with several generations of children and grandchildren is the measure of old age.[18] At one time, Jewish folk wisdom set this age at the biblical 120 years that Moses lived. The Talmud, citing the sage Rabbi Judah ben Tema, defined "the fullness of years" as coming by the age of 70, with true old age certainly arriving by one's nineties, when the person stands, as the rabbi put it, helplessly at the edge of the grave, when, because of one's helplessness, life has become a living death.[19]

> When my father's body had been taken away by the men of the burial society to be prepared for his funeral, we who remained behind found ourselves in a fog of bewilderment. In those first moments of our bereavement, we did not want to think about all that now stood before us: the funeral, the period of mourning to follow, the way our lives would change. That would come when the fog started to lift. In these initial moments when death could no longer be denied, we simply sought some consolation in our sorrow. And for that comfort we turned to one another, trying somehow to assure ourselves that this man who had meant so much to each of us had had a good death.
>
> "He died in his armchair, at home with his wife, who loved him deeply and cared for him selflessly at his side," I said to my mother and to myself, "not alone in a hospital, not in a coma in a nursing home. You recited the *Shema* with him."
>
> "He had been suffering since his stroke, and now he will not suffer any longer," someone else said, "and at last he was freed from his helpless body."
>
> "He lived to see and get to know his grandchildren, and he left them with a lasting loving memory."
>
> "He died on the eve of the Sabbath, and he will be buried just before twilight." The anguish of his death would be softened by the serenity of the Sabbath. He would enter the afterlife in the arms of the Sabbath Queen.
>
> "And he will be missed and mourned by people who loved him."

"Profound mourning, the reaction to the loss of a loved person," Freud tells us in his famous essay "Mourning and Melancholia," "contains the same feelings of pain, loss of interest in the outside world—in so far as it does not recall the dead one—loss of capacity to adopt a new object of love, which would mean a replacing of the one mourned, the same turning from every active effort that is not connected with thoughts of the dead."[20] Yet what distinguishes mourning from melancholia, Freud also informs us, is that unlike melancholia, in which the sad person in a sense loses his or her own life and becomes hopelessly impoverished emotionally, in mourning, normally those who grieve will "bit by bit, under great expense of time and . . . energy" at last return to reality and become strong, connected, "free and uninhibited again," even though "the existence of the lost object is continued in the mind." In short, "in grief the world becomes poor and empty; in melancholia it is the ego itself."[21] No less than any other bereaved person, the Jew is subject to such profound reactions at the moment of loss. Yet all that follows, so highly structured and exquisitely timed, moves the return to reality and personal freedom from mourning at an unyielding pace. The individual, the ego, is not left alone, while the grief is replaced by a world full of life's relationships.

Onen

Freshly Bereaved

. . . now you lie there mute and lifeless. Your mouth has ceased
speaking, your arm is paralyzed forever. O, dear me, what will
become of me?

> Rafael Karsten, *The Headhunters*
> *of the Western Amazonas*

I was exhausted from the grueling and extraordinarily slow journey from New
York to Boston on a train, packed to overflowing with passengers who had found
no other way north in the brutal March ice storm that, like my father's death,
seemed badly timed although not altogether unexpected. Finding no seats left
on the train, three of my sons and I had stood or sat on the floor in the narrow
aisle for most of the nearly five hours of a trip that usually took less than four.
Drained by the experience and the emotional distress that the news of my father's death had caused, I toppled into the house in which I had grown up and
from which my father's body had only a short time before been removed by the
Chevra Kaddisha. Although he was gone now, his spirit still undeniably lingered.
His absence from the armchair in which he had sat for years and in which at last
he had died was palpable.

So powerful was that presence that my mother now could not bear to go into
the room, and she sat in another, stunned and forlorn. We embraced and cried,
collapsing into each other. He was gone. Our lives were changed forever. But
even as we tried to absorb the reality of a world bereft of a man we had each
loved in our own way and for as long as we could remember and talked about
our loss, there were decisions to be made about what would happen next. Although my mother and I felt overwhelmed, the undeniable progression of events
and expectations was structured to lift us bit by bit out of our emotional torpor.
Jewish funerals follow swiftly on the heels of death. Everything would happen

quickly; the funeral would be the next day—early, both because of the storm and because it was the eve of Sabbath, and no burial could be done after sundown. Arrangements had to begin almost immediately.

Soon the rabbi would be coming to visit us for help in his preparations for a eulogy; on the eve of the funeral, he wanted to share our reflections and reminiscences about my father. As we confronted the reality of my father's death, we found ourselves paradoxically steeped in thoughts of his life and what it meant to us, as if trying to distill its complexity and richness into some discrete memories and understandings. How did we grasp the depth of this loss? How were we changed by having had him in our lives, and how would we be different in his absence? There was no thinking about anything else, and yet it seemed too soon to distill and order the inchoate feelings. How could we find adequate language?

Yet even in the midst of these thoughts about my father, the unyielding celerity of tomorrow's funeral and its preparations forced us to think also about the other people who were important to us and him. Who needed to be notified? What should the death notice in the paper say? Which papers did we want to notify? Then, too, there were the questions that came from the men of the burial society, who would help make the arrangements and needed to know where to prepare the body and schedule the funeral. Who would carry the coffin? How many did we think would come along to the cemetery? Should we arrange for a bus for those fearful of driving in the snow? We wanted people to be able to come, in spite of what was shaping up to be a significant snowfall. Could we wait until later in the day for the snow to let up, or would we have to schedule for the morning to be certain that the burial was completed in time? Who might want to speak? Who could and who should? Did I want to visit the funeral chapel that night, to stand for a few moments near my father's body?

Beyond all this, we were forced to think about how to prepare my father's dead body. The members of the burial society needed to know if we wanted them to wrap my father's body in his own prayer shawl, his tallit, in their preparations of his body. Should they dress him in his *kittel,* the white cassock he wore in his lifetime on Yom Kippur and at the Passover Seder, or should they use the standard one that came with the shrouds? Yes, we wanted him to have pieces of his life—his tallit and his *kittel*—cloak his body in death. We had to find and prepare them. His favorite tallit was still somewhere in the synagogue where he kept it. According to Jewish tradition, the silver mantle of father's tallit—the one I had bought him many years earlier as a birthday present—would have to be removed; the rich and the poor must go to burial alike. His *kittel,* with its special white cinch that I had brought from Israel, put away since the last Yom Kippur, needed to be located somewhere in the back of the closet.

As I searched for these items among my father's things, I could recognize the familiar smell of his clothes, the coats in which I had so often buried my face as a child. For a moment I lost myself in them, as I had long ago, and began to weep. In the drawer where he kept his things, I found a worn green velvet bag containing his phylacteries and weekday prayer cloth as well as his prayer book, worn smooth at the edges by his fingers. I held them close, as if I might find my father inside them. They were not just redolent of my father; he still inhabited them.

Then, too, I had to look for all sorts of papers, from cemetery deeds to wills and insurance documents. We needed to organize funds for the sudden expenses. I rummaged through my father's papers. He was still there in the perfect order of his files, the testament of a man who had been an accountant for nearly half a century. In the neat script of his penmanship, I saw his hand and longed to once again watch him writing, "doing his papers," as he called it, as I had for so many hours in the years I lived with him.

As we, the bereaved, became wrapped up with all these preparations, all else seemed to disappear. Time, at once rushing forward toward the burial was, no less than us, torn from its mooring. We were in another kind of existence. All else disappeared; nothing else mattered. In the terms of the Jewish tradition, we were *onenim*.

For Jews, the moment of death transforms. Those who were living a moment before and have suddenly become an inert body, skin and bones, are called *niftar*, literally "released" from this life. The *niftar*, regardless of what sort of a person he or she was in life—a saint or a sinner—as a corpse becomes the paradigm and epitome of impurity, *avi avot ha tuma*, capable of defiling all in its proximity and in need of ritual refinement and purification. At the same time, all those to whom the *niftar* was any one of seven relatives—father, mother, brother, sister, son, daughter, spouse—become *onenim*. This a special status for which no English terms exists: *onenim* are the bereaved before burial. Both the *niftar* and the *onenim* are powerless to avoid this change in status; both will need the help of others to get past it. Jewish death and mourning are ultimately an occasion of experiencing collective life, of being enfolded more closely into the "nurturing company of our Jewish fellowship."[1] All that follows the moment of death, then, is the story of these two parallel but opposite journeys carried on with the help of others: the *niftar* to the dead, the bereaved to the living.

In large measure, the coming together of life and death, the resulting transformative moment of the encounter that is followed by the subsequent reorganization of existence, is what the Jewish experience with death is all about. Onenim are the first to experience this encounter, but before the mourning is over, all those who have been touched by the death will in some way be transformed.

While the initial experience of being an *onen* is inchoate, in fact with the entry into this status a clock begins to tick, both for the bereaved and for the deceased. For both the *niftar* and the *onenim,* the time preceding burial is a betwixt-and-between transitional or liminal state during which they have become detached from their life's moorings and changed but not yet anchored to the new realities that the death has created. Both are "stricken"; the dead with the bottomless impurity of lifeless decay, and the *onenim* with profound grief and confusion. Both are here and there, among the living and dead. The *niftar* still inhabits the space of the living, though in a new relationship, and has not yet become pure spirit and memory. The bereaved *onen* is not yet able to mourn, although linked inextricably to death and therefore not expected to lead life as if nothing has happened. For Jews, this time is unlike any other in Jewish life, where even the normal quotidian religious obligations are suspended, including the anticipated demands of mourning.

Liminality, as students of this betwixt-and-between state have noted, is a situation fraught with both danger and potential. So, too, is being an *onen.* On the one hand, the *onenim* are in danger of being torn from life along with the dead for whom they grieve. The shock, the grief can overwhelm and hurl one to the depths of melancholia. The proximity of death can frighten one to death. Death almost seems contagious. To free one from its defiling grasp, to end the danger, Judaism makes this stage as brief as possible and moves toward purification, a swift burial and the healing structures of mourning.

On the other hand, the potential in that same liminal state offers *onenim* a chance to experience grief and become engaged by the mysteries of life and death that elevate them above profane everyday existence. Aside from seeing to the burial and other preparations of the dead, they need carry out no other Jewish obligations but may ponder what has happened to them, to the one they have lost, to life as they have known it. Bereavement is, after all, a moment in which consciousness about ultimate meaning and human existence is painfully but also extraordinarily heightened. This is a moment of high drama in life, almost never forgotten—a turning point in every biography.

The end of this brief and unstructured liminal period is the funeral, an event that will throw the bereaved from pure grief into the beginning of mourning.

No matter how expected or sudden death may be, its immediate aftermath thus retains a feeling of contingency.[2] Something else must, *will,* happen.

Recognizing the disorientation of the *onenim,* Jewish law frees them from almost all religious obligations. The *onen* is even freed from reciting the daily liturgy, the alpha and omega of the traditional day. Indeed, the *onen* is not even expected to be counted in the *minyan,* the ten who make up the quorum for public prayer.[3] The community cannot, does not, count on them now, for it knows they are captured in the melancholic limbo of the immediacy of loss. It is as if *onenim* are existentially "elsewhere" or, as we might put it these days, "out of it."

Onenim are not simply caught up in thoughts about a lost loved one or in preparations for a funeral. They are also caught, at least temporarily, in the suffocating embrace of death. As if in recognition of this, although prohibited from full-fledged mourning, *onenim* were enjoined by the rabbis from engaging in even the symbolic activity of life's joys, such as eating meat or drinking wine (which the rabbis saw as epitomes of life's physical pleasures), nor could they engage in sexual intercourse or lovemaking—the most powerful challenge to and antithesis of death. They could not go to make a living at their work, for living was suspended; and even Torah study was prohibited, for the rabbis the supreme pleasure in life, while "the corpse—who could not have these pleasures—lies unburied."[4] It is almost as if in restricting all these life-affirming activities, the *onenim* were somehow forced to mirror the dead, who likewise cannot do these things. Primitives, who were convinced that the newly dead still had feelings, understood these prohibitions in more psychological terms: they did not want to do anything that would arouse the jealousy of the dead who themselves could no longer engage in these activities. Moderns may not express these convictions, yet the tradition recognizes that they are still embedded in the unconscious. Hence the basic principle: Do not celebrate life in the face of the dead.

Nevertheless, Jewish tradition understood that this frozen social status could not be extended indefinitely. Indeed, because Jewish law requires burial on the selfsame day and as soon as possible after death, it expected that being *onenim* would be transient and that none of the bereft would have to remain for long in this betwixt-and-between situation.[5] Thus the same Jewish tradition that confirms the *onenim*'s disorientation and shock and frees them from so many quotidian religious obligations also presses them to busy themselves with the concerns of the *niftar* who "lies before them," as the rabbis put it. Or, in Freud's words, "deference for reality gains the day."[6] They are to see to the funeral; they are to remain busy although not fully socially engaged.[7]

But how can *onenim* remain discombobulated and still occupy themselves with their dead, remain concurrently in their transient and paradoxical state of emotional bewilderment and bent on conscientious activity? To do so, the *onenim* must become a kind of *Homo duplex,* simultaneously indulging themselves in an often personally paralyzing confusion while also looking to others with whom they share a collective life to help them deal with the dead and pull them out of grief and back into the community of the living. The sudden inability to act independently, the realization of how we are tied—both to the dead and to the living—is striking particularly to those who live in a modern Western society that stresses the individual and encourages personal autonomy. Perhaps this realization accounts in part for the frequent inability of this society to respond to and shape our encounter with death, and the consequent turn of the bereaved to the precincts of tradition—sometimes in spite of their own inclinations. Jews who have no personal rabbi or who know little, if anything, about Jewish religion may nevertheless find themselves turning to it and forced to shape their grief with its help. Poorly defined and often inchoate feelings that are raw and unfamiliar are put into the receptacles of tradition and custom, no less than are the dead. All this happens swiftly, because death does not wait.

While many moderns resent religious traditions because their ignorance of them arouses the unpleasant feelings of incompetence, they are often willing to turn to them at times of death because, at least for the Jews, this is a time when recognizing personal limitations and incompetence is not a failing; it is a ritual expectation. In a sense, sorrow is their cry for help.[8] Even those *onenim* who on their own want to do everything for their dead and themselves quickly discover that they need others to assist in the actual preparation and disposal of the body, to assemble the congregation that will bear witness to the funeral and respond to the eulogies and prayers, and to play out the role of consolers.

For Jews, no less so when they are *onenim,* "life is plural."[9] Indeed from the moment that they become *onenim* and until the end of their mourning, those who have lost a family member to death will be increasingly dependent on the help of others among the living. Perhaps that is why, even in the first shock of death, the Jew's thoughts must be and commonly are turned from the one who has been lost to whom among the living must be notified and whose help will be needed.[10]

Being an only child, I expected that I would have to do everything now that father was dead and mother was grieving. But from everywhere there came help. My son Uri and my friend David, who was also father's physician, had taken care

of seeing to the removal of the body, to calling the burial society. My son Adam
gathered up his other brothers and got them to Boston. My wife, Ellin, had made
the arrangements for the rabbi to come. Henry, the fellow with whom I had
played ball and run around the synagogue throughout many of my primary
school years, was now head of the volunteers of the burial society. Before I had
even had a chance to organize my thoughts, he was sitting with me in the
kitchen of my mother's house and patiently reviewing with me all the stages
that I would pass through in the next twenty-four hours. Quietly and tenderly,
he asked me questions for which he needed answers, coaching me when I was
stumped with examples of what others among the bereaved in our community
did. He knew this was my first time as one so bereaved.

The rabbi arrived to help; the community would provide for all the ritual and
material needs during the coming week, as we entered into the seven days of
mourning. Ellin would make sure they were able to get into the house. All
seemed prepared to suspend whatever else they were doing, to brave the elements, in order to be at my side and to extend themselves. Orphaned by my father's death, I was staggered by how much I needed others, and sustained by
how ready they were to help.

Some rabbinic commentators argue that the reason that *onenim* and others concerned with the dead are freed from other demands is related to the Judeo-
legal principle that "one already engaged in a *mitzvah* [religious obligation] is
thereby absolved of having to carry out another *mitzvah*." Others, however,
suggest that the tradition's liberating the *onenim* and those who assist them from
all other concerns beyond arranging a funeral comes from the special "honor
due to the dead." Psychologists could point, with Freud, to the inhibitions generated by grief. Sociologists might suggest that when a relationship that was
once with a living person turns into one with a corpse this necessarily creates a
kind of social paralysis that requires someone else's help to begin to move beyond it. Whatever the reasons, Judaism has long argued that almost nothing is
more important than setting into motion the activities that will allow the dead
to be laid to rest and the bereaved to begin the mourning.

Death will not be ignored. Not only are the *onenim* summoned. Those
whose job is to prepare the corpse and purify its departing spirit—the Chevra
Kaddisha, among the traditionalists—must come without delay to take up
their task, claiming the dead as their own. Those related to the dead or the immediately bereaved are likewise expected to defer all else and come from far
and near to attend the funeral. By Jewish tradition, this includes the entire

community and even those who happen upon a funeral procession, who must, regardless of what they are doing, turn their steps so that they follow it for a short distance (a custom still upheld in certain tradition-bound neighborhoods of Israel, where the dead are often carried through the streets to their place of burial). In our own society, the norm of allowing cars in a funeral procession the right of way is probably a faint echo of this custom, or of the desire to allow the spirit to depart as easily as possible. The claims of the dead may not be postponed (although at times brief allowances are made when close relatives must travel great distances to attend—here the imperatives of the living to be present balance the demands of the dead to be buried).

The decision of whom to notify (and hence to encumber with the responsibility to attend) is forced upon the bereaved. This need to organize a funeral does not allow for the *onen*'s social contraction. Because of the emotional difficulty inherent in this imperative, the actual funeral arrangements are sometimes handled by another family member who is not among the immediately bereaved or by friends in one's community, often through the offices of the synagogue or a local newspaper, the funeral parlor, or the Chevra Kaddisha. Yet for the unaffiliated, and even for those tightly bonded to Jewish institutional life, there can be no escape from having to personally notify a series of particular people. Those personally notified by the bereaved of course will have to attend the funeral and offer even more in the way of comfort and assistance— that is the "price" for such a personal notification. Those who receive the news via intermediaries or who read a notice in the newspaper or on a poster on the wall (the common method in Israel) or even via an announcement broadcast from a speaker atop a car that drives through the neighborhood (a practice used in the *haredi,* or ultra-Orthodox, precincts of Jerusalem) will have to decide for themselves the extent of their obligation to attend. The knowledge of death, however, stimulates a series of considerations about what the ties are between the living, the dead, and the bereaved. Is this a funeral at which I must be present? Should I expect this person to attend a funeral with which I am connected?

In effect, both for the bereaved and for all the rest of the living, these first moments after death and before the funeral define a time whose essence is to test the strength of the ties among those who survive, demonstrating in a dramatic and often unforgettable way who must be there for the dead and for the bereaved in extremis. Thus, from the earliest moments after death, the often invisible strands that link the dead and the living in a net of obligations and emotions begin to appear. Like a gauze pad, they will in time cover the tear of death.

Tahara

Purifying the Dead

It is an ancient custom to wash and purify the dead; some trace it
to Hillel the Elder.   Aaron Levine, *Sefer Zichron Meir*

Each and every Chevra Kaddisha shall act according to the
customs of its locality.   Responsa of Rabbenu Asher

"The living," as anthropologist Robert Hertz once put it, "owe all kinds of
care to the dead who reside among them."[1] While most Jews who die these
days are prepared for their last rites by professional undertakers, Jewish tradition considers these final concerns with the body as a matter of profound religious and community obligation—something that should not be transferred
to those who share neither faith nor fellowship with the dead. This preparation, called *tahara* (purification) for burial, which traditional Judaism considers the only appropriate disposal of the body, becomes the responsibility of the
women and men of the Chevra Kaddisha, literally the "holy fellowship."
These are Jews who, although not immediate relatives of the deceased, come
from the same (broadly defined) community as the dead or the bereaved. In
creating the Chevra, Jewish tradition has tried to ensure that each Jew's body
and the spirit that departs it will receive their final touch from the hands of
those for whom the disposition of his or her earthly remains has religious and
spiritual meaning, and that "this will not be a matter of luck, or chance, but a
deliberate and conscious commanded act, a promise on the part of the community, and an obligation on each."[2]

The Chevra Kaddisha offers what has been called "the last act of caring one
human being can give another."[3] That kindness consists of speeding the dead
to their new abode and returning the living to the web of community connections.[4] In Hebrew this is called *chesed shel emet* (true loving-kindness),
"true" because this a kindness for which the givers can expect no direct gratitude or gratuity; no recompense can come from the recipient to the giver.[5] In

general, the activities of the Chevra are free, its members all volunteers.[6] But why should someone perform this kindness?

While we all can hope for the kindness of strangers, in death we cannot always demand it. That is where Jewish law and practice play their part. For example, they mandate that the unidentified body found on the road must be buried by the elders of the city closest to where it was found, and they decree that a Chevra Kaddisha be found for everyone. This group serves as the agent for the immediate family, who, according to Jewish law, should not handle these preparations for burial personally but is responsible for seeing that they are done.

In its earliest days, during the Middle Ages, when Jews were not always gracefully treated in life or death by the surrounding society, the Chevra Kaddisha guaranteed dignity. It therefore could make demands on all members of the community to serve because "not to participate in the society was equivalent, from a communal perspective, to social exclusion and, from a spiritual perspective, to refuse to fulfill the laws or commandments, the primary basis for the practice of Judaism."[7] Moreover, as Sylvie-Anne Goldberg, who has studied this history, notes, "As an intermediary between the community and its members, [the Chevra Kaddisha] also seems to have been an intermediary between God and man."[8] In time, this religious and instrumental importance made membership in the Chevra far more exclusive, open only to the select and honorable. In effect, in return for doing what others might find onerous, the community gave the highest honor to those who did *tahara.*

Since then much has changed. Professional undertakers will bury everyone with dignity. The Jewish community today is no longer what it once was. Honor can be gained more easily in philanthropy, and finding volunteers for the Chevra Kaddisha is harder now than before. Even in the most Orthodox precincts, many of the people prefer fulfilling other religious obligations. Many believe that dealing with cadavers does not enhance their sense of self or worth. Others consider even the gathering of remains of those killed in Israel by terrorist bombs, among the most public and highly respected of Chevra Kaddisha duties, extraordinarily difficult. Still others in the modern world are simply troubled by the reality of mortality. They favor other religious activities: to give charity or to sit in the yeshiva and remain sheltered in the pages of sacred texts.

In the world outside these traditionalist enclaves of Orthodoxy, it is even harder to find volunteers. People have grown accustomed to having undertakers and professionals do the job. Few Jews with their feet planted in the secular world are ready to volunteer for this duty, however sacred it might be. Typical is a suburban New York Chevra, which covered five communities in two counties, that had only about fifty volunteers, and no one was knocking down the doors to join.

Hardest of all is finding women. The young are ineligible—in many an Orthodox Chevra, a woman who could still bear children was religiously prohibited from handling the dead and therefore was spiritually undesirable— even in the unlikely event that one found young women willing to do so. Young women commonly did not even want their husbands—who were permitted to serve—to come into contact with the dangers, both numinous and infernal, to say nothing of the risks of infection that they associated with the kingdom of the dead. Older traditionally Orthodox women who could serve were often too busy with their own lives, caring for their families or preparing their homes for the living, to be taken up with preparing the dead.

"The hardest day of the year to bury a woman," one volunteer suggested, "is the eve of Passover, when a woman is getting ready for the Seder and she is called to do a *tahara*." Friday afternoons, before the onset of the Sabbath, when last-minute preparations for the big Friday night dinners were being made, were also troublesome times.

As for modern women, they were frequently no less caught up in career and family than their male counterparts. The older ones among them often had the most responsibilities, in both their jobs and their personal lives. To expect them to add this volunteer duty, which was always unpredictable in its timing, to their roster of activities often seemed unreasonable. It was easier to find someone who would work on a testimonial dinner than one who would join the Chevra Kaddisha.

The demands of Judaism notwithstanding, most Jews today rely on the services of a "Jewish" funeral parlor, assuming the undertakers will do the job right. The "Jewish" character of these parlors often is little more than their Jewish-sounding name, ownership, or willingness to supply some Jewish amenities. In fact, in many cases the same undertaker serves both Jews and non-Jews. But, of course, while undertakers in these business establishments prepare bodies for burial, they do not carry out *tahara*—indeed, frequently their employees, the ones who actually work on the body or handle the details, are not Jews.

This is no small matter for, in a sense, implicit in *tahara* is the Jewish belief that in some important measure, our bodies and lives belong not just to us as individuals but also to the collective community of which we are a part. They are therefore not debris to be removed but the fragments of the collective human spirit that must be treated with the same respect and honor that we would give to the whole.[9] Furthermore, *tahara* implies that as the spirit departs from the corpse, that vessel in which it dwelled for a lifetime, it must be treated with extreme care. Finally, as the death of the body has engendered despair, so *tahara* begins the process of repair. It does this with a series of rituals by which these agents of the community mingle the individual with the collective, the corporeal with the numinous, the this-worldly with the otherworldly. It marks a new beginning of the recurrent human struggle against death and its desolation by trying to make pure what is quintessentially impure—the corruption of death and decay. In effect, *tahara* is an archetypal example of what ritual seeks to satisfy: "the deepest human yearnings for order, meaning, and structure in what would otherwise be utter chaos." [10] No understanding of what happens when a Jew dies can thus be complete without a careful look at *tahara*.

A thin description of the process is simple. Three to five volunteers—men for men and women for women—assemble on call to take charge of, cleanse, wash, perform purifying ablutions upon, and then dress the deceased in hand-sewn linen shrouds, accompanying this procedure with a series of scriptural verses and prayers that punctuate an otherwise governing silence. In those places where a coffin is used, the members of the Chevra place the purified and ritually garbed body into it. In some places, the men of the Chevra also bring the dead to burial, opening the grave, assisting in lowering the body into it, and closing it up.

A brief recital of the basic elements of the *tahara,* of course, does not capture its deeper meaning or Jewish significance, which requires a look that goes beyond surface descriptions. To achieve this, I shall make use of what I have learned from my nearly three years as a member of the Chevra Kaddisha. I have observed these activities primarily in a community near my home in suburban New York. Additionally, I have for limited periods been a participant-observer in a number of other burial societies—primarily in the New York area and in Jerusalem. What follows here is my effort ethnographically to translate those experiences into words. Unlike in the other chapters of this book, however, here the firsthand experiences from which I shall draw are of another order, for a son does not serve on the Chevra that prepares his father's body. Rather than review numerous burial preparations I have participated in, or try to imagine what my father underwent as his body was tended to by the Chevra Kaddisha in my hometown, I offer instead a thick description of the *tahara* of a man I shall call "Avraham," who was prepared for burial in Jerusalem. This will serve as a paradigm of the process. Where there are significant variations from this case study, I have tried to describe them as well. Where possible, I also endeavor to articulate some of the inner feelings that work on the Chevra engenders among its members.

Some may find the descriptions here overly graphic. The handling of corpses is, after all, something that we moderns have chosen to leave unobserved. Others may find the procedures repulsive or grotesque, even though everything I have witnessed was done with care and gentleness. Yet as we consider them, as well as so much else that happens when a Jew dies, it is worth recalling Emile Durkheim's admonition: "The most barbarous and the most fantastic rites and the strangest myths translate some human need, some aspect of life, either individual or social. The reasons with which the faithful justify them may be, and generally are erroneous; but the true reasons do not cease to exist."[11]

The last bodily remains of Avraham, a man in his eighties who for much of his life had lived and worked in Jerusalem, arrived by ambulance from Petach Tikva, a city on Israel's coastal plain, where he had met his appointment with death. Before the Chevra Kaddisha would bury him, one of its administrators, the one in the office who had answered the phone call from the family when they turned to him for help, checked the society's files to see whether Avraham had a burial plot registered with them. Someone manned the office phone at all hours; people's departure from this world—no less than their arrival—was not commonly subject to convenient scheduling. In the event that the deceased had a registered plot, there would be no need to make further inquiries. Only those who had the appropriate communal connections and rights to be interred by this particular burial society would have been allowed to purchase a plot. If there were no such record, further inquiries would be made to see if indeed there was a well-founded claim of a connection between the deceased or his family and the community that the Chevra served. If not, efforts would be made to find another suitable Chevra. The expansion of population and increased urbanization had created a society of individuals, and hence the contemporary search for a Chevra was often a pale reflection of the communal connections that once tied the living together. Still, at the very least, Jews prepared other Jews for burial, so some Chevra would be found.

This particular Chevra, founded in Jerusalem in 1897, operated according to time-honored traditions, local customs, and rituals and served the strictly Orthodox Ashkenazic community—so-called *haredim*—people that in their Yiddish vernacular they simply called *unsere yidn* (our Jews). In practice, *unsere yidn,* I was told, referred here to those who were religiously observant, who were particularly scrupulous about observing the Sabbath and the commandments, no less so than those who served on the Chevra. Avraham qualified. He was, as described by one of those who prepared him for burial and who knew him in life, "a Jew who observed the Torah and its commandments, who was careful to study the Torah each day and go to the synagogue morning and evening." Now, one last time, he needed the help of those Jews who shared his way of life to make the journey from death to burial. For although one may die alone, no one can lay himself to rest.[12] For the final journey, we must turn to those who will mourn for us, and they turn to the community. That is why, perhaps, "so many peoples believe that the greatest calamity that can befall an individual is to die far away and thus be separated from his kin forever."[13]

Having qualified for the full measure of social and communal care, at least in the minds of those who ran the Chevra, Avraham was now ready for *tahara,* the ceremony of purification, by which his cadaver, the embodiment of that which is considered most ritually unclean in Judaism, is transformed into a vessel ready to return to God and await the day of final judgment. *Tahara* was the Jewish version of the nearly universal belief among all peoples that "so long as the final rite has not been celebrated the corpse is exposed to grave perils."[14] The Chevra Kaddisha would protect him, and therefore also those who cared about and would mourn him, from those perils. This was also in a way the first step in the process whereby he would become an ancestor, separated from the here and now and moved into the there and then.

Just as a body in death loses control and discharges scum and impurities, so, too, the rabbis and mystics supposed, did the soul. One purifies the body, wrote the medieval North African rabbi Simeon ben Zemach Duran, "because when the soul departs the body and sees the face of the Divine Presence, the *Shechina,* out of dread it discharges impurity and must therefore be purified."[15]

In their religious imagination, the rabbis believed this discharge was something they could repair. As they washed the body, they could cleanse the soul. Here was evidence of the ancient religious conviction that "the intercession of the living could be accepted only if the dead were not immediately turned over to the torments of hell."[16]

Four volunteers had been assembled. In some Chevras, five were called; others made do with three. In extremity, even fewer would do. The men who had come to prepare Avraham's body were all *haredim.* Srulik belonged to the insular and rigidly Orthodox Reb Arelach Hasidim; Shlomo counted himself among those Hasidim who studied in and were connected with the Tshebin yeshiva; Moishe was part of the Lithuanian-style yeshiva world, the ideological antithesis of Hasidism. The last of the men, Lazar, simply defined himself as a "Jerusalemite," a strictly Orthodox Jew who moved among a number of religiously observant communities. While each of the volunteers had other occupations, most also had fathers and grandfathers who, like them, served as members of a burial society.

As always, each man had been expected to answer the summons to do a *tahara* without a moment's hesitation, simply leaving whatever he was doing to assist in these last rites. "This is a thing one cannot choose; we cannot choose the hour of death," as Shlomo put it.

I was at home in New York, wearied from a long day of teaching and about to grade some term papers when the call came around nine in the evening from a member of our community. One of the men in the synagogue had just passed away, and his family wanted him to be "cared for by our own people." Would I be prepared to join in a *tahara* later this night? I knew the man, a survivor of the Nazi death camps, whom I saw regularly in the synagogue. As a member of the Chevra Kaddisha, one did not lightly refuse such a call, even though I could always imagine some excuse for avoiding this activity which I found emotionally draining. Yes, I would be ready.

I was not always as ready to come. Sometimes Nina, who coordinated the volunteers, would preface a call with the warning "This is a hard one." "Hard ones" might be children or young people, with whom the emotional burden of *tahara* was especially heavy because we were dealing with a life so obviously cut short. "Hard ones" might also be bodies disfigured by a violent death, calls that came at times that were inconvenient, such as holiday periods. Or "hard ones" might be those sessions where only one other volunteer was available and the entire task had to be done by a Chevra made up of two. But this evening's call was relatively easy: an elderly man who had died at home after a short illness and whom we all knew.

The request came from the family, but it was as if the dead man himself was asking us. Of course we who knew him could not deny this assistance in this last act of his earthly existence. Three of us were there to meet his body when, around ten at night, still warm from the recently extinguished flame of life that had burned within, it arrived at the funeral home.

While we always treated every body we worked on with care and respect, remaining scrupulous in our adherence to ritual and custom, there was something different when the one we were preparing was someone we had known in life, someone from our local community. After all, we encountered these people not simply as dead bodies; we had known them as living persons, with biographies that intersected with our own. It was as if the bodies of these people still retained the social prerogatives that the persons who once inhabited them held. We might evidence the difference in the extra care we took to ask if the family wanted to use the deceased man's own prayer shawl or *kittel*. Or we might move his limbs and trunk a bit more tenderly as we dressed him in the shrouds or laid him in the coffin. At the outset, perhaps we might rush to the funeral parlor so as not to leave the body abandoned or unprepared a moment longer than absolutely necessary. It was all very personal.

This particular day, a weekday in early summer, the call to serve (which could come several times a week in Jerusalem, where the community served was large, but in other places, where fewer people made use of the Chevra, could come as seldom as once a month) was not especially difficult to answer. But there were times when it was not easy to drop everything and do the work of the Chevra.

"I remember sitting down at the festive meal at my son's bar mitzvah," one man reported, "and suddenly getting the call and having to depart just as we were about to begin eating and singing. No one wanted me to go." Yet such was the sense of obligation among those who joined the Chevra that even at the hardest times, they would answer the call. "Of course I had to go."

Yet those volunteers who came even at these problematic times did so because, as one explained, they saw themselves as "the vessels of a commandment." The dead were like a holy Torah scroll; neither could be left unattended. It was a parallelism that I would find recalled throughout the *tahara*.

By now, for most of those who served, this was a familiar activity—not as disquieting as when they had done it the first time. Nevertheless, there was something about that first time, the "awe and trembling," as one of them put it, that was unforgettable and that each volunteer tried to retain forever after.

When I came home that night after my first *tahara*, I was struck at how easily I had handled this dreaded first close encounter with a corpse. Before going to the funeral parlor, I had worried that I would be frozen with anxiety or repelled by the sights and smells. But while I had a hard time looking at the stiff body of the elderly gentleman whom I, along with two others, prepared for burial, and I was anxious as I poured the water over him, dressed him in his shrouds, and placed the broken shards upon his eyes—the tasks I had been assigned by the more experienced volunteers who took me through this evening—when I came home, I marveled at how easily I seemed to put the night's work behind me. Of course I discussed nothing with my family about the details of what I had done, in line with the accepted custom that the work of the Chevra Kaddisha was privileged. It detracted from the honor due the dead for us to talk about what we had done.

The hour was late, and I felt exhausted, maybe a bit drained, so I decided to go to bed. I did shower and douse myself liberally with cologne. But then, with surprising ease, I fell into a deep slumber almost as soon as my head touched the pillow. And then I began to dream. In my dream I found myself in the locker room of the local Jewish community center, where each day I went for a workout and a swim. In my dream, I was getting dressed; as usual, around me were the men whom I often saw on these daily visits. Most of them were retirees who came in the off-hours that I favored. Their faces were familiar, as were their jokes and small talk. But this time among the familiar faces was one older man; I thought I knew who he was, but I could not quite identify him. He was silent as he sat on the bench near me. As I dressed, I found myself watching him with furtive, sidelong glances. Who *was* that man? When he stood up, he seemed a bit stiff, but a lot of the old-timers did, especially when they were tired out from their exercise regimes or racquetball games. At last he sat down and opened his locker to start getting dressed. As he took the garments from the cubbyhole and began to put them on, I suddenly realized who he was. For instead of putting on clothes, like the rest of us, this man was dressing himself in the linen shrouds of the Jewish dead. This was the man whose body I had just prepared for burial.

"What's wrong?" my wife asked as she nudged me awake from what she told me was a shuddering in my sleep. "Nothing," I said, realizing I had not quite escaped the world of the dead untouched. "Just a dream."

"The book binders who prepare the holy books often step on those books, those who make the blessed tefillin often bang the table with them, and the doctors who take care of us—well, you know, they're not always so sensitive. So it can also be with those who do the work of the Chevra Kaddisha. But we try not to reach such a moment; we try to act as if each time we do the work, we are awestruck as we were that first time," one of the men explained as he took out the supplies he needed for the *tahara*.

The ceremonial preparations the Chevra carries out demonstrate that the death of an individual cannot by itself breach the tie to the group and the living. It makes clear that "there is a difference, an important difference, between when we die to our stethoscopes and encephalograms: *somatic* death; when we die to our nerve ends and molecules: *metabolic* death; and when we die to those around us—grandchildren and creditors, siblings and neighbors—an end we might call our *social* death." [17] From the moment the Chevra takes over the care of the dead, it illustrates the fact that the mourners and the community will determine the nature of their leaving, the disposition of the dead and the character of death. The actions of the Chevra represent a way that the living indicate

that when people die, "we want them back to let them go again—on our
terms, at our pace, to say you may not leave without permission, forgiveness,
or respects—to say we want our chance to say goodbye," as we see fit.[18]

The task had to be done with great care and ritual scrupulousness. "Death,"
as Hertz reminds us, "by striking the individual, has given him a new character; his body which . . . was in the realm of the ordinary, suddenly leaves it; it
can no longer be touched without danger."[19] Thomas Lynch, undertaker and
poet, calls fresh corpses "hatchlings of a new reality."[20] The task of the Chevra
is to help initiate that new reality by taking the new character, which is so
threatening and malevolent, and making it pure and beneficent.

To be sure, this belief is not unique to Judaism. "Spirituality," as Leon
Wieseltier perceptively notes, "is surrounded by superstition. It is a permanent
siege."[21] Anthropologists and folklorists have cataloged many groups that believe "that the body is at certain times particularly exposed to the attacks of evil
spirits and to all the harmful influences by which man is threatened"; the moments immediately following death are prominent among these, occasions
when the body's "diminished powers of resistance have to be reinforced" by
other means and other people.[22] Indeed, in many cultures, that is why people
believe that upon its demise, the corpse must be expeditiously "forearmed
against demons. This preoccupation inspires, at least partly, the ablutions and
various rites connected with the body immediately after death."[23]

"When death arrives," as the historian Philippe Ariès reminds us, "it is regarded as an accident, a sign of helplessness or clumsiness."[24] In response, the
Chevra tries to create a countersign. *Tahara* and its ablutions, which must be
accomplished as soon as possible after the demise, as such may be understood
as the markings of that countersign, a means of denying human helplessness and
death's malevolence. It aims to undo death's contaminations while ceremonially
neutralizing its jeopardy. It does so by providing the dead with (and thereby
proving the community's power to engender) a spiritual repair that was lost
when death first arrived. It is also possible to understand this repair as an expression of a lingering Jewish solicitude for the essential person who inhabited
that body. In much that is done by the Chevra Kaddisha there is the unmistakable inference that, even after the moment of death, the body still has that
person attached to it, one who will change form shortly thereafter but never
cease to exist.

The Chevra's assignment has a certain paradoxical quality. On the one hand,
handling the corpse requires the members of the Chevra to confront the reality
of its death. For those who look directly upon the deceased, there is no making
believe that what lies before them is not a cadaver. Yet at the same time, every-

thing that is done for this corpse points to a belief in the continuity of life and of some ongoing spiritual existence that includes the person whose dead body they must prepare. *Tahara* defines a sort of "supreme initiation" into "a new spiritual existence" where death has no dominion.[25] As this kind of transitional rite, *tahara*, the domain of the betwixt and between, tries to absorb the contradictions in the Jewish notion of death, which at once affirm the body's decay and end as well as the idea of some inevitable resurrection.

Tahara is thus not just a ceremony that marks the end of a life; it is no less an expression of collective confidence that even for the lifeless body, death is not final.[26] In traditional religious terms, the Chevra prepares the body not just for burial but also for its promised resurrection and the soul for its return to the divine source from whence it came.[27] While such a belief in the resurrection of the dead has been "disputed over the centuries," it remains a guiding principle behind the work of *tahara*.[28] The details of any physical rebirth are steeped in mystery. Will the dead be reborn into the body as it was at death or at its most vigorous? The theological texts are by no means uniform or clear on this matter. [29]

Even for the faithful, the belief is problematic, for if the righteous dead are offered an eternal life in a heavenly Garden of Eden, as the rabbis have asserted, then it is not at all clear why they would desire messianic resurrection. If, however, resurrection of the dead is the ultimate Jewish destiny, what is the eternity of Eden? While mystics, theologians, and believers have considered these matters and speculated about the ultimate reunion of body and spirit, the fact remains that we can describe very little about this sequel for the dead because it remains largely in the realm of belief and imagination, overlaid with syncretistic beliefs and traditions. Whatever Judaism means by it, the idea of resurrection clearly resonates with something other than a physical renaissance. It is perhaps most fundamentally an expression of the conviction that a continuing life force emanates from the dead. As such—even more than a belief in the immortality of the soul—resurrection, the silent partner of so much of what Judaism does in its treatment of the dead, is "the most literal and dogmatic and complete denial of death that is imaginable."[30]

To make certain that the transition is successful and that the rupture caused by the death is repaired, every action the Chevra takes becomes heavily freighted with symbolic meaning. The body, which will be the vessel from which the journey of spiritual rebirth begins, must be treated with extraordinary respect. No unnecessary manipulations may be performed; all is mandated by ritual (though local custom dictates much of this ritual, as if to remind us all that the particular place and community from which one comes determine the way one leaves life). Except for the words that are part of the service and those necessary to guide common actions, normally no other words are spoken.

> Throughout the evening, we were all careful to touch the body only to clean and clothe it. It remained covered—especially the face and the genitals (the parts that our culture assumed the person, if living, would have wanted to shield from another's gaze)—except when we washed or poured water over it. And when we turned or manipulated the corpse, we treated the dead man as if he were still sentient. Even if his lifeless body could feel no pain, we were careful not to treat it like a carcass. So, for example, we always cradled his head as we raised or lowered him, never allowing it to bang against any of the hard surfaces on which we worked. Although his cold body could itself no longer feel cold, we kept the water we poured over it tepid. Even if no one would ever see him again, we were careful to clean every part of his body, even under his toenails and fingernails and on the balls of his feet. In effect, we treated him as we wished someone would treat each of us when our turn to be purified would come—as it surely would. Later, as we prepared to make our exit, we would beg the dead man's indulgence if we had committed any offense against him in our handling of his body and his *tahara*. The last line we spoke in the liturgy we read said simply: "But we are alive." It was something we each needed to remember as we left this place. And then, following a long moment of silence, we would quietly leave the room, at last wishing one another, "*tizku l'mitzvot*" (may you continue to be worthy to perform mitzvahs).

Regardless of their particular affiliations and experiences, the Jerusalem volunteers and I would work together as a team this afternoon, to be joined later by five additional volunteers who, along with the young earlocked and bearded hearse driver, the only paid member of the team, would complete the *minyan*—the ten-man quorum—that this Chevra always sent to a funeral. The five others were older, gray in hair and beard—having done their stints in the more active role of *tahara* in days past. The four who handled today's *tahara* ranged in age from their thirties to their sixties; all were married and had children.

The four men and I each had come early for the *tahara*, arriving before the body at the *Beit Haleveiyot*, the "house of funerals," where most of the dead in Jerusalem began their final journey. In the summer heat, even a short delay in beginning the *tahara* could result in the body's beginning to decay, something everyone wanted to avoid. The *Beit Haleveiyot* had few facilities for storage. Awaiting the body's appearance, the members of the team stood together in the parking lot on a scorchingly hot June afternoon, trying to cool themselves in the shade. They chatted softly, circumspectly, ostensibly avoiding those subjects that might lead to *kalus rosh,* an attitude of levity inappropriate as a prologue to what they were about to do. But human beings being what they were, they could not altogether stop the normal flow of profane and simple conversations or the irreverent thoughts that—perhaps to break the tension—found their way into their talk. As soon as the body arrived, however, the men quickly shifted into action and chased away their other preoccupations. While the ambulance pulled into the parking lot, one of them radioed the central office to confirm the delivery, saying simply: "It has arrived, and we are dealing with it."

In America, the body commonly preceded our arrival. It lay on the tablet, sometimes for hours or overnight, while the family made arrangements for the funeral. When the family requested the most traditional and Orthodox of funerals, a *shomer* (guardian) was there. This man would sit with the body or in an antechamber all night and sometimes much of the day, reciting psalms. "You, who have shown me many and grievous troubles, restore me back to life, and bring me back from the depths of the earth" was a favorite refrain.

The tradition does not allow the dead to remain unaccompanied until they are finally put to rest in their graves. This would be ignominious, and it would add to the anxiety the living felt about death: that it meant abandonment and excruciating loneliness for both the survivors and the deceased. This mandate to stay near the freshly dead was, of course, not a custom limited to Jews. Most cultures imposed "on the survivors the duty of keeping the deceased company during this dreaded period, to keep watch by his side . . . in order to keep malignant spirits at bay."[31] Finding those who were ready and willing to fulfill this role in contemporary society, however, was not easy, for it required people able to take off large blocks of time from the rest of their active lives, and it demanded as well a discipline and calm that few seemed able to provide. Sitting alone with the dead and one's thoughts and whispering the words of the Psalmist for hours on end, in the dark of night in an often deserted funeral chapel, is not a task that many embrace. In these days, therefore, there were people who did this for a fee.

In other communities, where the preparations for burial were carried out by Jewish volunteers who did not necessarily hew to all the demands of strict Orthodoxy, *shmira* (guardianship) may become an opportunity for a community to display some of its core values. Thus, for example, in Mount Airy, a suburb of Philadelphia, where a liberal, Reconstructionist burial society operates, on occasion such vigils have been conducted by men and women together, a reflection of the community's deeply held commitment to egalitarianism and communalism.[32]

But in Jerusalem, in line with the traditional requirement to bring the dead to burial as soon as possible, there are seldom occasions that call for a *shomer*. Indeed, in Jerusalem, viewed by Jewish tradition as "the gateway to heaven," the Chevra will even bury the dead at night—something the nine-to-five Americans never do—and thus the body is hardly ever in a position to need a guardian.

Efficiently and with few words, the men of the Chevra took the gurney from the driver and wheeled it into the room where they and the body would now be alone. Papers were signed, and the metal door to the small *tahara* room clanged shut.

The room was barely wider than the raised tablet on which the body lay. Here, in this room so much shaped by the mundane realities of bodily concerns, religious metaphors, spiritual concerns, and ancient mysteries competed with the concrete decay of and concern with death for the minds and hearts of those present. Around the room's perimeter were lockers, pipes, hoses, and buckets. This chamber where the ritual transformation and purification of the body was to take place, where the dead were readied for their ultimate journey, was not constructed for spiritual meditation or beauty. Nor did it radiate with human dignity. Rather, it was simply a staging area where the physical aesthetic did not matter. What mattered was the ritual aesthetic; it had to be maintained: silence, dignity, order, seriousness, alacrity. This was not unusual. In even the most regal and ornate of American funeral parlors, places where I had prepared the dead with the local Chevra, the chamber where we did the work of *tahara* commonly radiated a profane ambience in which buckets and hoses, sinks and shrouds, sponges and washcloths, grapples and clasps, scissors and nail files, and all sorts of other implements by which the dead were cleaned, swaddled, and boxed stood out. It was as if the overwhelming profanity of these places challenged the ability of those who did the *tahara* to overcome their character, no less than *tahara* challenged the profanity of death. The beauty to be found here was that regardless of how things looked, spiritual and religious concerns would overwhelm the material. The care and the precise order in which the ritual would be carried out, for rich or poor, the powerful and the powerless, were to be identical.

We were to treat all our dead in exactly the same way. No step of the ritual was to be changed, and each year we would gather as a group and review the steps of our ritual to make certain we had not changed one iota of our accepted cus-

toms. But familiarity always threatened to foster, if not contempt, then a matter-
of-fact carelessness. We might be tired after the end of a long workday, wishing
we were elsewhere, or otherwise preoccupied. Yet there to remind us of what we
were doing were the words that accompanied our actions, the poetry of the
liturgy that got us past it all. And then, too, amid all the clutter, the barrels for
dirty sheets, and the paraphernalia of undertaking in the workroom behind the
funeral chapel someone had tacked a sign on the wall. "Remember you are handling someone's most precious loved one; act with respect." The sign might be
for those who were employed in undertaking. The rituals that guided our behavior in the Chevra Kaddisha guaranteed we would not forget.

Beginning the work, "Srulik" removed from the shelf a large metal case and
placed it on a side table. From here he would remove some of the materials
necessary for the *tahara:* a catch to hold the turned-over body while it was being washed on one side and then the other; sponges to soap it, combs for the
hair, files and toothpicks for cleaning under the nails, and unrefined flax to fill
what he called the "impure orifices." The men checked to make certain they
had enough of all the materials they would need.

The body had arrived naked, covered only by a large piece of blue crepe
paper; the dead were to be isolated "from the sight of the living, who must not
see the mystery of death."[33] It was now 2:30, and the funeral was called for 4:00
in the afternoon. Before that target time the body would be dressed, wrapped,
and moved out to the public hall where it would lie in state on a low catafalque,
as the mourners and their friends and relatives gathered for eulogies and a final
leave-taking before burial. During the *tahara* the men barely uttered a word,
using hand signals wherever they could, trying as much as possible to maintain
the dignity of silence in the presence of the dead, whose silence was perfect. To
be sure, they had each done this so many times before that they really needed
to say very little to one another. Every one of them knew just what to do.

There was always an overwhelming quiet as we entered the room in which the
body lay. We exchanged very few words, spoke only about our ritual activities or
to recite prayers. Occasionally, we would say a word or two to guide or coordinate our activities. But nothing else. We relied on pointing, shrugging of shoulders, and nods of heads to communicate what we needed done. Indeed, for years,
while I worked with a variety of other volunteers, I knew nothing about them
other than their names—and sometimes even these remained in doubt. We were
here to carry out a *mitzvah*, not to chat. And we followed that mandate strictly.

Before commencing their labors, the men washed their hands. Water, aqua vitae, remained an overarching Jewish symbol of life capable of obliterating its opposite, the decay and contamination of death. Ritually, the members of the Chevra poured a cupful of water over each hand three times, and then recited a prayer, enlisting the mercy and assistance of heaven. While washing their hands they recited no words of blessing, but the act itself echoed with the benedictions that commonly accompanied such ablutions when they were carried out on happier occasions. Each man in turn laved his hands, for no matter what he actually did in the procedure that followed—whether he washed the dead body or simply witnessed this activity by others, whether he turned the body or simply helped wrap it—he was included in the process. No one could assist in the process of purification if he himself were not pure.

The ritual reminded them that however coarse and vulgar what they would do next might seem, by associating it with matters of the spirit and God, they were elevating that which was most profane to the most sacred. In spite of what they did, they were neither undertakers nor gravediggers; they were instead pure instruments of the community, agents to the angels, conductors who sent the dead to a higher plane and helped protect those among the living who remained behind. Together, they began to pray:

Master of the Universe, have mercy upon Avraham the son of Solomon, the deceased before us, for he is the son of Abraham, Isaac, and Jacob your servants. May his soul and spirit rest with the righteous, for you resurrect the dead and also bring death to the living. Blessed art thou who replies to the supplications of your people Israel with pardon and forgiveness for their sins and transgressions. May it therefore be thy will, our God and the God of our forebears, that the angels of mercy surround the deceased, thy servant and the child of your maidservant. And thou, O Lord and God of our forebears, who gives wisdom to the wretched and delivers him from all trouble and a day of disaster and the empire of Gehenna, blessed art thou, great in kindness and master of mercy. Blessed art thou who makes peace on high for his servants, those in awe of his name. Blessed is he who mercifully redeems his people Israel from all sorts of calamities. May it therefore be thy will, our God and the God of our forebears, that you recall the merit of the holy covenant that marks his flesh, that it may serve to redeem him from a fiery hell and set him free. Blessed art thou who makes the covenant with mercy. With mercy conceal and shroud the sins of the deceased, your servant, save him from the fire, for he needs thy many mercies and thou our Lord are good and forgiving to all those who call unto you. Blessed art thou great of counsel and mighty and merciful deeds. May you lead him in the footsteps of the righteous to Eden, for it is the place of the upstanding, pre-serving the limbs of the righteous. Blessed art thou who bestows great mercies and forgiveness to the dead among thy people Israel.

On the surface these prayers aimed to somehow defuse the anger of God and those pernicious forces that the ancients surely associated with death and whose echoes remain embedded in traditional Jewish responses to it. But they also helped offset the possible feelings of impotence that the living feel when they see one of their own freshly dead. The prayer seems to imply that we, the living, can still save this one of our own from death's worst fate. Gone, too, in these words is the revulsion that the living might feel toward the dead.[34]

The content of the prayer was also significant. First was the echo of the primitive and perhaps essential fear of those who saw death, as indeed every-thing, as coming from the mighty hand of God, calculating that "if I am an-gry at Him and I express my anger, He will only reach out and smite me some more."[35] To offset this anger, they needed to publicly acknowledge their sub-servience to that same God, while enlisting his tender mercies. While the prayers were recited on behalf of the dead—an extension of the themes first raised in the deathbed confessional—they also could serve as a protective in-cantation for the living.

For some of the people who worked on the Chevra, these words and the others recited during the *tahara* were a refuge, a recitation that kept one oc-cupied emotionally and thereby prevented him or her from being over-whelmed by the stark actuality of the corpse and all it signified. Like so many other rituals that surrounded death and its aftermath, these prayers were what anthropologist Mary Douglas has called "focussing mechanisms" that helped direct one's attentions in the face of something that otherwise had the poten-tial for knocking over all the walls that separated the living from the dead.[36]

For me, particularly in the early days of my service on the Chevra, the book of prayers was a welcome sanctuary for my eyes, a place to which I would retreat whenever the sight of mortality was more than I could bear. I focused on my recitations keenly. When the edema-filled hands of the corpse, its alabaster pal-lor and absolute lifelessness, the oozing of bodily fluids, the powerful odor of death, or other such corporeal realities shook my confidence in immortality, I eagerly volunteered to be the one to recite the prayers, allowing the others on the team to wash the body and handle its reality. In time, however, like so many who had done this before me, I learned to manage the body, to hold its ice-cold hands, to turn it one way or the other, to close the eyes or mouth if they were opened, to wash, lift, and comb it, to clean carefully with a toothpick beneath the fingernails and toenails, to dress it and prepare it for the final journey. Hearing someone say the words before we began became a sufficient lift for my spirits that otherwise would have crumbled under the weight of the cadaver.

As they removed the covering sheet to expose the dead man for the first time, one of the men recited a verse from the third chapter of the book of Zachariah. These were "words from Heaven," first spoken by an angel of the Lord to Joshua the High Priest: "Remove the filthy garments from him. And to him he said, Behold, I have caused your iniquity to pass from you, and I will dress you in festive garments."

The choice of this verse, whose recitation as part of the *tahara* was first recommended by the author of the *Ma'aver Yabbok,* a popular seventeenth-century mortuary manual written by Aaron ben Moses Berachia of Modena (Italy), is not incidental.[37] In its original setting, the verse describes an encounter between the forces of God and Satan, and hints that this is not a final act on a decaying body but the first act of the drama of resurrection and toward final redemption.

And he showed me Joshua the high priest standing before the angel of the Lord, and Satan standing at his right hand to thwart him. And the Lord said to Satan, The Lord rebukes you, O Satan; the Lord that has chosen Jerusalem rebukes you. Is not this a brand plucked out of the fire? And Joshua was clothed with filthy garments, and stood before the angel. And he answered and spoke to those who stood before him, saying, remove the filthy garments from him. And to him he said, behold, I have caused your iniquity to pass from you, and I will dress you in festive garments. And I said, let them set a pure mitre upon his head. And they set a pure mitre upon his head, and dressed him with garments. And the angel of the Lord stood by. And the angel of the Lord warned Joshua, saying, thus says the Lord of hosts; If you will walk in my ways, and if you will keep my charge, and you will also judge my house, and will also guard my courts, then I will give you access among these who stand by. Hear now, O Joshua the high priest, you, and your friends who sit before you; for they are men of good omen; for, behold, I will bring my servant the Branch. For behold the stone that I have laid before Joshua. Upon one stone are seven facets; behold, I will engrave its inscription, says the Lord of hosts, and I will remove the iniquity of that land in one day. On that day, says the Lord of hosts, every one of you shall invite his neighbor under his vine and under his fig tree.

On the verge of the moment when the dead are to be laid to rest, this verse is a reminder (ostensibly for the dead but surely more for the living who handle the defiling corpse) that, dressed like priests, the dead will all arise again on that day at the end of time when everyone "shall invite his neighbor under his vine and under his fig tree." Just when one might be frightened away by the reality of death, here are verses that resonate with the promise of renewed life.

Why is the body washed? The religious would say that it is about raising the dead person from a "spiritual state of unworthiness."[38] But dirt, of course, as Mary Douglas has reminded us, "exists in the eye of the beholder"; there is no such thing as "absolute dirt." Thus, eliminating dirt "is not a negative movement, but a positive effort to organise the environment."[39] This washing is not about cleaning a body that in most cases arrived fairly unsoiled. Rather, it is about making order out of chaos, but not just order: the ultimate order of life, curving the line into a circle.

"Just as when one is born, we wash his body," wrote the Midrash on Ecclesiastes, "so too when one dies his body is washed."[40] Just as at birth one enters into this world, so at death "one is born into the world to come."[41] Echoing this Midrashic sentiment, Mircea Eliade notes: "In water, everything is 'dissolved,' every 'form' is broken up," so that "nothing that was before remains after immersion in water."[42] Just as in the volunteers' laving of their hands, here, too, the water is meant to somehow dissolve the defilement of death and assure a readiness for the rebirth of resurrection. That is to say, again to borrow from Eliade, immersion or its poured counterpart implied a capacity for "*starting time over again at its beginning*," a way to recover "the 'pure' time that existed at the moment of [the person's] creation."[43] In place of death comes an "eternal return."[44] Death is thus not linear, nor is life. They are made cyclical. Washing is not simply an instrumental task; it is to take a hand in the cycle of birth and death. It becomes the first concrete act in making death transitional to life.

Turning on the water and taking a hose in hand, Srulik, knowing that in America many volunteers were gowned and scrupulous about wearing latex gloves and all manner of protection against disease—my own Chevra even paid for our hepatitis inoculations—pointed out with what seemed pride: "In general, we don't use gloves," as if to say that this Chevra—more faithful than we who worked abroad—was willing to depend only on Heaven's protection, but then he added that even he wore protection "in cases where we receive some special instruction because the *mays* was sick."

He and the other men of the Chevra always used the word *mays* (the dead) when referring to the body.[45] From the moment they received Avraham, he was no longer a person but simply a *mays*. This reference was yet one more among many transformations that the Chevra accomplished. Yet speaking of it this way did not mean that this body could and would be treated with less than the utmost respect. Indeed, that was why, as he explained, Srulik used no gloves.

"This is a matter of conscience," he declared. To him this was an extension of the attitude he took when he ritually laved his hands before beginning: evidence that the body was not "a piece of meat" but rather like a "sheath of something holy."[46] Then he added, "You know, like the cover on a Torah scroll." Just as that covering, not inherently sacred in itself, earned a special sanctity by virtue of its serving as a covering for the holy Torah, so, too, the human body, in its death little more than flesh, retained a sanctity from its so recently having surrounded the soul that was just beginning its departure from it.

When they were finished washing the body and before they moved on to the actual purification process and the dressing, the volunteers would lave their hands again. Exposure to the contamination of death required repeated re-purifications. In some places, persons who did *tahara* were expected to first immerse themselves in a ritual bath, thereby purifying themselves before they went about the task of purifying another. But in the face of the involvements and time constraints of contemporary existence, this step frequently has been bypassed in favor of a simple laving of hands, a ritual shorthand for immersion. What remained, however, was the symbolism; the task of washing and preparing the dead was both a dangerously defiling and a sacred activity; those who did it therefore needed to purify themselves before and afterward. The washing was a ritual ordering that seemed to battle both the idea of the corruption of the dead body and the disequilibrium it had brought about. The washing sought to set everything right, clean up the mess that death had wrought in life, restore the dead via the efforts of the living.[47] One could argue that this effort was in fact an effort to somehow effect a "transfer of properties by sympathy or likeness" to the dead man.[48] As they made themselves pure, so they could make him pure. Or, alternatively, the defilement around them was so powerful, the pollution of death so spiritually frightening, that they had to repeatedly engage in purification exercises. Whatever the case, "the union of opposites," as Douglas suggests, is a common "vehicle for religious themes."[49] One might understand the entire ritual exercise here as an effort at what Douglas calls an act of "at-one-ment,"[50] bringing death and life, chaos and order into one whole.

After they had laved their hands and before they began the actual treatment of the dead body, the men recited aloud the following verse from the Seventy-eighth chapter of Psalms, a line that is ubiquitous in the liturgy of atonement: "And He is full of compassion, forgiveth iniquity, and destroyeth not, and many times has turned His anger away, and did not arouse all of His wrath." Once again, here was an invocation of the malignancy of death and a concurrent effort to mitigate it by making certain that in their activities the men did not carelessly awaken the anger of the forces of evil or the divine.

Next they set out the shrouds in which the body would be dressed and wrapped before burial. These garments, the last earthly clothing this body would have, were—here as everywhere the Jewish traditions were practiced—hand-sewn panels of white linen. Linen, probably the first vegetable fiber known to mankind (linens more than thirty-five hundred years old have been recovered from Egyptian tombs), was not always the burial garment of choice. At one time Jewish "grave-clothes were often elaborate and ornate, but this convention tended to strain the resources of the bereaved and to introduce invidious distinctions between rich and poor. In the first century, therefore, the great Gamaliel the Elder set an example by enjoining on his disciples that they bury him only in plain white linen garments, and ever since, traditionally minded Jews have followed this precedent."[51]

These white linen garments, "patterned after those worn in ancient times by the high priest when he entered the holy of holies on the Day of Atonement," would be the "celestial garb" from which the soul was "transferred to heaven," and in which on the day of resurrection this body and all those like him would "arise."[52] That miraculous day would begin, according to Jewish tradition, here in Jerusalem, and as one buried in its soil, Avraham would presumably be among the first to rise to eternal life.

Outside of Israel, where bodies were buried in coffins, the Chevra would at this point prepare the box as well, filling it with straw, taking a small sack made of the same fabric as the shrouds set aside to be a pillow and filling it with some of that straw, along with a few grains of sand from the Holy Land. But here in Israel, except in the case of soldiers or those whose bodies had been mangled in death, the dead were buried only in their shrouds and covered in a sheet (and, in the case of males, a tallit). In some places, women are covered by a *parochet,* the mantle that is used to cover the ark holding the Torah scrolls. In communities where *tahara* is handled by non-Orthodox Jews for whom egalitarianism has become a core Jewish value, accommodations are sometimes made for enfolding a woman in a tallit no different from a man's.[53]

Those who followed the ancient customs of Hillel the Elder, the talmudic sage who had established a routine for how *tahara* was to be performed, saw to it that two people handled the washing. One would pour the water, and the other would do the washing. Each section of the body was to be cleaned with water from a separate vessel. At the end, there were to be seven ablutions. For each of these steps there were special accompanying recitations. While much had changed since Hillel's time, the basic pattern of the washing and purifications remained the same generations later among those who served on the Chevra Kaddisha, although each group hewed to its own established customs, which adapted this basic ritual.

Reliance on custom and scrupulosity in all its details may be seen as yet another antidote to the anarchy of death. Custom, moreover, is the way each community puts its imprimatur on its own encounter with death's disorder. It allows the community thereby to "fill in the cracks" left by the written law and ensure a solid response to the trauma that death engendered among its own.[54] That was why the idea that each Chevra Kaddisha had its own customary way of preparing the body was deeply entrenched in Jewish tradition and supported by generations of rabbinic responsa.[55] A responsum from the nineteenth-century Austro-Hungarian rabbi Moses Schick is typical: "The Chevra Kaddisha must not change any of its customs for to do so would show contempt for all those dead who have earlier been prepared in different ways."[56] Each community needed to feel secure that it was restoring its order by doing right by its dead. The conservative tendencies with regard to maintaining local customs are probably connected to the fact that rituals surrounding death are deeply rooted in a community's sense of itself. That is, as already noted, the way a community deals with the death of its members is a reflection of how it deals not only with the fact that death has robbed it of one of its members but also with the uncomfortable reminder of the inevitability of death, the warning to the living of the limits of their control.

So deeply ingrained are these folkways and attitudes on behalf of maintaining local traditions among the Chevra Kaddisha that more often than not even those who have been doing this job for years will know *what* they must do but will not necessarily know *why* they do it. For them it is sufficient to know the custom. Deeper reasons are not needed; the reference to sacred texts and time-honored customs is more than enough. They are simply the faithful bearers of tradition; it is left to a few specialists and scholars to explain the reasons. To be sure, this kind of unquestioning trust in the supremacy of tradition is strongest among the Orthodox. Yet even among those who appear to embrace modernity and change, who try to guide their lives by reason and understanding, when it comes to death and responses to it, the willingness to embrace traditions—even those not completely understood—is stronger than at other times.

Yet while each community has its customs, ultimately every generation needs to find its own meaning in them if they are to survive. As William Graham Sumner put it, "The father dies, and the son who he has educated, even if he continues the ritual and repeats the formulae, does not think and feel the same ideas and sentiments as his father." [57]

The custom of the Jerusalem Chevra was to begin with a thorough cleansing. Following their time-honored practice, Shlomo and Moishe stood at the head and foot of the body, while Srulik, with the help of Lazar, washed it vigorously in the customary order: first the head, then the face, the neck, then on the right side the hand, chest, abdomen, the area over the kidneys, thigh, leg, and feet. The procedure was then repeated for the left side. Srulik lathered everywhere energetically. When he had covered every part of the body with soap, he took the hose and rinsed everything off. Then the others turned the body to the left side, and he did everything again. Finally, he began what was called the "internal cleansing," during which he poured water into the anus to flush out any remaining bodily waste. Srulik was scrupulous about this purging. He would not stop until he was certain there was nothing left inside. At last, when he could stream the water in three times with no bodily discharge, he was satisfied that he had fulfilled his duty.

Next, he took several strands of unrefined flax, the same fiber that Jews used to protect the precious *etrog,* the citron with which they celebrated the festival of Sukkot, and began gently to insert it into the body's cavities. Explaining this practice, he noted, "This is written in the Gemara Shabbos." He quoted the Babylonian Talmud: "And they [those who prepare the dead for burial] stop up his orifices so that no air may enter them." [58]

Why the entrance of air was a bad thing, why flax was used, how much needed to be inserted—all these were questions that did not concern him or any of the others, although one man explained that it was to separate the air of life from the ether of death. What mattered to these men, however, was simply that the Chevra was acting precisely in accordance with its venerable rules and procedures, customs that stretched back beyond memory and that those who regarded themselves as guardians of that tradition dared not change, especially in the face of death. For Srulik and others on his team, it was sufficient to cite the Talmud's unexplained injunction to stop up the orifices, to note that in Jerusalem they always checked three times to make certain all the waste was removed from the bowel cavity—knowing the reasons was not necessary.

"The mouth, too, must be closed," Lazar added. For generations people have believed that the soul survives the body and departs along with the last breath, and hence the place from where this spirit passed on must now be closed forever.[59] "The door of the soul's home for a lifetime cannot be left ajar." Here was a suggestion that, as human beings, "we see life vanish but we express this fact by the use of a special language: it is the soul, we say, which departs for another world where it will join its forefathers."[60]

Once again the body was washed to remove any remaining impurities. At the same time two of the men used toothpicks to scrape the barely visible dirt from under the fingernails and toenails. The body of one who is about to meet the creator must shine. As they completed each digit, the men counted together using the letters of the Hebrew alphabet. Just as letters and numbers were interchangeable in the Kabbalah, so here, too, the spiritual and corporeal overlapped. In this second washing, recitations accompanied each step. As the Chevra turned to each part of the body and rinsed it off, the men repeated verses from the fifth chapter of the Song of Songs, that most mysterious of all Scriptures that the rabbis themselves were not certain about whether to insert into the holy canon but which at last they did, declaring it the holiest of books because it metaphorically described a love relationship between God and the Jewish people. In this day's recitation, however, this scriptural love poem was freighted with new meanings, for the dialogue was not between two lovers but instead between the living and the dead. For the head, the men intoned the verse: "His head is as the most fine gold, his locks as bushy and black as a raven's." For the eyes: "His eyes are the eyes of doves along the riverbeds, awash with milk and fitly set." For the visage: "His cheeks are a bed of spices, as sweet as flowers, his lips like lilies dropping sweet-smelling myrrh." For the neck: "Your neck is like a tower of ivory; your eyes like the pools in Heshbon, by the gate of Bath-Rabbim." For the hands: "His hands are like circlets of gold set with emeralds. . . . " For the chest: "Your two breasts are like two fawns, twins of a gazelle." For the abdomen and lower regions: "Your belly is like a heap of wheat set about with lilies." "His entrails are like polished ivory overlaid with sapphires." The thigh: "His legs are like pillars of marble, set upon sockets of fine gold; his countenance is like Lebanon, excellent like the cedars." And then they concluded: "His mouth is most sweet; and he is altogether lovely. This is my beloved, and this is my friend, O daughters of Jerusalem."

There are many Jewish explanations for this custom, most coming from the realm of mysticism. Others see in this poetry an effort to recall the love between God and the Jews at a moment when a Jew was preparing to meet with God, which of course was one of the theological reasons for this preliminary purification. But one may no less explain this recitation as an inversion of reality, an antidote to the repulsion the living and the dead have always been assumed to feel toward each other. So as each part of the dead body is lifted or approached, the appropriate verse from this poem is recited, and hence what is repulsive is transformed into the attractive. And if, as should be the case with all sacred speech, the speaker transforms him- or herself to believe that which is being said, the incantation will work. That, without question, would turn disgust into honor, the profane into the sacred—precisely the goal of *tahara*. To be sure, there is embedded here as well the primitive fears of the dead whose wrath and malevolence this flattery is meant to annul.

While all the activities of the Chevra are generally referred to as *tahara,* the essential process of "purification" begins when the body is immersed in the *mikveh* (ritual bath) or, when no *mikveh* is available, it is rinsed for a final time by a measure of nine *kavin* of water—approximately three large buckets full, or about seven to eight gallons. [61] This must be poured over the body in one unending stream, as if the body were passing through a ritual bath. Where "nine *kavin*" are used, to make certain that the corpse is entirely covered by this water, it is raised from the large sink on which it was washed and laid upon several boards (themselves first rinsed by water). Thus every part of the body is touched by the purifying water.

Behind the tablet on which Avraham's body lay was what at first glance looked like a door leading down under the floor. When opened, though, it turned out to be a *mikveh* in which, after being washed, the body would ritually be immersed. Now the door was opened. With a swift and seemingly effortless movement, the men lifted the freshly washed body from where it lay and immersed it in the "living waters" of the ritual bath. For a moment it was almost as if the corpse had sprung to life as Avraham seemed suddenly to stand and then fall gracefully backward into the pool of clear water. Two members of the Chevra saw to it that he was completely submerged. Seven times they plunged his body into the depths.

During his life, Avraham may have immersed himself in the waters of the *mikveh* many times.[62] Perhaps he had gone for a dip before Yom Kippur, before the prayers of Rosh Hashanah, or regularly on the eve of the Sabbath or before other holidays. Perchance he was one of those who went after a nocturnal emission or following a troubling dream. But these "purifications" could only be temporary. Like any living person, Avraham would inevitably succumb to ubiquitous defilement that, according to Jewish law, accompanied human existence—and then he would need to immerse himself again in the purifying "living waters" of the *mikveh*. Now, as a cadaver, he had helplessly become *avi avot ha'tumah,* the epitome of what is defiled, just at the moment when he was about to join the ethereally pure in the world beyond. That was why he had need of an immersion that would be his last upon earth. For this *hesed shel emet,* he needed the help of the Chevra Kaddisha, the holy community, the living.

Once again actions were accompanied by a sympathetic recitation integral to the purification process. With each of the last three immersions, the men intoned verses from Scripture: "O Hope of Israel, its Savior in time of trouble, why should you be like a stranger in the land, and like a wayfaring man that turns aside to stay for a night?" (Jeremiah 14:8). This line played on the words *mikveh Yisrael,* which in addition to meaning "a ritual bath for the Jews" could also be translated as "hope of Israel."

With the next dip they repeated God's biblical injunction to the Jewish people: "You shall sanctify yourselves and you shall be holy, for I am holy" (Leviticus 11:44).

Finally, concluding with words meant to safeguard the soul, on the verge of its liberation from its physical restrictions and about to journey forth from the body whose immersions were now complete, they echoed the prophet Isaiah's promise of consolation: "No weapon that is made against you shall prosper; and every tongue that shall rise against you in judgment you shall condemn. This is the heritage of the servants of the Lord, and the reward of their righteousness appointed by me, says the Lord" (Isaiah 54:17). The immersion complete, the men repeated the words of the talmudic sage and Jewish martyr Rabbi Akiva:

> *Fortunate are you O Israel. Before whom are you purified and who is it that purifies you? Your father in heaven. For it is written: "Then I will sprinkle clean water upon you, and you shall be clean from all your filthiness; and from all your idols, will I cleanse you." And it says: "O hope [mikveh] of Israel is the Lord." As a mikveh purifies the defiled so does the Holy One Blessed be He purify Israel. (Ezekiel 36:25)*

The message was clear. The living were agents of God, the dead their beneficiary. Good triumphs over evil, life over death.

> In our Chevra we were always careful to see to it that we poured the nine *kavin* in an unending stream. Timing was everything, and this was the essential moment of *tahara;* the nine *kavin* had to cover the dead without an interruption in the flow. If there was even the tiniest gap between one bucket and the next, we would dry the corpse, cover it (or at least the face and privates), and begin again, with both the pouring and our recitations. If we did it wrong, we would have left

the dead impure; we would have failed to repair death's spiritual damage. We would have failed in our role as religious emissaries of the community and God.

As we went about the task, we tried to maintain a kind of dignity. While one of us recited the verses, the other two would handle the ablutions. As one of the pourers neared the calves of the corpse, he would nod his head to signal his accomplice to get ready so that just as the last drops of the first bucket dribbled onto the toes, the second would begin to be poured onto the head. Finally, as that volunteer reached the calf, he would signal for the third bucket to begin at the top. If we got it wrong, if one man finished pouring before the other began, so that there was not an uninterrupted flow of water over the corpse, or if we found that some part of the body had not had water run over it, we would start our ablutions again. In rituals, motives surely matter, but details are crucial. As members of the Chevra Kaddisha, we learned and accepted the idea that in the preparation of the dead, the solemn responsibilities of *tahara*, details were not trifles.

With the immersions complete, the men raised the body out of the *mikveh* and in a few rapid motions stood it erect for one last time, not allowing the feet to touch the "impure" floor but placing them on a wooden plank. Again covering its private parts and then drying it with a sheet, they called out as all Chevras do after the final ablution: *"Tahor hu, tahor hu, tahor hu"* (He is pure. He is pure. He is pure).

With this, the Chevra Kaddisha had created one of the conundrums of Jewish ritual. It had purified a dead body, which nevertheless remained the incarnation of all that could ritually contaminate. The answer to that enigma was that what the volunteers had accomplished was an internal purity, a purification of the *nefesh*, or eternal soul, even as their ministrations were made upon the decaying body. This was the order they established in the face of chaos. They purified the soul so that the empty body could be buried.

The dead, with its spirit purified but not yet freed (that would take a year), hovered somewhere in the liminal ether between ritual contamination and purity, between the profane and the sacred, between body and spirit, between an end and a beginning, death and life. Like so much else about these circumstances when death is fresh, it was enfolded in contradiction and ambiguity.[63]

In a dramatic enactment of this ambiguity, for a brief moment, the dead man seemed to stand among the living. Animated by the power of those who held him up and readied him for the donning of his shrouds, with which he would be "transferred to the side of the divine and therefore . . . no longer [be] an object of impurity."[64] It was an extraordinary sight, serving to remind all those in the room that this was someone who once lived and breathed and was counted among the members of the community. One of the volunteers proclaimed the words of Isaiah, the prophet of hope and messianic redemption: "For as the earth brings forth her bud, and as the garden causes the things that are sown in it to spring forth; so the Lord God will cause righteousness and praise to spring forth before all the nations" (Isaiah 61:11).

At this point in the *tahara*, those readying a body in accordance with Jewish traditions outside of Israel—where Jews remained a minority—would prepare a mixture of vinegar and the white of an egg in a small bowl and anoint the forehead of the dead man with it.[65] The origins of this custom were said to be rooted in the desire of Jews to be able to distinguish their dead from those of others and hence avoid the possibility that a non-Jew might be wrongly buried as a Jew, a concern that grew over the centuries in the Diaspora as the idea of special Jewish places of interment became rooted in custom. The distinctive odor and sticky texture of the mixture would serve as a silent sign to the informed. In Israel, however, where Jews control the entire process of preparation of the dead and burial, this custom is no longer practiced.

Each time we came to do a *tahara*, someone was asked to bring along an egg, which we later used in preparing the special mixture for anointing the head of the deceased. There was something oddly tragic in the cracking of the raw chicken egg, as its contents—symbolic of life—were broken into the bitter vinegar. In the metaphor of the ritual, the broken egg was the broken life, and the vinegar was the bitter exile that had replaced the sweet wine of a homeland and Jewish national sovereignty. We commingled them and rubbed a few drops of the mixture on his forehead. Then we opened a tiny sack of sacred soil from the Land of Israel, poured a few grains of its contents into the coffin and then later, after the dead man was placed inside it, over his eyes, heart, and genitals—the vital centers. The precious grains would accompany the dead in burial, as if connecting him wherever he remained in the Diaspora to the Holy Land from whence resurrection in the end of days would take place.

Next began the enrobing of the body. As they worked, the men once again recited a verse from Isaiah: "I will greatly rejoice in the Lord, my soul shall be joyful in my God; for he has clothed me with the garments of salvation, he has covered me with the robe of righteousness, as a bridegroom decks himself with a garland, and as a bride adorns herself with her jewels" (Isaiah 61:10). Just as the rabbis were wont to point out that on the days of joy a Jew "should keep in mind the day of death," so on this day so obviously sad, they now invoked moments of joy.[66] The invocation of joy and wedlock while dealing with the corpse was, of course, a way of neutralizing the disquieting and painful character of death, an incantational analogue to whistling in the dark. It was also a way of emphasizing that death was an initiation rather than a termination. Inversion remains one of the most powerful means we have of dealing with what otherwise would defeat us.

With swift movements the men now seized a deep white linen hat, a semicircular cap, called the *mitznefet*—the same term used in the Bible for the priest's mitre. In this ritual, the dressing of the dead man would parallel the robing of the priest before his participation in the temple service. In both cases, the profane was being made holy. In both, the one wearing the mitre was seeking atonement for himself, his family, and the Jewish people.

Taking the hat in hand, the men quoted the appropriate Scripture: "And I said, Let them set a pure mitre upon his head. And they set a pure mitre upon his head, and dressed him with garments. And the angel of the Lord stood by" (Zachariah 3:5). They pulled the hat snugly over the dead man's head, covering his entire face and down to his neck. Lazar declared, "And with the linen mitre shall he be attired" (Leviticus 16:4).

Next they clothed the *mays* in a *tallit katan,* a garment meant to mirror the undergarment of ritual fringes worn by Jewish males in line with the biblical injunction (Numbers 15:39) to "look upon them and remember all the commandments of the Lord." But there were no fringes on this garment, no strings tied with knots and loops, for the dead man can no longer observe these commandments. There were no real knots in any of the shrouds, nothing that would symbolically bind the body or prevent the soul from escaping to heaven.[67] This was, after all, a robing that carried a symbolic meaning, a preparation for an encounter of the spirit. For all the care taken in dressing the body, the fact remained that almost no living person other than those who entered this room would ever see this sight.

Swiftly, two members of the Chevra reached for the matching white trousers, which were sewn shut at the bottom. Each man took one of the dead man's legs and slipped it into the long pants that enclosed his legs all the way to his toes. In a single rapid motion, they pulled them up and wrapped a white band around the waist, tying it with a simple slipknot. Outside of Israel, the Chevra would also bind the pants near the ankles with two slender straps, but here there were no such bindings. "And his linen breeches shall he put upon his flesh," Lazar said, continuing with the verses from *Torat Kohanim,* the text of Leviticus (6:3).

Except for the verses they recited, the men of the Chevra remained eerily silent, which made the chafing of the linen sound strikingly loud as they took hold of the *kutonet,* a large white tunic, that they pulled over the *tallit katan.* The two who had put on the trousers now raised the arms of the dead man and slipped them into the sleeves, which came down to about his fingertips.

Shlomo announced, "And he shall don a tunic of linen" (Leviticus 16:3).

Next came the *kittel,* the white outer coat that traditional Jewish men wore on various occasions during their lifetimes. A man would don it for the first time under the wedding canopy and then wear it in the synagogue on the Day of Atonement. Others put it on at the Passover Seder table, to commemorate the liberation of the Jewish people from Egypt and their rebirth as a nation. In each case, the *kittel* was meant to remind the wearer that persons could slip on a new coat, liberate themselves from their past, cover whatever sins or defilement they had engendered, and hence purify themselves. Donning a *kittel* at the *tahara* and end of life was thus a way to put on a new garment and begin again one last time. It was a way to redefine death as liberation, an exodus from the bondage and confinements of this world.

> For years on Yom Kippur, my father would tell me, as he put on his white *kittel,* before singing the opening words of the haunting Kol Nidre, that he wore this garment, as his father had before him and as I would from the day I married, as a reminder of his mortality. "We are all only human when we stand before our Maker," he once told me. But when he saw how this thought frightened me when I was young, he would add that this same *kittel* also gave him comfort in the sure knowledge that in this coat, in which for so many years he had prayed for atonement, he would "meet the Almighty" when his time came. And when that day of his death did at last come, we who mourned him sent his *kittel* to the Chevra Kaddisha, which saw that he was buried in it—its buttons removed in line with the tradition so that his soul could soar out freely to its heavenly abode.

In the Jerusalem Chevra, the custom was to array the dead only in a linen *kittel* that came with and matched the rest of the shrouds. It extended fully three-quarters down the body and had long sleeves that completely enveloped the wearer's arms. In some places the *kittel* was already stitched shut; in others, it needed to be closed. When put on, the right side was folded over the left, so that the coat was closed atop the heart.

The coat was now bound with the *avnet* or, as it was commonly called in Yiddish, the *gartel,* a simple white belt. Three times around they wrapped it while intoning the verse from Leviticus: "And he shall be girded with a linen girdle" (16:4).

In America, the Chevra tied an elaborate thirteen-tiered knot at this point, with two persons twisting it as they both repeated the first thirteen letters of the Hebrew alphabet and topping it off with three loops to form the Hebrew letter ש: *shin,* a letter used as a mnemonic for one of the mystical names of God, Shaddai.[68]

"We do none of that here," Srulik commented when we compared notes. Then he added, "When we get a body from America for burial here, we take all those knots out right away."

For women, the entire process of the *tahara* was largely the same—with some important differences, foremost among them the fact that women were bathed, purified, and dressed by other women. Only when it came time for the actual procession to the burial did the women of the Chevra turn the body over to their male counterparts for the final steps. Then the dead woman, her hair unbound but covered with the *mitznefet,* had her face covered with a special veil. "But they shall not go in to see when the holy things are covered, lest they die," the members of the Chevra would say as they placed the veil on the woman's face, drawing the parallel between the sanctums of the Holy Temple—"the most holy things"—and the face of a dead woman (Numbers 4:20).

In place of the *tallit katan,* an item of clothing they would never have worn in life, women were instead garbed in an *ephod,* a long apron. Their trousers were bound at the bottom, and then all the other shrouds that the men wore were also placed upon them: the *kutonet, kittel,* and the *avnet.*

Fully garbed at last, Avraham's body was once again placed on the table over which the *sovev,* a large linen winding-sheet, had been placed. As they laid him down this last time, the men of the Chevra echoed their forefather Jacob's parting words to his sons on that day generations earlier when they took their youngest brother, Benjamin, down to Egypt for what would be a dramatic and eventful meeting with their long-lost brother Joseph. These were also, it turned out, the words that accompanied them on their descent from the promised land on the fateful journey that would lead to Jewish exile, slavery, and ultimately redemption: "And may God Almighty give you mercy" (Genesis 43:14).

Jacob's encounter with death served as a scriptural paradigm for much of what Jews did. Perhaps more than with any other biblical character, Scripture had described Jacob's death and its aftermath. That story had become a kind of subtext to much that Jews did when death was near. Echoes of it still reverberated in many of the practices that had become part of Jewish tradition and contemporary custom.

By punctuating each of their own steps and the overwhelming silence in the room with these verses from Scripture, whether from the love poem in the Song of Songs, the description of the garbing of the high priest, the prophesies of Isaiah and Zachariah, or the narrative of Jacob and his sons, the first Israelites, the members of the Chevra Kaddisha were not only maintaining their sense of awe in the face of death. They were symbolically placing this death, and their own activities, into a long Jewish chain of being and venerated setting of hallowed words and events. By framing the repetition from a sacred text, they could avoid the capacity of death to make them feel "overwhelmed by the meaninglessness of profane existence."[69] They were putting this death into the sacred order of Scripture. Repeating the sacred words and echoing the sacred myths, they were in effect also recalling—sharing in—the patrimony of Jewish tradition. Thus, in the presence of death, with all its attendant anxieties and unknowns, these ritualized repetitions were demonstrating not only that "there is nothing new under the sun" and that "things repeat themselves forever," but also that through this repetition, some of the anxiety engendered by the uncanny, the unique, and the unknown can be quieted and that the relentlessness of time and even the virulence of death may somehow be diminished.[70] Repetition serves as a corrective to the finality of death.

The body was swaddled in the cream-colored *sovev,* wrapped at an angle so as to enclose it entirely from head to foot, again folding the right side over the left. This sheet completely covered all that had been left exposed: the hands and a small portion of the chest. The sheathing was loosely bound so that at the grave it could be opened, allowing the soul to "slip" out easily from the body that lay in the ground.

Later, before bringing the body outside the room, they would place a tallit around it. Since no coffins were used in Israel, the tallit for men and the *sovev* for women were all that the world outside this room would see before burial.

Our dressing of the dead was complete. We placed the *sovev* diagonally over the open casket with a tallit on top so that when we lowered the dead man into it, he would become enfolded into these. First the head, then the left side, and next the right, with the feet wrapped last—the customary order was never to be changed. One of the ritually tied fringes, with their knots and circles used to stand for the letters of the divine name, had been cut so as to make this prayer shawl unfit for use in prayer, for the dead did not pray in the same way as did the living. In some cases, the remaining fringes on the corners were tied to one another, to further invalidate the garment for use in normal prayer. Where possible, the tallit used, like the *kittel,* was to be the dead man's own. But before burial, all its special adornments—for example, the silver or embroidered collars that some people liked to put on—were removed. As with the shrouds, the intention was to erase in death all the distinctions between the rich and the poor. Before God, after all, everyone was to be judged by the quality of their lives, not by the charm of their possessions. We wrapped the *sovev,* and it covered everything.

Whenever we closed the coffin in which we placed the dead, it always struck me that I and the others who had prepared him for burial would be the last to ever see this body. But of course these thoughts contradicted the doctrine, which suggested that we were only preparing him for a temporary period: that he would once again arise, throw off his deathly slumber, and join the reborn at the end of time. Eternal death and eternal life mingled mysteriously in all we did. Even though we in the Chevra Kaddisha handled these preparations, ultimately we really did not know what exactly it was for which we were preparing our inert charges.

Throughout their preparations, all the men of the Chevra Kaddisha had worked alone. Now, when Avraham's body was completely swaddled, a new drama would unfold. This ceremony was far from universal, but it was customary in this Jerusalem society. One of the men of the Chevra opened the door to the room and called in the dead man's son, who had been waiting outside. What he would be called upon to do was not easy, yet because "father and son are but one body," as the ancient *Sefer Hasidim* put it, "the sons must be saddened."[71] It was time for the son to close the dead man's eyes and to sprinkle a bit of dust from the soil of the Holy Land upon them. The son came hesitantly into the room. A large man in his forties, still shaken by the fresh shock of his father's death, he was led by hand for the few steps in from the door to the prone and wrapped corpse. For surely the last time, he was face-to-face with his father as a dead man. Had there been other sons, they, too, would have been called into the room (and had there been only daughters or no children at all, Srulik or someone else from the Chevra would have done and said all this), and each would repeat precisely the same movements and words. Avraham, the son of Solomon, however, had only one son. With his eyes awash in tears and blinded by grief, the son seemed unable to move on his own. Quietly, Lazar took him to the sink, where he handed him a cup to lave his hands; three times he poured the contents of the cup first on his left hand, then on his right. Lazar gently nudged him back to stand facing his father.

Once, no doubt, the father had come in to see his newborn son swaddled in a blanket and watched him open his eyes to the world and to life. Now his son had come in to see his father swaddled in the garments of death and to close his eyes to the world and to life. The circle was complete.

Poised now near the head of the body, the son swayed back and forth as if he were at prayer. His eyes tightly closed, he seemed to try to avoid staring at his father or to lose himself in devotions. Even though his father was swathed in shrouds and only his eyes were visible, surely this was not the way the son wished to remember him. But there was no escaping the reality there before him. Lazar cued him softly; he knew how difficult this was. He could still recall his own feelings when he began working on the Chevra—"It was very hard, impossible to forget," as he put it. To look upon the face of the dead, to be reminded of mortality, and to do that in the presence of a parent's body, was surely among the more haunting experiences that Jewish custom provoked. Lazar gently pushed up the *mitznefet* so that the dead man's eyes were revealed. Next he opened a small sealed pouch in which was a small measure of fine grains of Jerusalem sandstone. He passed it to the son and indicated he should take a small portion with his fingers.

Srulik now took over. He addressed the son: "Repeat what I say." And now he intoned the famous words from Genesis, the declaration of God to Adam that human beings would forever be mortal, "for dust you are, and to dust shall you return" (Genesis 3:19). [72] Srulik shifted the son's hand and tapped it so that he could sprinkle a pinch of the grains into the corner of his father's lifeless eyes. When the dust had dropped, Srulik guided the son's hands to close the eyes. The words he spoke next were those, according to Scripture, which God spoke to Jacob when urging him to follow his sons down to Egypt. The rabbinic commentators had seen these words as comforting for a Jacob who, they believed, had prophetically envisioned the bondage and suffering to come in Egypt even as he also foresaw the liberation of the Exodus and the return it promised. According to the account in Genesis, God had met Jacob's reluctance to be the last of his family to leave the promised land to join his children, with the assurance that he should "fear not." But the last pledge he made before parting was that "Joseph shall put his hand upon your eyes" (Genesis 46:4). It was a declaration made by God to put the dying father's mind at ease. Joseph, a free man, would be there to bury his father; he would close his father's eyes and bring the body back to Hebron in the Holy Land of his birth and the cave of Machpelah to be buried with his forebears.

As Jews had for generations, Avraham's son repeated the words of God's promise to Jacob, placing his hand on and closing his father's eyes. In that original pledge, God had concluded, "I will also surely bring you up again." These words, resonant with the echoes of redemption and resurrection, remained unspoken, but, for those who knew the texts, they were doubtlessly embedded in the moment's drama and filled the ensuing silence.

As the son closed his father's eyes, from which the light of life had been extinguished, the eyes that some have called the "habitation of the spirit," the eyes that in death some believed perhaps had already glimpsed a vision of the divine, his act reflected a recognition that with this he brought to a close that life from which he himself had come.[73] The act was heavy with collective memory. It recalled the great chain of Jewish being from Jacob/Israel to now. It recalled the passing of one generation to the other. And perhaps most important, it provided the mourner with the words to deny an otherwise deathly silence in the face of death.

Outside of Israel, no children were ever called upon to close the eyes and sprinkle the dust, for such a drama would be counterfeit and incomplete, a mockery of the scriptural promise that, after all, was tied to the bringing of Jacob's body back to the land of his fathers, the land that took his name, Israel. Within the Holy Land the dead were buried in and hence surrounded by sacred earth, and the few grains in the eye were simply a symbolic reminder of that ancient redemptive promise. Outside it, however, in "the lands of Jewish exile," the hallowed dust was a replacement for the Holy Land, and sprinkling it remained the responsibility of the Chevra alone. And the volunteers scattered it in a variety of places, not simply on the eyes. They put it on the forehead, heart, and navel; for men, they also put it in the area of their circumcision—the "holy *brit*," or covenant, as this reminder of the covenant between God and Abraham is called—and throughout the coffin and into the straw-filled pillow placed beneath the head. This was meant not only to focus on those parts of the body associated with the essence of life—seeing, thinking, feeling, and sexuality—but also to make it seem as if the dead "were actually buried in the holy land of Israel."[74] And then they closed the eyes with little ceremony, for the promise of a return to the Holy Land had not yet been kept.

In time, other reasons were given for this scattering of the dust. Rabbi Shabbetai ben Meir HaCohen, a seventeenth-century Polish-Lithuanian authority, saw the custom as an exercise in humility, a way of reminding the living (the volunteers of the Chevra) that all they rush after in life will in the end come to dust and that they would do best to conquer their vainglorious desires.[75] Here was evidence that, as Abraham Heschel once put it, "death is not understood as the end of being but rather as the end of doing."[76]

Placed as well over the eyes and mouth were earthenware shards that had been broken as a sign of mourning; the earthenware represented the human effort to improve upon nature, to make something substantial out of the dust of the earth. That creativity, however, died with a man, and the shards on his eyes were reminders that we were all, as proposed in the liturgy on the Days of Awe—Rosh Hashanah and Yom Kippur—"like a broken clay vessel . . . and a fleeting dream." The work of our hands was no less likely to crumble than the pottery was to break.

Once again, at one level the *tahara* was on behalf of the dead, but at another it aimed no less to instruct and caution the living about what awaits us all and how therefore we should live. While it is primarily the members of the Chevra Kaddisha that, via their actions and recitations, would be exposed directly to these messages, they were meant to represent the living, the community that they serve. As such, whatever they might learn would trickle through the entire society.

Avraham's son was ushered out into the hall, and the Chevra bound Avraham's eyes with a white ribbon, turning it toward the left, and covered the dead man's face again. As the men did so, they echoed in chorus the words that described how the biblical Moses covered his own visage: "And he put a veil on his face" (Exodus 34:33). With this they had completed dressing the body.

Now came a recitation that could perhaps be understood as a dialogue between the dead man and those who had prepared him for burial. Although the members of the Chevra spoke the words, it was as if they were playing the parts of both the living and the dead. The dead man spoke first: "I will greatly rejoice in the Lord, my soul shall be joyful in my God; for he has clothed me with the garments of salvation, he has covered me with the robe of righteousness, as a bridegroom decks himself with a garland, and as a bride adorns herself with her jewels" (Isaiah 61:10).

Next the living spoke: "And I said, Let them set a pure mitre upon his head. And they set a pure mitre upon his head, and dressed him with garments. And the angel of the Lord stood by" (Zachariah 3:5). This reiteration of this verse invoked once again, as they were about to hand the body over to the mourners, the presence of a guardian angel. In Jewish tradition, at the time of demise angels were not simply the messengers of death; they were no less protectors who accompanied both the living and the dead, shielding them against the wrath of forces from the netherworld. In the ritual, this verse was meant to recall that the dead man, dressed like a priest in his mitre and white garments, still not assigned to his place in the kingdom of dead, was hoping for such protection. And so the men of the Chevra concluded in unison, as if offering the dead man its final consolation, repeating the promises of redemption from the prophet Isaiah: "And the Lord shall guide you continually, and satisfy your soul in drought, and make strong your bones; and you shall be like a watered garden, and like a spring of water, whose waters fail not" (Isaiah 58:11).

Everywhere but in Israel, the enshrouded body would now be placed into a plain wood coffin, a mandate going back at least as far as the twelfth-century philosopher, rabbi, and codifier Maimonides. Some found a hint for this custom in the Midrash associated with the verse in Genesis which noted that after their original sin of eating the forbidden fruit, the transgression that would lead to human mortality and expulsion from Eden, "Adam and his wife hid themselves from the presence of the Lord God among the trees of the garden" (3:8). The Midrash saw this reference to "the trees of the garden" as a hint that Adam and Eve's progeny were forever after to be buried in wood.[77] This simple box, like the shrouds, was meant to blur the distinctions between the wealthy and the indigent. "The rich used to be carried to burial on a grand bed, and the poor in a box, but the poor were ashamed, and so the rabbis instituted that everyone should be carried to burial in a box," as one medieval funeral manual puts it.[78] Yet, while economic disparities were muted, discrimination between the scholar and the unlearned *was* maintained in the custom of using the former's study table for making his coffin, while the latter was placed in the standard wooden box.[79]

The corpse was left with the hands by its side, and if possible the fingers were uncurled, as if to show that the dead took nothing material along from this world.[80] Here, too, the lesson was no less for the living, who were to understand from this custom that in the end we can take nothing with us other than the history of what we have done in life.

Yet even among those who choose to have the Chevra Kaddisha prepare them for burial, some people—most commonly a wish of the bereaved rather than the last will of the deceased—want to have special articles placed inside the coffin. Commonly these are items like a yarmulke from a family wedding or a bar or bat mitzvah, a personal Bible or prayer book, or even some sort of certificate vaguely associated with acts of religious significance—everything from tributes from synagogues or other charities to certifications of the deceased having visited some holy site in Israel. The Chevras treated these requests in a variety of ways, with some placing the items into the box and others leaving them for disposition by the funeral home.

The first time I was confronted with the prayer book and yarmulke the family of the dead man had asked to be buried with him, I was a bit startled. Yet as we placed these remnants of someone's life inside the coffin alongside the body, I could imagine the comfort that the family would feel in the belief that somehow the dead *could* take along something with them. When those items were the relics of their religion, putting them into the coffin seemed quite in order. There were, of course, those who wanted to add all sorts of other items, some of which were deeply personal and few of which most traditional Chevras would have included.

What every Chevra *did* do was to insert into the casket any cloths used to absorb whatever blood might have trickled out of the body. This was not just a case of cleaning up; it was a religious duty. The biblical assertion that "the life of all flesh is its blood" had been interpreted by the rabbis as a sign that all traces of blood—the "life"—could not remain unburied (Leviticus 17:14). That was why following accidents or at the site of bombings where the Chevra Kaddisha is put in charge of collecting the Jewish victims for burial, the volunteers were always scrupulous about collecting every last drop of blood. Whatever contained that blood was therefore interred with the dead. Where coffins were used, the box with the body inside was closed, preferably with wooden dowels, and then covered either with a large tallit for males or a simple velvet cloth of the sort used for covering the table on which the Torah scrolls were read.

Then, as a parting gesture, for this was the point at which many Chevras abroad completed their work, they turned to the dead person as they closed the coffin and petitioned him: "Avraham the son of Solomon, we ask for forgiveness from you if we have not handled you according to the respect owed you, but we have acted in accord with the customs of this place. Be thou for us and all of the people of Israel an advocate on high."

For those who went on to bury the dead, such pleas for forgiveness would come later, at the closed grave when the Chevra had completed the last of its duties. Indeed, forgiveness was something these attendants of the dead begged for repeatedly. Each year, on the seventh of the Hebrew month of Adar, the traditional anniversary of Moses' death, they would all declare a fast day, gather at the morning services in a particular synagogue, recite *slichot,* the penitential prayers, and then—at least in Jerusalem—repair to the ancient Jewish cemetery on the Mount of Olives, according to tradition, the site of the promised resurrection, and then to the other cemeteries where during the preceding year they had interred the dead. There, standing before the graves, they would appeal one last time for forgiveness from those they had served, repeating the same words they used each time they completed a burial. In so doing, of course, they not only discharged a religious obligation but also affirmed a faith in the immortality of the soul and the role of the dead as intermediaries on behalf of the living, as patrons who could save the living from their own premature deaths.

This request was not just a religious nicety. Rather, it expressed once again, albeit in somewhat camouflaged form, the abiding dread that the living have of the dead and of the unending desire to mitigate this anxiety. *Tahara,* the purification rituals that, as representatives of the community of the living, the Chevra Kaddisha engaged in was aimed not just to provide the last respects and prepare the dead for burial and resurrection. It also sought to transform what was worrying into a source of reassurance, to turn the dead person from one who held a grudge against or was jealous of the living into a *guter beiter,* as the Yiddish phrase put it, or *meylitz yosher,* in the Hebrew expression. These changed dead would then pray and make the best case in the heavenly court for the benefit of those who survived and cared for them in life. At this time, when the accounts for the year were being closed, the members of the Chevra wanted to be certain that the malignant dead were replaced by supporting spirits. Later in the afternoon, to make certain that they were enlisting the dead on behalf of the living, they would return to the synagogue for brief words of eulogy for all those buried during the year.

"He was a person of great kindness; she gave much charity; he was careful never to hurt anyone's feelings; she was constant in her faith"—the words of praise were like epitaphs. This was meant, as Lazar explained, not just to recall the dead but also to arouse the spirits of the living, to make the people of the Chevra reflect on what remains of a person after he is no longer among the living, and perhaps to think to themselves, "would that I were thus," and to remember what is truly important in life. Of course, they were also a way of providing a reminder for the dead to reciprocate in their advocacy on behalf of the living. If I speak well of the dead, was the implicit message, then they will speak well of me, and I shall live and not die. The spiritual remains a mix of the religious sensibility and sympathetic magic.

Then, at last, these people who came so close to death so often and wanted not to be tainted or harmed by it would recite the afternoon and evening prayers, finally breaking the daylong fast together with a festive meal meant to bring them back to life and the living. All that, however, was for another time. Now the wrapped body was swiftly moved to the place of eulogy.

With our preparations of the *mays* complete, I and the other volunteers quietly exited into the night from a side door of the funeral parlor and reassembled near a small tap, where each of us filled a cup with water to lave our hands. This time, however, unlike before, each man would not pour its contents over his own hands but rather perform this last "service" for one of his living partners, as if to demonstrate that we could serve the living and not just the dead. Between each ablution the cup was set down so that each man could start the process on his own. When we had finished, and each man's hands were wet, following our community's custom, none of us wiped the moisture because, as our rabbi had put it, "Those drops on our hands reflect the tears of all the Jewish people over the loss of one of our people." Only God, we were told, and time could dry those tears. Then, as we silently departed, each man whispered to the others: *"Tizku l'mitzvot."*

"We are strict about removing the body immediately following the *tahara*," Lazar explained as the men of the Chevra now placed the enshrouded body on the eighteen metal rungs that hung between two long wooden poles—some people called it a *kelicha*—they used to carry the dead. Like so much else in the preparation of the dead for burial, this simple device, used for at least two thousand years and the local equivalent of the plain pine box in which Jews outside of Israel were to be buried, served to blur the distinctions among all Jews who died. We are, the ceremony of *tahara* from start to finish seems to say, all one, regardless of what each of us has accomplished in life.

> Thus have our rabbis taught: Formerly, they used to unveil the face of the [deceased] rich and cover the face of the poor for they appeared blackened by scarcity, and the poor were thereby embarrassed. Therefore, a law was passed that everyone's face would be covered, in deference to the poor.
>
> Formerly, they used to bring out the deceased for burial, the rich on a tall bed ornamented with rich covers, the poor on a *kelicha;* and the poor felt ashamed. Therefore, a law was passed that all should be brought out on a *kelicha,* in deference to the poor. . . .
>
> Formerly, the expense of burying the dead was harder for a family to bear than the death itself, so that sometimes family members fled to escape the expense. This was so until Rabban Gamaliel [himself a wealthy man and head of the yeshiva] ordered that he be buried in a plain linen shroud instead of in expensive garments. Since then, people have buried their dead in simple shrouds.[81]

The ceremony of *tahara* is clearly rich with meaning, trying to begin the healing that must follow death. But, of course, since few people other than those who do *tahara* ever get to see these rituals, their capacity to help the living has remained limited to those few who learned about the rituals from the codebooks and manuals. Perhaps that is why, these days, the Chevra Kaddisha is no longer as active as it once was. So elite did it become that it failed to share its work and its rich symbolism with the people, leading to a Jewry that largely remained ignorant of what the ceremony had to offer and what it could teach about life in death.

There would be more for this Chevra Kaddisha to do. The funeral procession and the burial were theirs to carry out. But the *tahara*, the first step in the transition from life through death, from sadness to solace, from social breach to collective healing, had been completed. In just about half an hour, Avraham, the son of Solomon, had been transformed from a lifeless cadaver to a Jew, purified and ready for his body's burial and his soul's escape. And the first malignancies of death's disorder had been brought under control and replaced by sacred order.

Leveiya

The Funeral and Its Accompaniment

> The meaning of our lives, and the memories of them, belong to
> the living, just as our funerals do.
>
> Thomas Lynch, *The Undertaking*

In the words of an old Syrian Jewish proverb, "Birth is the messenger of
death." Or, as the anthropologist Bronislaw Malinowski once observed: "Man
has to live his life in the shadow of death, and he who clings to life and enjoys
its fullness must dread the menace of its end." Perhaps as an antidote to this
dread, Malinowski continued, when at last persons are actually "faced by
death," they turn almost immediately instead "to the promise of life." In other
words, "death and its denial—immortality"—coincide.[1] We have seen this
vividly in the ceremony and rituals of *tahara;* we see it no less in the Jewish funeral. Whereas the burial (or other disposal), particularly in the traditional
Jewish rush to be rid of the body and its impurities, confirms the reality and
finality of the death, almost everything else about the funeral asserts immortality: of the soul, of the community, and of faith in the future.

"There are two parties to the suffering that death inflicts," Arnold Toynbee
notes, "and in the apportionment of this suffering, the survivor takes the
brunt."[2] "Weep for the mourners," urges the Talmud, "and not for what was
lost, for it has gone to its rest but we who grieve have come to lamentation."[3]
Yet the immediately bereaved are not alone. Although the orphaned, wid-
owed, and immediately bereaved surely feel the sting of a relative's death most
directly, the larger group among whom they count themselves is also powerfully affected. As such, both must determine "what to do about death."[4]

The question of what to do about death is in many ways more uncomfortable for society than for the individual, for society "feels itself immortal and wants to be so; it cannot normally believe that its members . . . should be fated to die."[5] Death's capacity to tear anyone and everyone away throws a challenge at the very heart of society's claim of continued existence by reminding us of the limits of even the most powerful collective forces to hold onto even those who matter most to it. Death carries off the leader as easily as the led. Indeed, death threatens to make the sense of community evanescent. Thus, according to Robert Hertz, "when a man dies, society loses in him much more than a unit; it is stricken in the very principle of its life, in the faith it has in itself."[6] Perhaps that is why death in all societies is never just the concern of the immediately bereaved nor only the affliction of those who have died.

Moreover, at the time of death, when the bereaved, stricken by pain and diminished by a sense of loss, might be moved to withdraw into themselves, be alone with their sorrow, and tear themselves away from the fabric of the living—no less than the dead person—or, in extreme cases, even to follow those who have died, society forces them to plan a funeral, a ceremony of departure for the dead at which everyone who knew the deceased or who has a relationship with the bereaved must be assembled.[7] In effect, the onset of death among Jews forces the living to recall all sorts of associations they have with one another. The departure of the one initiates the reunion of the many. And all this must be done posthaste—according to Jewish custom, within the day of death or as close as possible to it. Only if some of the bereaved in the immediate family cannot get to the funeral in time may the burial be postponed (and among the strictly Orthodox even these allowances are extremely limited). It is as if through the funeral, which ostensibly is for the one who has died, the many must swiftly reassure themselves and prove that they are still strong and able to gather themselves together. Nothing is more distressing than a poorly attended funeral; it compounds the pain.

According to the Talmud, *leviyas hamayt* (accompanying the dead), the traditional term for a Jewish funeral, is among the most compelling of Jewish commandments, one of those acts of kindness for which one receives rewards both in this world and in the one to come.[8] In other words, it is enormously important. So decisive is the mandate to attend to a funeral that the *Shulchan Aruch,* the authoritative Code of Jewish Law published in the sixteenth century by Rabbi Joseph Caro, asserts that even Torah study, which otherwise is a supreme, ceaseless, and continuous Jewish obligation, should be suspended to allow one to take part in a funeral and its preparations.[9] This is because funerals simply cannot be complete without an audience, without a congregation come to mark the end. "We need our witnesses and archivists to say we lived, we died, we made this difference," as Thomas Lynch puts it.[10] Moreover, those who are bereaved (really all of us who still live) should not be left alone.

While the Jewish funeral, then, is overwhelmingly a death-defying gathering of the living, in its ceremonial and ritual ordering of experience it also manages significantly to separate the realm of death irrevocably from that of the living.[11] At its successful conclusion, the dead must be buried completely while the living are ushered away, with an enhanced sense of solidarity and capacity to mourn and console one another back to life. A religious retreat from the edge of anguish and ultimate abandonment, the Jewish funeral transforms what might otherwise just mark annihilation into a rite of passage, during which persons begin by being confronted by something unfathomable and end with a sense of meaningful closure in which the dead go one way and the all the rest begin a return to the company of the living.[12] In so doing, the funeral—"extremely complex and even contradictory"—acts not simply to separate the domains of death and life but, in effect, no less than *tahara,* to create order in the face of chaos and breach.[13] Yet unlike *tahara,* which accomplishes this goal almost in secret, in funerals the chaos engendered by death is publicly replaced by order. In the process, the funeral reiterates and makes prominent some of the most fundamental beliefs about life and the concerns of society, making visible what we at other times take for granted.[14]

In the Jewish case, this entails rituals that aim to confront death with repeated assertions of life, as well as expressions and ceremonial displays that make the bereaved feel that they are not completely abandoned.[15] Like the *tahara* before it, but again far more publicly, the funeral repeatedly affirms that, in the midst of death, life still goes on and we are not alone. The mortality of one person does not presage or guarantee the death and disintegration of all. The funeral seeks to reflect the Jewish people's fundamental realization that, although they die and feel the precariousness of their existence, they also continue and survive, that they have lost one connection but remain bonded to others.[16] With weeping and the general atmosphere of sadness serving as the emotional and social glue by which those in attendance "hold to one another," the funeral also helps the living maintain their attachment to one another and to life, both collective and individual, in spite of death's blows.[17] As Raymond Firth explains, "The death of every person must be followed by a reaffirmation of the social character of human existence."[18]

Finally, the funeral tries to make the living appreciate that death is not the end of being but simply the end of doing. It allows Jews to avoid having to think of death as "complete cessation" or total annihilation.[19] While ostensibly carried out for the dead person, the funeral rites in fact have important effects and benefits for the living, both as individuals and a group. All of society participates in the lamentation, and all will share in the consolation.

The author of Ecclesiastes ruefully advises us that "there is no mastery on the day of death." But the funeral is a social response that seems to assert that, on the contrary, there is at least *some* mastery on the day of death. Jewish funerary services and the mourning they initiate ease the apprehension that accompanies bereavement and the dread of not knowing what will happen next. At its best, the funeral allows all those present—from those who have lost someone close to them, a family member or intimate friend, to those who barely knew the deceased—to begin their escape from the overwhelming uncertainty and helplessness that accompany death.

To be sure, when a society is undergoing change or when the bereaved, for whatever reason, do not feel themselves bonded to the group with whom they are forced to deal with their dead, many of these rituals and ceremonies may not work well. Under such circumstances, "traditional rites are not always sufficient for the occasion and its stress."[20] Rather than providing a ready vessel into which inchoate feelings of grief may be poured, saving the mourners from the need to suddenly improvise their responses to this breach in life, the funeral and all that occurs around it can actually become a disruptive and most uncomfortable experience. Jews who feel little if any connection with the Jewish people, its traditions, and its customs or those who are ideologically committed to secular ideals may find many of the Jewish responses to death worse than meaningless, even distressing. Rather than being able to draw upon the resources implicit in the Jewish funeral, such people often try to create alternatives to it, looking for other kinds of passages. Not infrequently, these Jews choose a course of behavior that draws its essential meaning from their cultural opposition to many of the traditional Jewish norms. These alternative choices are often made either because people are alienated from their Jewish origins and traditions or because, from their point of view, the Jewish funeral remains culturally opaque and spiritually cryptic. The description and analysis that follow aim to exchange clarity for opacity.

PRELIMINARIES

However much we realize that death is inevitable, its arrival—even when coming as a resolution to prolonged illness, the conclusion to suffering, or after many years of life—is commonly accompanied by anxiety and tension. We may ask, "What happens next?" "What do we do now?" While Jewish tradition and practice as already described offer answers, the funeral—more publicly than anything that precedes it and perhaps most dramatically—demonstrates what happens next and what we, the living, are supposed to do in order to move past death.

Most contemporary observers would probably fix the beginning of the Jewish funeral with the formal service that starts when people have assembled for prayers and eulogies. Careful scrutiny of most such gatherings reveals that in fact much happens beforehand. The memorial service is indeed often the focus of the funeral and the burial its denouement, but practices that occur prior to both are essential to what it is meant to accomplish.[21]

First, perhaps, is the public placement of the "prepared" body, which in effect begins the funerary proceedings. The public placement of the dead body among the living is always temporary. In some cultures this display may last several days—what we sometimes call "lying in state." In others this is called the "viewing," and often the body is covered, wrapped, adorned, or otherwise "improved" so that the repulsion of death does not overwhelm the living. As we have seen, for Jews, this stage is quite brief, since burial must come quickly. Moreover, the "improvement" to the corpse that the Jews perform (tahara), although physical, is primarily spiritual and in any event is kept largely hidden. In effect, Jews seek to keep the actual view of the body to a minimum so that it remains present yet also concealed. According to Jewish tradition, the body—and in particular the face—must always remain obscured in public.

Many reasons have been offered to explain this practice, including the most common, which sees in it the lingering horror that the ancients felt when looking at the face of the dead, as if they were looking at the Face of Death. Yet because Judaism views the funeral and the preparations for it as ceremonies of transition, one also may see in this religious requirement to keep the face of the dead from view a means of fostering that belief in transition. To see the deceased face-to-face before they have been formally relegated to the realm of death is to deny the funeral its efficacy as a rite of passage. The dead, like death itself, must not be seen. As Hertz explains, "To make an object or living being pass from this world into the next, to free or create the soul, it must be destroyed"; then, only as the "visible object vanishes" and becomes invisible can it be "reconstructed in the beyond, transformed to a greater or lesser degree."[22] To look directly at the face and body of the dead, on the contrary, is to be struck hard by the undeniability of the corpse's passivity, which makes it difficult to believe that a passage to another kind of existence has begun. So the Jewish dead are brought for a brief period before the burial, placed in a

casket or enshrouded on a catafalque before all those assembled at the funeral—unmistakably dead yet not altogether visible.

As for those who choose to embalm and somehow restore the corpse to
make it look as if the deceased is only asleep, they, too, display a desire not to
look upon the true face of death, preferring instead to create an image of life,
as if the dead body were not dead, as if the face of death were simply a face
asleep. Yet such a sight fools no one; the counterfeit is seen for what it is. Similarly, the increasingly popular common practice of cremation prior to the funeral aims at the same goal—yet here the absence of an object impairs the ability of the funeral to act as a send-off.

The dead and the living have a hard time sharing a space, for they seem to
be endowed with valences that oppose each other. "The survivors are drawn
toward the deceased by their affection for him, repelled from him by the dreadful transformation wrought by death."[23] The temporariness of the propinquity
may also be understood as a symbolic expression of the transitional character
of the entire proceedings, a reminder that this disorder in which the dead and
living are mixed together must be resolved, with each going off in a separate
direction. But just where is the body placed?

In some cases, the casket is placed near the immediate mourners, as the family stands to accept the consolations of those who have come to the funeral.
The presence of this hidden yet present corpse among the family is a message
that the deceased is still a part of their circle, albeit unable to interact with
them. By offering them consolation, moreover, those who have come are also
"paying respect" to the dead who is near them.[24] Some people may actually lay
a hand on the casket, though never on a body that is only in its shroud.

Sometimes the casket is camouflaged as a part of the furniture. This is easily done when the casket is a rich-looking, polished wood. In this case it often literally blends in with the woodwork, and all attention instead flows to the
living, both the grieving and those who have come to console them. But of
course that is one of the latent motives of choosing such a fine-looking coffin,
to camouflage the frightening presence of death within.

On occasion, the casket is placed in another room, and those who come to
the funeral may then divide this preliminary time between the bereaved and
the corpse. The living are offered condolences, gestures of support—anything
that can establish an emotional connection between the grieving and those
who have come to console them. Some of these visitors share their own grief
at this loss, in a display of empathy. Others offer the message that they are available for whatever support is needed. People enter the circle of the grieving
and float out again, in the eddies of human circulation that flow about the

grieving. Subsequently, some of these same "comforting guests" will move away from the bereaved and focus their attention on the others in the crowd, renewing ties that this occasion has once again recalled. This huddling of the living dramatically displays their need to be with one another in the face of death, a theme that will be replayed throughout the funeral. Finally, they may gather about the corpse.

In the bureaucratization that has taken over so much of modern society, some of those who wish to demonstrate this willingness to console and desire to be counted among the comforting guests will sign an attendance sheet provided by a funeral "director." These lists are then given to the grieving family as a written record of who came to be with them in their time of need. "You haven't been at the funeral," one American Jew once suggested to me, "unless you've signed the sheet." What she meant, of course, was that one's presence alone did not count; it was having a tangible record of it that mattered.

According to the strict dictates of Jewish law, greetings generally are not to be exchanged at a funeral.[25] In practice, however, all that remains of this requirement, even among the most observant, is the avoidance of expressions of salutation and welcome. The fact is that greetings are largely unnecessary, for the funeral is one of those occasions on which no opening comment is required, when the bereaved are in a continuous standing of public access. At this time a display of silence or a touch, a look into the eyes or a sigh is sufficient.

In effect the conversations at these preliminaries are less *about* something than they are talk aimed at "the fulfillment of a relation that wants to be nothing but relation," discourse in the service of solace and sociability.[26] Even when they are taken up with questions about the cause of death or whispers about the last hours of life, or when they seem to be overtures of encouragement, they seek in their deeper structure above all else to communicate and reestablish a sense of connection and social equilibrium, a feeling among the living that they are not abandoned or alone, that this trauma, too, shall pass, and all will return to some modicum of normalcy wherein the living will not be conquered by the dead. Even when the chatter is ordinary, it implicitly asserts with its very ordinariness that life still goes on as before the death. Indeed, this pattern of social interaction first established at the preliminaries to the funeral often repeats itself throughout the period set aside for comforting the mourners, in which much that happens seems aimed at undoing the changes wrought by death.

Others guests will assemble near the dead body or settle into the room where it lies. That these rooms have come to be called "chapels" in America reflects how the dominant metaphor of the funeral assembly is a religious one. Here those in attendance quietly await the formal start of the proceedings. With whispered snippets of conversation, by staring off into space, or even with tears, they put themselves into a kind of suspended animation.

Some, finding this sort of waiting difficult to sustain, may move toward the dead body and take on some of the responsibilities of a *shomer,* or guardian of the deceased. This role calls for the recitation of Psalms, whose protective power is seen as warding off the malevolence that surrounds death. For Jews the recitation of Psalms has often served as a religious activity that simultaneously allows persons to feel as if they are actively doing something and makes them feel that they are subject to the superior power of the Creator to whom these Psalms are ultimately addressed. As such, the Psalms capture much of the ambiguity of the funeral, which likewise expresses the effort at human control even as it highlights human helplessness. Not incidentally, this part prayer and part incantation provides a way of handling the otherwise awkward, ambiguous situation of being in the presence of a newly dead person. If several people are carrying on a recitation of Psalms at the same time, one person may take the initiative to lead a common reading, among the most popular being selections from chapter 119, the Grand Alpha Beta. Stanzas that begin with the letters that spell out the deceased's Hebrew name are then recited aloud, as if to suggest that the dead is interwoven into sacred liturgy and text. The fact that the casket at the front of the room is covered by either a *parochet* or a tallit, and therefore looks a bit like the table on which a Torah scroll might be placed, helps camouflage the presence of death and enhances this practice by making it seem like the far less anxiety-provoking synagogue activity.

In those cases where the body is not in a casket but only in a shroud, it quietly but unmistakably radiates its presence and effectively overwhelms all else, including the bereaved and their supporters. The outlines of the human form clearly visible, there is no ignoring it, no talking it away, no making believe it is a piece of furniture or a synagogue prop. If in the "family rooms" of the American funeral parlor, with their polished or separated coffins, the living manage to dominate at least the preliminaries to the funeral, in this bare chamber, the dead hold on more powerfully to the living. Indeed, this proximity of the dead and living in the raw surroundings of the Israeli *Beit Haleveiyot,* a place that stresses their juxtaposition, hints at a tacit contest, a striving between these two opposites, as if to see which will triumph. Moreover, because there are rabbinic authorities who concluded that the law demanded that "one cannot and should not comfort the mourners while their dead lie before them," this arrangement seems to help ensure that at least at the outset the dead will dominate. This is my last moment to hold on to you, the body of the deceased seems to say. In a sense, all that follows in the funeral allows the living to over-come that dominance of the dead.[27]

In the traditional Jewish funeral, the end of the preliminaries is the time for those who have lost an intimate relative to perform *keriah*, the ritualized rending of a garment in a violent display of mourning (although in some places the custom is to do this at the grave site, while other customs suggest that it be done at the moment one learns of the death of a family member or if one is present at the moment of demise). Much has been written about the symbolism of the tear—about its being a "substitute for the ancient pagan cus-tom of tearing the flesh and the hair" meant to effect a sympathy with the loss of death, or about its being a way to show how death tears apart life.[28] This practice of tearing garments was common not only among the ancient He-brews but also among the Canaanites and later the Romans.[29] Menachem HaMeiri, the medieval Provençal rabbi, said it most directly: "When the gar-ments are rent, the hearts will be rent." Moreover, just as the death of a once intimate relative results in the world of the bereaved becoming irrevocably torn and never fully mended, so, by tradition, the tear that marks that recog-nition is never to be completely repaired. Among the traditionally observant, the torn garment is worn throughout the shivah, the seven-day mourning pe-riod that follows burial. This garment becomes the attire of bereavement, which one must wear as an outward sign of being rent by grief. "Life rips you up, so look ripped up," as Wieseltier summarizes it.[30] In its destructive gesture, the *keriah* likewise reenacts the central drama of the funeral: the fact that the dead has been torn from the fabric of the living.[31]

Originally, *keriah* was to have taken place when one witnessed death, at the instant when feelings of anguish and grief were vividly experienced and the bereaved were torn asunder, when the act of ripping one's garments would seem a most natural reaction—a tearing down of the bereaved's veneer of ci-vility and order which death itself has initiated. But to give in to this emotion without restraint would be to give in to chaos, to allow death to destroy civil-ity and its correlate, modesty. It would unsettle those who are tearing and those who bear witness. That, however, would be the opposite of what Jew-ish traditions have tried to accomplish in the face of death. Indeed, the Jerusalem Talmud explains that some people—"mockers," it calls them—made too much of the practice of rending garments and carried it to excess, and hence the practice had to be limited.[32] Accordingly, *keriah* has been trans-formed as well from its chaotic and impulsive roots into a ceremonial, tamed, almost stylized, reenactment. That is why practitioners tend to exercise a kind of "emotional self-control" when they perform the act.[33] Of course, by making it a ceremony, the tradition emotionally reined in the act and thereby assisted in this self-control and to an extent almost depersonalized the practice.

Commonly limited to those who have lost an immediate family member— defined by Judaism as a parent, sibling, child, or spouse[34]—*keriah* thus at one and the same time seeks to express and limit grief. Mandated by the ancient rabbinic sages, this practice—which is the remaining custom of a number of outward signs of Jewish mourning that once included wrapping heads in a dark cloth—was said by them to refer back to the biblical story of Jacob, which serves as a leitmotif in so much of the Jewish response to death.[35] It reproduces Jacob's reaction upon seeing his son Joseph's coat of many colors drenched in blood and thinking him dead. This is the same response that, generations later, is attributed to King David, upon learning of the death of his predecessor, King Saul, along with his son, Jonathan, David's closest friend. As rabbis put it: *ma'aseh avot, siman l'banim* (the acts of the fathers are to be emulated by their children). The response to death of today's Jews must be an echo of those made by their biblical forebears.

In line with the need to contain its emotional contagion, *keriah* is normally done today with the assistance of a rabbi or a member of the Chevra Kaddisha, who, with blade in hand, makes an incision in the grief-torn person's garment, usually a shirt, suit jacket, or sweater. For parents the tear is traditionally made on the left side, over the heart (the Mishnah demands that the tear should go down as far as the heart), while for all others it is made on the right.[36] Grasping the cut garment, the bereaved person now publicly rips his clothes in a downward motion while reciting the benediction to which the assembled must respond "amen." This word, whose original meaning, "yes it is true," resonates with the need of others to bear witness to the mourners' willingness to accept the destiny and propriety of death as coming from out of God's judgment. By accompanying the tearing with the ritually obligatory invocation "Blessed art thou O Lord our God, the true judge," *keriah* further tames those powerful emotions of grief, anger, fear, and loss that stand behind it. This ceremony—expressing pain and its restraint—sets the tone for and epitomizes the purpose of the entire funeral: to display the grief and yet to contain it.

Often, *keriah* is performed in the anteroom, just before the beginning of the service, where the family waits after everyone else has already repaired to the chapel. Indeed, in some instances, the funeral directors or rabbis will usher guests out of these antechambers to allow the *keriah* to take place. Among some Jews of Sephardic origins, the tearing is done in an even more sheltered environment, only upon their return home from the cemetery as they sit down for a first meal.[37] The sheltering of this gesture from a fully public view, of course, is yet one more way in which its emotional power to unsettle the living is contained.

Yet containment can also become so dominant a drive that it finally empties the gesture of all its original meaning. Thus, the more assimilated American Jews—those who have tried to emulate the less emotionally expressive Protestant ideal, which eschews such displays of grief, or who reflect what Mark Zborowski has called the American cultural tendency to "avoid provoking pity"—commonly skip the *keriah* ceremony entirely. Some instead opt to put on a black button to which a partially torn ribbon is attached.[38] This American sign of mourning, probably derived from Protestant English usage and later incorporated into the American custom of wearing a black band, is often donned at the time when *keriah* would take place. While putting on this badge of mourning may arouse some of the same feelings of publicly acknowledging mourning, it lacks the symbolism and emotional charge of the tearing.

As practiced in Israel, however, where funerals are still largely governed by Jewish traditions and private emotion is often absorbed by collective experience, the *keriah* takes place in the presence of the deceased and the public, commonly in the *Beit Haleveiyot*, where no private antechambers separate the mourners from the public. This ritualized performance of anguish is part of the social drama of the funeral. Here, as the procession behind the body is about to leave for the graveyard, the tearing takes place as everyone huddles around the mourners who, with the help of one of the Chevra Kaddisha, rend their garments in full view of everyone, reciting the blessing loud enough for all to hear and to respond with the obligatory "amen."

Just as we were about to move from the anteroom into the chapel for the beginning of the service, the rabbi walked slowly toward my mother and me, penetrating the protective circle formed by my wife, our four sons, and a few of our closest friends. "It's time," he said as he withdrew a small blade from his pocket, "but first you need to mark yourselves as mourners." We stopped talking, and I watched silently as he reached over and made a small incision in my mother's blouse. Next he turned toward me and made two cuts: one on the left collar of my shirt and a second on the left lapel of my suit jacket. Now he gave us directions: at his signal, my mother and I were to pull downward on the cuts while reciting the benedictions of bereavement, which he would repeat with us. I began, and my right hand seemed to take on a life of its own as I tremblingly

reached across my chest and began the ripping. The fabric gave way with surprising ease, and the tear went quite far, exposing my breast. It looked white
against the brown suit, almost deathly pale. The sight of the flesh, the sound of
the ripping, the recitation of the words so heavily freighted with the associations
of death all seemed to undo me. The violence of the motion, the need to pro-
claim God as the true judge, a benediction I had never before recited, combined
suddenly, startlingly, to break my composure. The calm I had managed to marshal
since the arrival of the funeral "guests" was shattered. Surrendering to death,
pulled down into mourning, I felt unexpectedly alone, as if falling into chaos.
Yet if the *keriah* tore me from my moorings, the spoken "amens" around me
that came in response to my benediction were like voices in the wilderness of
my loneliness, reminding me that someone was out there to help pull me back to
life. The voices were those of my wife, children, the rabbi, and those friends who
stayed nearby, voices that in this moment out of time helped me feel that I was
still tied to this world. Regaining my composure, I held on to those around me,
and together we walked into the chapel.

THE SERVICE

A final breath, a moment of crushing violence, a heart stopped, a hemorrhaged
blood vessel—death arrives in an instant. We speak of the "moment of death."
In stopping to reflect upon and mark the death by means of a funeral, the living in effect hold off its finality. To be sure, there are limits to how long the
end can be delayed or denied. Jewish law encourages brevity in funerals because of the requirement to bury the dead as expeditiously as possible. Moreover, precisely because funerals are social occasions, restraints upon them
flow from the presence of others and from social and cultural mores. These
commonly carry the day—to say nothing of the requirements of funeral directors, burial societies, and gravediggers, whose schedules often determine
the amount of time that even the most passionately bereaved may devote to a
service and to holding off the final farewell to the one who has died.

While the actual service is considered by many the central element of the
funeral, its basic structure remains quite flexible—perhaps more so than any
other of the Jewish rites of passage. In its essentials, it consists very simply of a
chance to say some words. Commonly these are made in tribute to the deceased, although some of that praise may be shared with the surviving family,
whose treatment of the person who has died is singled out for attention. According to one time-honored tradition, Jews continue to talk with the dead,

and therefore the bereaved must use this occasion to ask the one who has died and whose spirit is assumed to hover nearby for forgiveness for any slights or affronts that those gathered at the funeral may have committed during his or her lifetime. There is even a hoary custom in which some speakers face the assembled as they offer their eulogies but at the same time lay a hand on or turn to the casket.[39] Essential to all these is the witness borne by all those gathered at the funeral. They are both audience and people who share in the bereavement. As such, they are a bulwark against the feelings of overwhelming loneliness that death engenders in us all. Finally, in a show of solidarity, the assembled are expected to recite prayers on behalf of the departing spirit and leave all those present feeling as if they have "done right by the dead." In all this, one discovers, as Robert Hertz long ago observed, "funerary ritual in general acts for the good of both the survivors and the deceased."[40]

There are no set pieces with which the traditional Jewish service opens. Yet, among the most common beginnings is the recitation of a psalm, often the twenty-third, with its well-known line that seems to echo with the sentiments meant to offer comfort both to the dead and to the grieving: "Even though I walk through the valley of the shadow of death, I fear no evil for thou art with me."[41] Concluding with the confidence that "surely goodness and mercy shall follow me" and the assurance that "I shall abide in the house of the Lord forever," these verses, like the funeral itself, offer a double message. When focused on the dead, they clearly offer comfort, as all incantations do, that what is described in the psalm somehow rehearses the experience of the deceased. But when applied to the living, who actually recite the words, these assurances from the "Lord who is my Shepherd" and who "revives my soul" and in whose house the living shall continue to abide, come what may, surely offer respite from the terror and chaos of death, a promise of escape from its malevolence and a restoration of order in life. Moreover, although the "thou" in the psalm refers to God, in the context of the funeral, it resonates with references to ongoing relationships between the dead and the living.

The traditional funeral—a kind of extension of the prayer service—may offer additional recitations from other psalms, each making an implicit statement about the deceased or those who grieve for him. In contemporary practice a number of other readings—poems, favorite stories, or even personal writings of either the deceased or the eulogizer—are increasingly inserted into the service here. The selected readings often reflect the religious and cultural location of the dead and the community that grieves the loss. In some cases, the readings aim to celebrate a life lived. In this they also suggest a model for the living, for that which we celebrate in one person we intrinsically call for in another.

There are also readings meant to remind everyone of what is surely among the most common messages at funerals: the fleeting nature of life. "A person is like nothing, his days like a passing shadow," as the Psalmist put it (Psalms 144:4). That realization is meant to lead the living to repair themselves, to improve their lives, to make each of their remaining moments count, for at every funeral, death must be perceived not simply as one person's end but also as a lesson of caution for those who survive. In a funerary custom cited by a German rabbinic commentator of the nineteenth century, when standing before the casket, persons are to turn to one another and remark: "Look at where you are going, and you have still not changed your ways. . . ." [42] To be sure, this is undoubtedly a universal sentiment that the living share when they confront the reality of death.

Sometimes people will use the time of the eulogy to allow the voice that has now been stilled one last chance to be heard, enabling the dead to communicate with the living. Letters or last testaments from the "departed" are read; the "moral will," which offers guidance from the deceased for those left behind and was once quite common, was sometimes read at this time. [43] In perhaps one of his most frequently quoted stories, "Four Generations—Four Wills," the Yiddish writer Y. L. Peretz re-creates four such wills. Each gives voice to the changing nature of the moral universe in which the Jews who wrote them lived. Thus, the first will, a brief note found under the deceased's pillow, requests that "my children shall continue as partners in my lumber-business" and "have a gate made for the Jewish cemetery and the roof of the synagogue repaired." The second records the wishes of a dead father who announces his recognition that "I go from this world . . . without sadness and with absolute faith in the God of Mercy," and who adds, among other expressions of his moral will, that "my children . . . continue the custom of deducting each year before the Jewish New Year one-tenth of the profit of the preceding twelve months for the benefit of the poor and, even if (God forbid!) there should ever be a loss, let them nevertheless give charity, since the loss is doubtless a trial sent from heaven." In Peretz's narrative, the wishes of each generation as communicated to the next reflect a recognition of the changes that time has wrought, as well as an understanding by those who have died of what they need to say to those they have left behind. [44] It is this understanding, along with a willingness of those at a funeral, at least for this one moment, to defer to the spiritual authority of the deceased and hear them out, that is at the heart of a moral will's power (or the lack of understanding and an unwillingness to thus defer that is the mark of its weakness).

Nowadays, the oral reading or even the composition of such moral wills is rare. Instead, eulogizers recount stories from the life of the one mourned, as if in the details of the biographical narrative one could discover embedded moral messages and keys to summing up the essentials of a life. In such eulogies lives are turned into moral tales reenacted. Their substance is what allows people in some quarters paradoxically or euphemistically to call a funeral a "celebration of life." Some eulogies endeavor to place the deceased into the great chain of Jewish being, trying thereby to unravel the inexplicable mystery that both life and death represent. The public review of a life or its perceived "highlights" is offered as a message to the living, implicitly informing them of what sort of life they, too, must lead to be as praiseworthy as the person being eulogized. This is an opportunity for a public reaffirmation of common values, providing a counterweight to the collective shock and vulnerability that death engenders. On other occasions, in place of a life story, the eulogist offers an array of quotable quotes, favorite memories, or best-loved poems meant to capture the essence of the person being recalled. In all the goal is to make present the absent, to bring the deceased back from the oblivion of death—if only for a few moments and only in spirit.

Of course, implicit in all eulogies is the assumption that what is said will put the deceased in a positive light. In a eulogy, no one is a nobody after death. There are, however, always bound to be those who die for whom the survivors find it difficult to say something positive. Here, in line with the antediluvian yet still-powerful assumption that one must not speak ill of the dead lest they reciprocate and, with their now superior spiritual power (an inversion of their obviously *inferior* bodily power), curse those who fail to grieve for them, the effort must be made to nevertheless find some kind words.[45]

For several generations, the eulogy, as indeed the entire funeral, has become the domain of rabbis, the religious virtuosi who have taken over so much of Jewish ritual life in the modern world. The enlisting of rabbis to provide the meaning at a time of death is connected to the need of the bereaved to receive superhuman assurance, words that come from an extraordinary realm above that of those who suffer mortality. The recourse, particularly but not only at tragic funerals, to rabbis or preachers for eulogies—as indeed to "officiate" at a funeral in general—is probably a reflection of the fact that these "people of God," as they have sometimes been called, were once (and in some quarters still are) thought of as endowed with precisely this sort of charisma, spiritual authority, knowledge, and a share of the numinous. They who speak with God, as the old-time believer in rabbis might have put it, can fathom the meaning of life and death. And even now, when perhaps this sort of confidence in rabbis is no longer widely held, the dependence on them at the moment of bereavement resounds with the echoes of a once-powerful faith in those who have devoted their lives to religion.

There is also the matter of status. The presence of rabbis and others of special high distinction, as well as their communal and religious stature, serves as a social monument both to the deceased and to the mourners. The more rabbis, the more prominent or respected the eulogizers are, the more their presence redounds to the social—if not necessarily always to the spiritual—benefit of those who have been touched by this death. And indeed, the fact that these immortals have come and prepared their eulogies on short notice—for Jewish funerals are always a matter of short notice—adds to the power of their presence.

So dependent have Jews become on the rabbi that those who find themselves planning funerals and who have no synagogue affiliation or no personal rabbi often turn to funeral parlors for a kind of generic rabbi, who is provided general background information about the deceased and then expected to offer a eulogy. When a rabbi displays little or no knowledge of the deceased, little or no benefit is derived from such a eulogy. Eulogies that are generic and lack the detail that brings the dead to life one last time at best often demean both the dead and their memory, and at worst turn a time of solemn remembrance into a trifling occasion. In fact, such rabbinic expressions have often been the subject of morbid humor.

Increasingly, the bereaved, many of whom, because of declining affiliations with Judaism and institutional Jewish life, have been forced to choose between such a generic and often impersonal eulogy and none, are choosing instead to offer their own words to take hold of the funeral and make it their own. In these eulogies, the restraint on displaying personal grief has been loosened, and in typically American fashion the personal becomes public as the drama of family life is played out. This also publicly expresses the pain of loss, a kind of confessional for the living to experience and share. While in some sense this personalism goes against the collectivist ethos of Jewish tradition and the traditional demand to restrain personal pain, the desire to display and enact the personal in front of the community may also be understood as a desire to adapt and merge the personal and the collective. Not by coincidence is this practice common in contemporary American culture, where the blurring of the line between private and public is nearly complete. It is in tune, moreover, with the contemporary American ethos of "do-it-yourself" and "self-reliance" that asserts that those who lived with and loved the deceased can also eulogize them best.

Nevertheless, these eulogies, even when they lack eloquence and are only raw expressions of grief, may more actively engage those who have come to share in the sorrow or offer comfort. The tears that flood a speaker often arouse a sympathetic reaction in others, especially those who identify in some way with the grief.

There also are people who struggle to maintain composure, whose goal is to master fear, calm anger, hold back sobs.[46] These are the ones who represent the motive force that refuses to give in to the pain. If the "active sadness" of tears is an expression of "impotence," of an inability to get beyond the pain and the anxiety, then the restraint is an expression of a desire for mastery.[47] The speaker who tries to muffle tears displays both these tendencies. Recognizing the difficulty of this double imperative, Jewish custom often divided the labor, assigning eulogies to rabbis and the task of mournful crying to a hired chorus of women who could turn on the tears at will.[48] Recognizing the limitations of this practice, the sages simply discouraged "excessive weeping" and urged the mourners to get to the graveyard as expeditiously as possible.[49]

Wherever legalist rabbinic scholars believed people would be defeated by emotion, they created imperatives that would force people to move away from death. That was why, based on the cultural assumption that certain people were more tender-hearted and more deeply touched by the pain of loss, some Jewish communities, guided by these rabbinic dicta, established a custom of keeping women and children away from the corpse or the cemetery, where death always threatened to overwhelm life. Needless to say, as such rabbinic legalism has waned in its authority in Jewish life and as male, patriarchal society has declined as well, these restrictions on women and children have likewise been loosened.

Tragic deaths, those that seem particularly premature or untimely, and those that take place in such a way that the body cannot be retrieved or offered proper burial tend to engender greater trauma.[50] These deaths may require a more vigorous defense against the unbearable and hence often engender public justification and explanation, a eulogy of theodicy. This is so because tragic deaths not only question God's justice but also threaten more vividly the sense of control that human beings and the community have over life. In such cases, the eulogy may seek to repair the damage by offering the consolation that we, the survivors, "are not alone"; that "all this is part of a master plan which will only be revealed to us in the end"; or that the living are being tested, "but if we are good and brave and true all will be well."[51] The messages try to assure the living that the frightening chaos that this death has pointed to is not really there, that instead there is some hidden order, and therefore, even in the face of this gruesome death, there is no need to be anxious. The greater the tragedy of the death, the greater the need to restore order and life. Only God knows why this terrible thing has happened—but God does know, as this case might be made by the traditionally religious.

To be sure, to achieve all these ends, the eulogy must be crafted perfectly.

This is also why we often wish the distinguished or charismatic to compose a eulogy. We attribute to them a capacity beyond that of mere mortals.

While I had no doubt that my sons and I would eulogize my father at his funeral—we wanted to bear witness to how much and what he had meant to us—
there was also no question that we would want his rabbi to speak as well. It was,
after all, a religious service, and rabbis were the ones who endowed such occasions with a special sanctity. We chose two rabbis. One was the rabbi of the synagogue, but the other was a close friend. We asked him to chant the final prayer,
the mournful tune that would invoke God's mercies upon the soul of the departed. Knowing that this rabbi had personal ties to my father, and presumably
stronger ones to God, the family chose to call upon him for this expression of
caring. I suppose the bereaved and faithful son in me also imagined that if there
was to be a heavenly fulfillment of this plea, then having it come from the lips
of a rabbi whose piety and Jewish learning were remarkable and well known in
the community would ensure it.

For an additional eulogy we selected the rabbi from my father's synagogue
because he represented the spiritual voice of the community. His words not only
would ratify that my father belonged to that community but also would echo
the sentiments and cast back the impression that he had left behind. He was
relatively new in town and had not known my father more than a few years. But
the rabbis who knew him and could have waxed poetic about his courage and his
kindness, his gentle spirit and his love of family, his keen wit and sharp intelligence were beyond reach and far from Boston on this snowy March afternoon.
So as the rabbi finished his remarks, concluding with the only words that truly
touched me, the words *yehi zichro baruch* (may his memory be a blessing), which
reminded me that my father now was truly among the dead, I realized that it
was up to me and my sons to stand as public witnesses to who this man truly
was and what we all had lost that day.

"My father was a gentle man," I began, and then reviewed his capacity to love
all that was human, to rebuild his life, to smile, even after having survived the
greatest inhumanity of this century, even after years of suffering the demeaning
horror of his fellow man, and even after the shattering experience of his five
years as a stroke victim. Expressing my feelings and love for him, barely holding
back my tears, and trying to sum up his life, I felt in some small way that I was

beginning the healing, putting at least some part of my father's life into the past
tense, accepting the reality of his death. And, of course, by doing so before the
community and my family, in public, I was also turning outward from myself and
hence toward life.

The traditional Jewish eulogy often tries to connect the event of the death or
the person who is mourned to the season, to the biblical portion read that
week in the synagogue, or to other Scriptures. It is as if by making these connections, the living are somehow rendered less vulnerable: this was the deceased one's time, not ours. Or, alternatively, the day of death was special, and
its timing reveals something distinguished and uniquely revealing about the
one who has died, a kind of Jewish cosmic plan. All this implies that there is
some key to understanding why the person has died at this particular time.
Death is not capricious or completely beyond our comprehension.

Some eulogies, uncommon today but still offered in some places where familiarity with Scripture is abundant, recite a stream of verses from Torah, a
personal book of Lamentations. Each verse is meant to hint at some aspect of
the deceased's biography or personal qualities. This sort of panegyric not only
illustrates the erudition of the eulogizer (and tests the literary knowledge of
those listening) but also implies that the life being recalled was one subsumed
by the Torah, as if to say that the one who has died was part of the sacred
canon.[52] In the absence of such an elaborate litany, eulogizers sometimes select
a verse or two—commonly from the week's Torah reading or from the liturgy
of the particular season—and weave a connection between the one who has
died and the verse. Whatever the nature of the textual gloss, however, it makes
of the funeral an occasion to plumb holy Scriptures, an opportunity for a text-
based moral teaching.

The substance and style of the eulogy are open. Jewish law is far less concerned
with *what* is said than with *when* it is said. In particular, the rabbis noted the
occasions on which eulogies should be *not* be given. There were many. At funerals occurring on festival days and a variety of other holidays, including the
first day of the new Hebrew month, and even on the afternoons preceding
these special days, as well as on the eve of the Sabbath, no eulogies are to be
spoken—all this in line with the principle that "the joyous spirit of the holiday, which devolves on the entire community, overrides the obligation and desire for lamentation by individuals."[53] That is to say, the order of life here
among the living, with its demands and seasons, is what matters most, not the

chaos to which a eulogy is the response. The living and their order—not the dead and their chaos—are in charge here. The requirements of Jewish life must take precedence. Nothing occupies Jewish concerns more insistently and with greater legitimate authority than holy days. So powerful is their claim, which is a claim of life over death, that gradually more and more days have been added to those on which no eulogies are to be offered. Thus, for example, Rabbi David HaLevi Segal, the seventeenth-century Polish author of the *Turei Zahav* (better known as the *Taz*), an authoritative and widely cited gloss on the Code of Jewish Law, has—with the concurrence of a number of other codifiers—extended the exclusion of eulogies to the entire Hebrew month of Nissan, the month in which Passover occurs.[54] Still others also added the first eight days of the month of Sivan, when the festival of Shavuot, commemorating the receipt of the Torah, is celebrated. In time, the list grew to include the Ninth of Av, a fast day commemorating the destruction of the Holy Temple in Jerusalem; the five days between Yom Kippur and the festival of Sukkot; Hanukkah; Purim; Lag B'Omer, a minor holiday in late spring; Tu B'Shvat, the so-called New Year for Trees; and some days whose festive character is largely a shadow of what it was when the Temple was still standing and sacrifices were still brought. In brief, whenever Jewish demands were made on the lives of Jews—even if those demands are in "abeyance" while the Temple remains but a memory and "not yet rebuilt"—eulogies, those homages to the dead, are to be canceled.

In sum, these customs demonstrate that even in death, collective needs take precedence over individual ones. Whereas the individual might have a legitimate claim to receive a eulogy—it is not my fault I died when I did—and the bereaved have the need for it, too, this homage must be set aside because of the festivals and holidays that belong to the Jewish people as a whole. The tension between the needs of the individual and the collective hovers over the funeral, just as the tragedy that one experiences has the capacity to undermine the confidence of all. This tension must be controlled, but in the end it must always be life—which is associated with the collective, the Jewish people who can "never die"—that triumphs.

Does this mean that at funerals falling on these special days no words can be said about the deceased? In fact, among even the most traditionally observant of Jews, the occasion of a funeral does not pass without so-called words of praise for the dead. But the aim of these words, according to the commentators, is to provide "moral teaching" meant to inspire the living rather than words of homage to the dead or words that will elicit tears and regret about the loss of a life.[55] Thus, what might seem to be a eulogy for the dead is, as

these codes affirm, really a service to the living. The prohibitions are circum-
vented because it is by the leave of the living that the dead are praised. In practice, of course, such words of praise are impossible to distinguish from full-
blown eulogies. But, in principle, the distinction must be recognized.

As I stood to deliver the eulogy for my father—forced to be brief, for this was the
eve of the Sabbath—my heart pounded so powerfully, I thought I might collapse
from its force or that all those whose faces I now looked out upon from my
perch next to his casket would not listen to what I said but instead would notice
only my quivering chest. But once I began to speak, they looked directly into my
eyes and never left them. I had spoken to many audiences before—it was what I
did for a living—but never had I experienced the trepidation bordering on panic
that gripped me now. It was not that I worried about holding the listeners'
interest or that they might question my authority to speak before them. As my
father's only child, my right to offer these words would not be questioned. Nor
was I concerned about my remarks comparing unfavorably with those of the
two rabbis who had spoken before me. One had read movingly from Psalms, his
voice solemn and dignified, his choice of verses appropriate; the other had given
the sort of eulogy that everyone expected, with references to my father's biography, to the man that most of those who now came to see him off remembered
from the synagogue. He talked about my father's attachment to and importance
in the community they all shared, about his place in Jewish history as a death
camp survivor, and about his attachment to and pride in his family. For each of
these points, the rabbi offered an appropriate verse from Torah sources that connected my father's life with the sacred Scriptures and traditions that sustained
the Jewish people.

    But when I stood up to speak in a quavering voice, I knew this was not just
another speech. For hours during the previous night, as I waited impatiently for
the dawn of the day he would be buried, I had tried to collect my thoughts
about a life that had been so close to mine. Was it possible to sum up so much
in just a few words? Could I share with others the intimate nature of the tie between him and me? Although I did not think of it in these terms, in all this, I was
of course forced to consider not simply my father or my relationship with him
but how all this could be explained to others, how that which was in the realm
of feeling could be translated. Had I not planned on giving a eulogy, I still would
have had to explain all this to the rabbi or to whomever I would have asked to

speak—there was no avoiding the need to shape feelings into public words and making a life sensible to others. That was what eulogies were.

Now, as I began to search for the right words, I tried to find those that would describe his essential qualities. I reminded everyone, and myself, of how my father was a gentle man who would be remembered by most of those at his funeral and others who knew him as always having a face brightened by a smile. To have seen the horrors of inhumanity, as he had during his years in the Crakow ghetto and later in the several concentration camps where he spent the war, and still be able to smile, to recall not just the horror but also the humanity he had encountered in that terrible time—this, I testified, was the special gift of my father. I shared the story of how, in the ghetto, he had risked his life to ensure that as many people as possible received enough coal to keep warm throughout the bitter winter and the increasing restrictions of the Nazi regime.

I talked about how much he had taught me in his last years of suffering, as his body crumbled under the burden of successive strokes. I admitted that through-out that hell, he still retained the ability to find pleasure in what remained of life, to smile and to share his love. It was a power at which I could only marvel, even as I watched and hated the torment of his tragically broken body.

I talked about how my mother and father had been united throughout sixty years of marriage and all they had been through in the dark years of Nazism, which began just as they were ending their honeymoon year. I spoke about how many times my mother had succeeded in saving his life, first in the concentra-tion camps when she got his name on to the lifesaving list in Oskar Schindler's camp where they were both internees. I reminded all those listening how, in the last five years, she had saved him again by caring for him at home, restoring what little was left of his life, but how at last even she had been crushed by the overwhelming power of age and mortality and could no longer save him. I re-called how she had held his hand as she watched powerlessly when, sitting in his armchair at home, he breathed his last.

But as I spoke these last words, I felt myself losing my composure—as I had lost it when I had first been confronted by my father's plain pine casket, covered by the same tallit that not so long before had been draped over the coffin of the great Rabbi Joseph Dov Soloveitchik, with whom my father shared not only a generation but a community. From some wellspring deep within, a weeping seemed to rise up relentlessly, shaking me. Yet even as I felt the tears well up in-side, and as my efforts to control them became increasingly obvious in my shak-ing voice and the breaths and long pauses that punctuated my uneven staccato rhythm, the very display of frailty, my struggle to control the uncontrollable, I realize now, provided those who watched and listened precisely the experience they had come to share. "All who weep for the dead are forgiven their sins because of the honor they have given the dead."[56] I collected myself, turned to my father's casket, and asked for forgiveness.

In Jewish tradition, whereas God can offer forgiveness for those transgressions committed against Heaven, only one's fellow human beings can pardon those sins that stem from actions within the realm of human relations. Once a year, on the eve of the Days of Awe and the Day of Atonement, Yom Kippur, Jews may turn to one another and ask for forgiveness for the inevitable slights and violations they have committed. Only those who have made their peace with their fellows can then ask God to wipe their slate clean as well. In this worldview, life is an incessant series of human breakdowns of civility and kindness, for which there is no less an endless set of opportunities for repair. And then comes death—and the accounts remain unsettled. How, then, can any of us clear our human debts and on our own judgment day hope for absolution? Only if we gain forgiveness from those who have died can we hope to go on with our own lives and ultimately clear the ledger of our inevitable crimes and misdemeanors. So at the funeral, when the spirits of the newly dead still "hover" about, the mourners turn to them and ask for forgiveness for any and all our offenses against them.[57] These pleas, to close all outstanding grievances, are the last words to be addressed to the dead before they are buried. No less than it does for the Chevra Kaddisha, this appeal tries to turn any possible malevolence in the relationship between the dead and the living into feelings of patronage and forgiveness.

In the drama of this turning to address the casket or the shroud, there is, however, more. It shifts the attention of those assembled back to the inert cadaver but at the same time reminds them that the one whose body is wrapped and boxed for the final journey still retains a relationship to the living.

With that realization, and having asked for forgiveness, the mourners may then also invoke a favor and request in full view of the community that the dead serve as a *meilitz yosher*, an advocate at the Court on High, on behalf of those who grieve and those who have come to the funeral. This is a key moment in the transformation that is inherent in the funeral. A once-living relative or friend now has become a patron saint for the living, all those who recall and turn to him or her for help. The angry dead are now the helpful dead, guardian angels, and the dread that came with their death is diminished.

"These fears of the living can only end completely when the soul has lost the painful and disquieting character that it has after death."[58]

Traditionally, the service is punctuated by prayer. In this context, prayer may be understood as a move from the powerlessness of grief to the empowerment of enlisting God's grace, an echo of the request to the dead for forgiveness, which evolved into a plea for advocacy. The adjuration is the *El Moleh Rachamim,* Lord of Many Mercies, among the most common prayers at funerals, which asks to send the spirit of the dead on its way and appeals to God to accept it upon its arrival at its divine destiny. There are various versions of this prayer, some particular to Jews of Ashkenazic or European origins and others associated with Jews who trace their connections to Sephardic traditions. What all these variants have in common is their insertion of the name of the deceased into the prayer, which thus personalizes the request. That name, followed for the first time publicly in prayer by the words "who has gone to his eternity," associates the one being mourned with this new classification and identity. Unlike the expression "of blessed memory," the tag added in many a eulogy, this phrasing, like the rest of the prayer, is chanted in a mournful melody that echoes with the sounds of generations of Jewish grief. Like all chants, it has a capacity to touch beyond the power of words alone.

Like so much else that marks the way Jewish tradition deals with death, *El Moleh Rachamim* is steeped in the mysteries of Kabbalah, depicting the dead as departing on "the wings of the *Shechina,*" the Godly Spirit, to be "hidden forever in the secret of her wings" and "bound up in the bond of life" in "the Garden of Eden," where the deceased will at last find a "peaceful rest." Few who listen to these words, even those who understand the Hebrew, can fully comprehend them, although the notion that one yearns for a "peaceful rest" implies that the journey is something other than peaceful or restful. This mystery helps turn the prayer, even for those who can follow the words, into something bordering on incantation, yet another reason that *El Moleh Rachamim* looms so large in the encounter with death which remains, after all, the greatest of all mysteries.

Not all services end with this prayer. Although commonly saved for the graveside, in some cases, a Kaddish, the recitation of mourners, is proclaimed at the end of the service (this is common in Jerusalem, where all the offspring of a man are discouraged from accompanying his body to the cemetery and therefore must make their final parting here).[59] With its well-known cadences and rhythms that echo with generations of Jewish memory, the Kaddish—no less than the sung *El Moleh Rachamim*—also has a transformative power (about which more later).

With the concluding prayers, a deference to reality gains the day. Announcements are made about the interment, the period of mourning, and where (and sometimes for how long) it will take place. Ostensibly meant simply to provide information, these proclamations remind all those present that there is more grief work to be done before life will be able to return to its normal patterns. While only some of those at the funeral may choose to accompany the mourners and the dead further, even those who leave do so with the knowledge that they have not necessarily fulfilled either their social or their religious obligations, for the dead and the bereaved are still in transit.

THE PROCESSION TO BURIAL

The time now comes to move the corpse toward its ultimate disposition. Perhaps more than at any other moment during the funeral, this activity forces all those present to confront the corpse. Here local customs are particularly conspicuous. In some funerals, the casket containing the body is lifted and carried through the crowd of mourners, some of whom follow behind it. In others, it is simply removed through a side door and placed in a hearse, while the mourners exit elsewhere and reassemble for some sort of procession later. What is key, however, is the fact that the dead cannot—should not—go to their ultimate repose alone. Like a Torah scroll or, earlier in Jewish history, the Holy Ark of the Covenant, and indeed like any object endowed with exceptional sanctity, in their ceremonial existence the dead must never move unaccompanied.[60] This is because one who is dead, no less than what is sacred, is not only "a reality of a wholly different order from 'natural' realities"; it also is dependent upon those who hold it in esteem to display that honor which otherwise remains obscured.[61]

In the traditional procession, the coffin or enshrouded body is borne from inside the chapel. Carried feet first, the body is oriented in the way it will be laid into the grave, with the feet facing toward the Temple Mount in Jerusalem so that the first steps taken upon resurrection will be toward this sanctum sanctorum. The pallbearers, in an action freighted with meaning, along with those who stand to show honor to the dead, are agents of this sacred duty. Ideally, those who bear the Jewish dead should also be Jews, for in this way the body remains enfolded within the religious community. Undoubtedly, the historic association of impurity with non-Jews (by a Jewish people who traditionally identified themselves as a "kingdom of priests"), as well as the desire somehow to maintain the virtual purity of the corpse that the *tahara* accomplished, is also embedded in this chauvinistic custom.

In Israel, where burial remains within the overall control of the religious establishment, this is not an issue, for these are the men of the Chevra Kaddisha. As they remove the body for burial, the Israelis raise it once again on the *kelicha,* while those elsewhere carry a coffin and the assembled follow behind it. Traditionally, the pallbearers would raise the dead up to their shoulders—a reference to the biblical verse "For the holy service is upon them, to be carried upon their shoulders." The members of the Chevra, who frequently serve as pallbearers, are sometimes known simply as "those who carry on the shoulders."[62] This practice was also meant symbolically to demonstrate for all to see that the dead could rest assured on them.[63] In Hebrew, the term for this action, *lismoch,* also carries the same double meaning: to rest and to rely upon.

There is another reason, some say, for carrying the dead on one's shoulders. Because the word for coffin—*aron*—is the same "as that used in the Bible for the Ark of the Covenant," it became customary, "in conveying it to the cemetery, to carry it on the shoulders, in the manner of that sacred receptacle," which it was thought to parallel.[64] As the ark carried the material objects dedicated to the service of God and sharing a special relationship with the divine, so, too, the coffin (or the cerements) contained a body once dedicated to the service of and created in the image of the divine.

Traditional customs notwithstanding, outside of Israel, this task increasingly has been given over to employees of the funeral chapel, who frequently are not Jews and have no personal relationship with either the deceased, the mourners, or the Jewish community, nor do they have anything but the most instrumental understanding of Jewish ritual. More and more they are likely to move the casket on a rolling wagon, as if to show that the dead can rest and rely on wheels and not people. This shifting of the task to the employees of a funeral chapel and use of a little wagon typify the increasing secularization, depersonalization, and profanation that characterize the contemporary American Jewish funeral and Jewish life.

But in those cases where the pallbearers are drawn from the community, from those who had some relationship with the dead or with those who are grieving, the meaning of this activity is enhanced. In this case, moving the body becomes an expression of a relationship, as well as a display of codependence. Moreover, when those who normally would not take on such "manual labor" instead do so, they do not just bear the dead but also give honor to them and to those who grieve.

Borne aloft and passing close to the living, the body threatens, by its proximity and its sheer physicality, to overwhelm. People move aside, fall behind, give way. But then they follow it. No longer do those in line behind the coffin repeat the medieval formula that Menachem HaMeiri offered, a whispered admission that "I die next."[65] Yet surely these thoughts of mortality are in the air, for the procession behind the coffin is potentially quite frightening. After all, the one who leads the procession is going to be buried, and so one could suppose that all who follow in line will also be swallowed up in the pit. Indeed, there are those who now whisper, in a kind of counterforce of life, verse 10 of Psalm 30: "What profit is there in my blood, if I go down to the pit? Shall the dust praise you? Shall it declare your truth?" More widespread is the quiet recitation of the so-called Golden Poem of David, Psalm 16, a common refrain throughout the period of most intense mourning, which is ordinarily led by whoever is officiating; those who know it join in:

> Preserve me, O God; for in you I put my trust.
> I have said to God, You are my Lord; I have nothing good apart from you;
> As for the holy, who are in the earth, they are the excellent, in whom is all my delight.
> And as for those who follow another god, their sorrows shall be multiplied; their drink offerings of blood I will not offer, nor take up their names upon my lips.
> God is the portion of my inheritance and of my cup; You maintain my lot.
> The lines [of my life] are fallen for me in pleasant places; I have a goodly heritage.
> I will bless the Lord, who has given me counsel; my intuition instructs me in the season of night.
> Always I have set the Lord before me; as long as He is at my right hand, I shall not be moved.
> Therefore my heart is glad, and my honor can rejoice; my flesh also dwells secure.
> For You will not abandon my soul to Sheol; nor will You suffer your pious one to see the pit.
> You will show me the path of life; in Your presence is fullness of joy; at your right hand there are pleasures for evermore.

These are the words of hope, of a desire to avoid the pit of death and the horrors of Sheol. Using the words of the Psalmist, this prayer ostensibly serves as an opportunity for the living to invoke God on behalf of the deceased. Yet it could as easily express the hopes of the living, praying also for themselves and giving thanks for the miracle of their survival. The more people who know the words of the Psalm (one that appears often in the liturgy) are present, the louder becomes the murmur of their voices, the more one gets the sense that it is as much for them as for the dead that they recite these words.

Now, in the open air, when carried out according to tradition, the body leads a procession that is a striking ballet of paradoxes, mirroring the ambivalent feelings inherent in the funeral. In this march to the grave, the steps forward are offset by standstills (seven in some places, three in others) called *ma'amadot,* dramatic displays of hesitation, of an unwillingness to part utterly and finally from those who were so recently among the living, of a desire to delay the burial and implicitly the finality of death, to hold on to the person of the deceased while still moving toward disposing of the decaying corpse.

At the first of these, what is perhaps the single most sensational moment in the service occurs. Someone (often the same person who has led the recitation of Psalm 16) takes a piece of crockery, raises it up, and then casts it to the ground, where it shatters. As he does this, he shouts a line from Psalm 124: "The snare is broken, and we have escaped!" [66]

This gesture, accompanied by the extraordinary outcry and the crash of the breaking pottery, carries a twofold message that cannot help but touch those who understand the words, and even more so those who know the reference. On the one hand, it echoes the Psalmist's description of the soul escaping like a bird from the snare of fowlers. The allegory describes the soul of the dead person, which, until now imprisoned in the body, crashes out of its all-too-human trap and suddenly takes flight just as it is brought out of doors, rising into heaven, liberated from the snare of bodily needs and frailties, a spirit freed from the corpse. It is an image of fleeing from death, of being free as a bird. Life may have an end, the ceremony seems to say, but that end does not necessarily coincide with physical death.

Yet, as already noted, this same moment also echoes the anxieties of all those at the funeral who have been near a death that touched their lives. As they walk into the outside air, often into the light of day from the funereal darkness of the chapel, they must surely feel that "there is but a step between me and death" (1 Samuel 20:3). This is what psychoanalyst Erik Erikson has called an "ego chill," a "shudder which comes from the sudden awareness that . . . nonexistence . . . is possible." [67] Then, as they take a breath of life, they may think as well: the snare is broken, and we have escaped. We have been in the room with death, but *we* are still alive. The Psalmist's outcry becomes a sigh of relief. The transition from eulogy to this moment is a transition "from death as an awareness and summation of *a* life, to death as an awareness and desperate love of *this* life." [68]

The choice of pottery is not incidental. According to Jewish law, all earthenware that comes in contact with death becomes "impure" and must be destroyed. And, of course, it is broken earthenware that covers the eyes and mouth of the corpse. Finally, the destruction of this ancient human creation, the stuff that separates the human intelligence from the animal, is a reminder that regardless of our accomplishments here on earth, nothing that we make is eternal.[69]

> As my family and I stepped out of the chapel, we were at once struck by a gust of cold wind from the late-winter storm and the blinding whiteness of the snow. My eyes began to tear. I was crying; I was blinded; I was cold. But the sharp reality of the outside world—so different from the melancholy darkness of the chapel out of which we had just come—somehow gave me a new breath. And then I heard someone recite the striking words of the Psalmist, "The snare is broken, and we have escaped!" I shivered when I heard them, but there was a truth in them that I could not deny. My father's suffering was over; he had escaped his broken body; and we could now mourn him—we who were still among the living. I took a deep breath of the cold air and began to walk behind the slowly moving hearse that carried his coffin to the grave.

In some funerals, particularly those that take place in the traditionalist precincts of Orthodoxy, it is not uncommon to find alms collectors who, drawing on these desires of the living to avoid death, suddenly appear. Then, often whispering in Hebrew the declaration that "charity will save one from death," a reference to the well-known verse of the High Holy Days' liturgy that asserts that "penitence, prayer and charity controvert the evil decree," they ask for money. The crowd is ready to oblige. Because Judaism views poverty as a kind of death, the giving of charity is seen as a means of giving life, something that those accompanying a body to burial are surely disposed to believe. Good deeds and acts of charity are eternal. If we have escaped the snare of death, let us give the gift of life. The desire to mitigate deeply felt "primitive forebodings of providence" by what is a kind of sympathetic magic retains its power into the present.[70]

Others have suggested that the disposition of the mourners to give to the poor at a time of grieving shifts their attention from themselves back to the community. It makes them "aware of other people's troubles" at a time when they would otherwise be "absorbed" by their own.[71] Perhaps only this underlying dynamic can explain the tolerance that tradition has shown over generations to this infringement of the pain of others on such a personal occasion.[72]

Much could be said about the symbolism of this hesitant march of the living with the dead.[73] To the observer it may seem as if it is simply the words of Scripture as pronounced by the living that ultimately accompany the dead to their tomb, but of course it is the hopes and fears of the living that determine the pace of the journey. They are its inner dynamic. The words of Scripture have been chosen because they reflect the deep structure of the procession's meaning, the dual intention to dispose of the corpse but also to hold on to the life and protect the spirit that once animated it. The symbolism of the march, like so much else during the funeral, awakens individual experience and transmutes "it into a spiritual act, into a metaphysical comprehension" of what it means to accompany the dead to their grave.[74] This is where the talk, that expression of an inner feeling of ambivalence, turns into the walk, its choreography.

The snare broken, those who now choose to leave the funeral—for not all the people, nor even most of those who attend the service, necessarily accompany the dead to burial—may try personally to connect to the mourners and offer some brief expression of comfort. A whispered word, a caress, perhaps even an embrace may be all the occasion demands. Others, particularly those power- fully attached to Jewish tradition, may follow the body for a short distance, as if continuing in the procession. A custom has arisen, particularly (but not ex- clusively) among the Orthodox, to walk slowly behind the body (or the slow- moving vehicle carrying it) for a short distance or to wait until the body has been taken out of sight. While burial must come soon after death, the proces- sion itself should go slowly to show how reluctant the survivors are to part from the one whom they have lost. Some funeral manuals urge those who de- cide to leave at this point to murmur their requests to the dead for forgiveness, while others suggest simply that they whisper the Hebrew farewell: "Go in peace and rest in peace, and arise for your destiny at the end of days." The words of the prophet Daniel echo here: ". . . those who sleep in the dust of the earth shall awake, some to everlasting life" (12:2).

In those funerals—particularly in America—where most of those present remain ignorant of or untouched by the traditions, this moment often loses much of its drama. Instead, the body is removed from the front of the chapel— as already noted, often by the undertakers—and slipped unnoticed into a hearse, while the assembled file out in silence, only to linger out-of-doors, re- orienting themselves to where they must go next: whether to travel on to the grave site or to depart and go on with their own lives. As they stand about, os- tensibly making small talk or perhaps saying their good-byes to friends and family whom they may not have seen in a long time and with whom they have reconnected because of their mutual attachments to the deceased or other mourners (the funeral, after all, *is* an occasion for individuals who share a social network to make contact with one another), they may assert the wish that they meet again, "but only on happy occasions." This is one of those expressions that probably taps the most genuine of feelings, which may account for its universal appeal.

Traditionally a circuitous route to the cemetery was selected "in order to give as many persons as possible an opportunity to join the procession."[75] Here the *ma'amadot* serve to slow down the movement and originally probably offered passersby an opportunity to join, if only briefly, the funeral procession. In some places the procession takes a turn through the streets of the community where the deceased lived, and most frequently at the synagogue, offering a last good-bye. Even when the neighborhood itself is not the actual place in which the deceased lived, the trip is made through the places that are understood to be the home of the Jews. Thus, for example, in Venice, Italy, as recently as the 1970s, funeral processions went through the old Jewish ghetto area, allowing the deceased to pass in front of its five synagogues for one last time. Moreover, the door of the synagogue in which the deceased used to pray was kept open while the procession passed, allowing for a stop there in case a eulogy was to be given.[76]

On those rare occasions when the funeral procession is carried out on foot—these days, that occurs when the funeral takes place on a holy day or when the person being buried is an outstanding public figure (and the cemetery is within walking distance)—the *ma'amadot* can be performed along the route and provide a chance for the column of mourners to expand or even for sharing the privilege of shouldering the corpse.[77] And even those who do not join at the procession can, at the very least, offer a prayer or a recitation of Psalms.[78]

In most instances, however, these days the bodies are taken by car over longer distances. Even here, although recognizing the need for such a conveyance to bring the body to burial, some traditionalists have urged that whatever vehicle is used should somehow be distinguishable from those used by non-Jews or that the driver be a Jew.[79] In most funerals outside of Israel, however, these restrictions are seldom enforced, although hearses used for Jewish funerals are never the flower-bedecked open cars that other religious groups favor, and in many cases, whoever the chauffeur of the hearse is, some member of the family or funeral party (presumably a Jew) rides along (an option that some of the traditionalist rabbis endorsed).[80]

When the body is carried by a motor vehicle, the *ma'amadot* must be carried out either in the few steps between the chapel and the hearse or else later at the cemetery as the body is removed from the hearse and carried to burial.

In those few yards, the broken rhythm of the cortege, along with its recitations and prayers, returns as the procession inches toward the waiting grave. Yet what of the ride in between? In our day in America and most other places, the journey to the cemetery at least partially suspends the funeral, which in the past was a long procession during which Psalm 91 was recited and the body carried to its grave. Now, as the journey to the grave involves a drive, something must be done to bridge the first and second parts of the funeral. But this is difficult. As people enter their cars, they break into small groups or even continue as solitary individuals. In so doing, they in effect leave the funeral gathering, with all its social and spiritual overtones. The time in transit is spent with the living, often focused on matters quite unconnected to the funeral, offering a chance to forget, if only briefly, where one has been and is now going. This is true even when individual cars follow along in parade. Even those who travel in the limousines provided by funeral parlors, while more likely to remain in the funereal atmosphere in part because of the unique character and circumstances of their ride, are nevertheless physically separated from the dead and hence given an opportunity to regenerate themselves as a family of those still among the living.

In Israel, however, not only do the entire funeral services often take place at the cemetery or close to it; when there is a need to convey the body, it travels in a large van attended by ten men of the Chevra Kaddisha. It is a singular expedition.

I clambered aboard the blue van along with the ten members of the Chevra Kaddisha and a couple of relatives of the deceased who squeezed inside with us. We sat along two benches attached to the walls of the small truck while between us, on four metal shafts and still suspended between the poles on which it had been carried from the *Beit Haleveiyot*, rested the enshrouded body of the man we were escorting to his grave. Only a few centimeters separated him from us, and as the van bumped over the rutted streets of Jerusalem, and especially after we drove onto the stony paths in the cemetery on Mount Menuchot, just outside the city limits, we could see the lifeless corpse swaying from side to side or back and forth, the fringes of the tallit in which it was wrapped often grazing our knees.

The immediacy of death was apparent not just in the sight of the corpse; it was in the sound of the rattling poles and chains of the *kelicha* on which the body rested and no less in the words we recited throughout the journey. They

came from *Pirkei Avot*, that section of the Mishnah in which the sages offered
their greatest wisdom to the ages. The particular Mishnah we repeated aloud was
the first of the third chapter, a gloss by one of the sages on the first verse of
chapter 12 of Ecclesiastes, "Remember your Creator."

Dolefully, the recitation began as we stopped dead in our tracks on our way
to the van. In an almost conversational inflection, one of the men intoned:
"Akavya ben Mehalalel says, 'Consider three things and you will not come to sin.
Know from whence you came, where you are going, and before whom you will
have to give an account and reckoning. From whence have you come? From a
putrid drop. Where are you going? To a place of dust, decay, and maggots. Before
whom are you destined to give account and reckoning? Before the Supreme King
of Kings, the Holy One Blessed be He.'" Several times the words of the Mishnah,
so striking in their directness, were repeated, each time followed by the more
hopeful verse from Psalms: "But he, being full of compassion, forgave their iniquity, and did not destroy them; often he turned away his anger, and did not stir
up all his wrath" (78:38). Then one of the mourners repeated the Kaddish. When
he came to the words "may our redemption bloom and our redeemer come
soon," everyone seemed to answer "amen" with particular fervor.

To whom was this addressed, to the dead man we were bringing to grave or
to those of us among the living who accompanied him and could not help but
think that soon enough we would be following the same route? It was a sobering
thought that ensured there would be no small talk—no respite of life—while we
accompanied the dead in the burial van. In line with the code of behavior demanded by the *Gesher HaChayim* manual, no extra words were spoken. From the
moment we had loaded the body into the vehicle and jumped in behind it until
we arrived at the site of the grave—and even while we waited in the closed,
stifling truck while the rest of the cars filled with mourners lined up behind us—
we repeated only the words of Psalm 91, "The Song against Plagues," as some
called it. Once the door to the van slammed shut, the world outside seemed to
evaporate, while inside the sound of this endlessly repeated psalm filled the air.
The atmosphere was smothering me. For the first time, I understood why some
pallbearers chose to recite the *Shema*, that credo of Jewish belief that was also
to be recited by a person as he encountered his own death. I felt like crying out
its words, if only to assure myself that I still lived. But instead, I simply joined in
the chorus of recitation.

Like an endless mantra in an exaggerated monotone, all those in the van
chanted as one its words:

He who dwells in the secret place of the most High, who abides under the shadow
of the Almighty,

Will say to the Lord, my refuge and my fortress, my God, in whom I trust,

For he shall save you from the snare of the fowler, and from the noisome pestilence. He shall cover you with his feathers, and under his wings shall you find
refuge; his truth shall be your shield and buckler.

You shall not be afraid of the terror by night; nor of the arrow that flies by day;

Nor of the pestilence that walks in darkness; nor of the destruction that wastes
at noonday.

A thousand shall fall at your side, and ten thousand at your right hand; but it
shall not come near you.

Only with your eyes shall you behold and see the reward of the wicked.

Because you, O Lord, are my refuge. You have made the most High your
habitation;

No evil shall befall you, nor shall any plague come near your dwelling.

For he shall give his angels charge over you, to keep you in all your ways.

They shall carry you up in their hands, lest you dash your foot against a stone.

You shall tread on the lion and on the adder; the young lion and the crocodile
shall you trample under foot.

Because he has set his love upon me, therefore I will save him; I will set him on
high, because he knows my name.

He shall call upon me, and I will answer him; I will be with him in trouble; I will
save him, and honor him.

With long life I will satisfy him, and show him my salvation.

Like those of the others, my eyes glazed over quickly, looking but seeing nothing. I hung in some in-between world, not dead but not fully engaged by life.
When at last the van reached the cemetery and someone opened the door, I
tumbled out, silently gasping for fresh air, as if trying to breathe in life. Then, the
words of Akavya ben Mehalalel were repeated, and a third and last Kaddish was
recited, just in case any of us might forget where we came from and where we
were yet to go.

AT THE CEMETERY

While the rites at the grave may properly be understood as the culmination
of the Jewish funeral, these days, because the procession to the cemetery is
carried on in automobiles, the interment often seems like a separate reality.
Consequently, activities at the cemetery require, at least in their first moments,
some sort of reorientation to death and a renewal of the funerary ambience.
The sight of the coffin or the enshrouded body and the focused attention upon

it, perhaps more than anything else, accomplish this. The closer one stands to it, the more powerful is its effect. If that is not enough, the sight of the open grave will do the job. The hole is even more striking because it often contrasts starkly with the appearance of the surrounding graves. While the older graves, often neatly covered by earth or manicured grass, demonstrate that even this terrible breach eventually will disappear, that comforting thought usually is not what occurs to mourners looking down at the gaping pit of an open grave.

The traditional Jewish funeral does not, however, depend on these sights alone. Rather, it organizes a variety of rituals and customs to absorb every-one—rituals and customs that also serve to distinguish the occasion as a Jew-ish one. First comes the final processional to the grave. As the pallbearers take up the body for these final steps, Psalm 91 is again invoked. This repetition of the actions and words that marked the funeral just before the ride to the place of burial is meant to arouse feelings of continuity. Now, however, as the body is brought closer to the grave, Psalm 91 is no longer recited in its entirety. In-stead, it becomes truncated, as if the living cannot bring themselves to recite it all the way to the end, just as they cannot bring themselves to the grave and there finally be separated from the person whose body will inhabit it. Seven times the psalm is recited, with each repetition suspended just before the verse "For he shall give his angels charge over you, to keep you in all your ways." Then the procession stops, and with each standstill—closer and closer to the grave—additional words of that last verse are chanted. At the first stop, "For"; at the second, "For he shall give his angels"; at the third, "For he shall give his angels charge"; and so on until at last the entire verse is spoken just as the body reaches the grave. The message is unmistakable: only when the dead and the living stand together at the edge of the abyss are those who still live ready to give "the angels charge" to keep the dead in all their ways.

For the living the encounter with death opened with an expression of confidence in God's justice—Blessed is the True Judge. Now, as the journey to the grave is about to close, it does so with the same sentiment. I refer here to the *Tzidduk HaDin*, the so-called justification of the decree.[81] This is an in-vocation in which the assembled testify to their belief in a God who is power-ful, just, and omnipresent; a God who, regardless of whatever else absorbs his attention, is not uninvolved with the particular but concerns himself with keeping an account of each person's life and death. This is a God—"the Rock," in the opening metaphor of this prayer—who is "perfect in his work and just in all his ways," and hence his decrees of death must also be perfect and just. "Who can say to Him, 'what do you do?'" the invocation continues, admit-ting here at the grave the limits of human power in the face of death. For human beings, who are necessarily feeling relatively powerless and vulnerable at this time, these references are clearly echoes of a desire to lean on a rock, to be secure, to feel that all is still right with the world. So they add that "there is no complaining about the measure of your judgments."

But as with so much else spoken on this day, all this is said not just for the sake of the dead; it is no less an entreaty for the living. "Please take pity and please spare parents and children," the assembled cry out as they move closer to the grave, finding yet another expression for those who have survived, all of whom are surely either parents or children. The words seek hope, recalling the power to "resurrect and give life" from the one who has the capacity for "safe-keeping all the spirits." Finally *Tzidduk HaDin* concludes with the blessing of God, "the true judge," and the line from Job: "The Lord giveth, the Lord taketh, blessed be the name of the Lord." And with that, Kaddish, with its praises of God, is recited, to which all the assembled answer "amen," again and again. Amen, they believe in God's justice. Amen, they believe in his power. Amen, they believe he will spare the righteous and all of the house of Israel.

At the funerals of adult males, particularly in Jerusalem, one discovers a rarely practiced but quite revealing custom in which the Chevra Kaddisha makes seven slow circuits around the body before placing it in the grave. Steeped in hoary belief and mysticism, these seven deliberate revolutions, like the seven pauses on the way to the cemetery, are meant as a protective ritual. Yet here the protection is expressly against the hovering presence of jealous demons, spirits ejaculated with the dead man's nocturnal emissions or seeds otherwise spilled during his lifetime. In the veiled language of the Jewish tradition, these are "the children of the concubines," the "offspring of Lilith," Eve's evil predecessor, who, having adopted these motherless children, still hopes for the offspring she never had to take their vengeance for never having lived. At this moment, they are ready to retaliate against both the living who took their rightful place (which is why the man's living offspring were discouraged from appearing at the graveyard) and the dead. The human circle that surrounds the dead man who is laid upon the ground next to his grave is meant to keep these demons at bay.

Of course, the idea of demons works on a variety of levels and is not unique to Jewish thinking; it is a fixed feature of most primitive people's beliefs.[82] Jewish belief in demons became more highly developed during and after the period of the Babylonian exile (sixth to fifth centuries B.C.E.), when contacts were made with Zoroastrianism, which relied on belief in these evil or fallen angels.[83] In the tradition, however, Jewish demons are traced to Jewish sources, in Scripture, Midrash, and Kabbalah. According to these sources, at the time of death, the demons' goal is to impede the soul's passage to the next world and to capture it. In folk belief the demons also want to capture the souls of the living, which is possible only if the living likewise die. That was why, in Jewish folk belief, demons operated at night (the sleeping are like the dead just as the dead are like those sleeping) and were active at graveyards and around corpses left too long without burial who would attract them.

In the language of Jewish law, this demonization is expressed in terms of the ritual impurity of the cadaver, which remains the aboriginal and ultimate source of all contamination. Even after it has undergone *tahara,* after all, the corpse, as I have noted, remains capable of defiling the living by its proximity and its contact with them. "Death," as John Donne put it, "gets 'twixt soules and bodies such a place as sin insinuates 'twixt just men and grace."[84] As the living must separate themselves from sin, so they must retreat from death and cadavers. To bury the dead as expeditiously as possible is very simply to separate the impurities and demons of death from the living.[85]

Yet the belief in demons also has a psychological dimension that retains its hold long after people have found the belief in the spirit world difficult to sustain. These are the demons that Freud and others have shown us reside in the deeply ambivalent feelings we harbor toward those we mourn and which we project at the time of death as coming from the dead toward the living who have "unfairly" survived them.[86] Recognizing these feelings embedded somewhere inside the relationship between son and father (even before Freud's discovery of the Oedipal relationship), the tradition projected them onto these demonic pretenders for the true living son's role—hence they were called the "children of the concubines." In this circle dance, an eerie replay of the Jewish dances of joy, the demons of guilt are barred from staying in this place (and in the holy city they are even "tricked" by the son's not appearing at the grave of his father, where they await him).

Perhaps this demon dance is also a gestural expression of the Psalmist's declaration: "You have turned my mourning into dancing" (Psalms 30:12). The dance, associated with life, the seven circuits an echo of those made on the holy day of the Rejoicing of the Law, of the bride on her wedding day, is now slow but still resonant with life in the face of death. It is no less an expression of the common practice of inversion, in which the dangerous and malevolent is replaced by its opposite. As Jews refer to the cemetery in Hebrew as the *Beit HaChayim,* the house of life, so they refer to this dance of death as a dance of life.

But, like the existential angst that they represent, the demons cannot simply be kept at bay; they must be placated and dispatched to another place. To accomplish this, custom has a plan. On the dead man's abdomen, seven tiny pieces of silver are placed (for the distinguished, the pieces are larger, sometimes coins or even gold; for those lacking resources, seven pieces of copper or some other metal or even seven stones will do). The ten men of the Chevra Kaddisha join hands—careful not to allow for a breach in the circle through which the demons might enter—and recite Psalm 91 again, always ending each circuit with the plea: "Master of the Universe, take pity and show mercy on the soul of this man for he is the son of Abraham, Isaac and Jacob, Reuben, Simeon, Levi, Judah, Issachar, Zebulun, Joseph, Benjamin, Dan, Naftali, Gad, and Asher." And having mentioned the dead man's family heritage, all these children of Israel, they now conclude with the sixth verse of the twenty-fifth chapter of Genesis: "But to the sons of the concubines, Abraham gave gifts, and sent them away from Isaac his son, while he yet lived, eastward, to the east country." In so doing, they verbally reenact an ancient archetypal gesture that lies deep in the collective memory, a kind of eternal return to the virtues of Father Abraham, and associate themselves with his actions.[87]

After the last circuit has been made, the seven tiny pieces of silver are thrown to the wind.[88] Some have seen this custom as a symbol of the effort to give the gifts to the offspring of the concubines, the evil spirits who will follow the wind. Others hear an echo of a far more ancient belief that the dead must be sent off with a sufficient "fare" that will allow them to pass through the toll gates on the way to heaven. Thus, with words, gifts, and a slow dance are the dead forearmed for the "dangerous" journey that the living believe they are about to take.[89] One might simply say that the living "pay off" the demons of death to be rid of them.[90]

Demons are, of course, also the incarnation of all that is antisocial. Unlike living persons who can share in collective life, demons represent the spirit that plunders and shreds collective existence. They are the tricksters, the evil twins, the accursed, the incorrigibly uncivilized. They are the ones who would dupe the living but in the end are always duped themselves, as life triumphs over death.[91] As these demons are duped and "paid off" in this ceremony, the evil feelings and the destructive impulses they represent are symbolically banished to the winds.[92] At the end, the dead and the mourners are left encircled only by the protective communal display of solicitude and love.

Placing the dead into the grave is probably the most dramatic moment of every funeral. For those Jews who have followed the guidelines of the tradition, who have handled and prepared the body for these last rites from the moment of its demise, the possibility that a "stranger," one outside the faith community, should be responsible for this final phase of the funeral is unthinkable.[93]

This imperative reflects not only the extent to which Judaism sees death as a concern of the community—so much so that the codes prohibit non-Jews from even incidental contact with the corpse—but also the religious sensibility that sees the corpse as an object of both dread and sanctity, which only the select must handle.

In Jerusalem, as the body is laid into the earth, a member of the Chevra, with his own shoes removed, steps into the grave to accept it and swiftly unties all the slipknots that bind the shrouds to the body. This is done to make the departure of the soul swift and easy, to loosen the ties that bind us to our earthly form and context. Then the one who has eased the dead into the ground places a series of cement bricks around and over the prone body, encasing it almost like a coffin. Only then is earth thrown into the hole and the grave covered over. Elsewhere, the coffin or corpse is simply lowered into the ground and then buried.[94]

Whether by burial or some other kind of disposal, the dead at last become invisible. Once they do so, they enter the domain of mystery, that which is beyond the senses and must be treated exclusively with the language of mystery: ritual and rite. Being invisible, the dead in a sense now become more powerful than they ever were in life or even just after death.[95] After all, the dead body, no matter how much it is purified, is still a corrupting influence. But the invisible spirit of the dead, although capable of malevolence, can be, if dealt with in a spiritually positive manner, according to rites prescribed by hallowed tradition and time-honored custom, made altogether holy and pure. The ritual, beginning with *tahara* and continuing at the funeral and throughout the period of mourning, penetrates the mystery of death and makes the spirit of the dead beneficent. It turns the dead into a *meilitz yosher,* an ally, a memory that becomes a blessing. That is precisely what Jews pray for as they commend the body to its rest.

As my father's coffin was carried up the narrow path upon the shoulders of his grandsons and the few of his friends who still had sufficient strength to bear this load through the driving snow that blanketed the graveyard, it passed between rows of monuments of those who had preceded him in death. On the left lay one of his cousins; nearby were his uncle and aunt, the only ones of that generation to have marked graves—all the others having been either murdered and burned by the Nazis or their gravestones torn down by them. Now they awaited him here in this earth of his adopted America. For a moment, I almost forgot that my father was dead and felt like rushing over to him and telling him, "Look, Father, look who's here with you."

In the field in which he would be buried, there were the men and women of his synagogue, people who had worshiped with him and now awaited him in the congregation of the dead. Although my father's body was now a lifeless receptacle in a plain pine box, I still imagined him as being comforted by the knowledge that he was not going to lie alone tonight and forever among strangers, that friends and family lay nearby, that the limitless loneliness of the grave would be mitigated by monuments with familiar names on them. It was probably more a comfort for me, the one who could not feel easy about leaving someone I loved alone in the cold ground, than for him.

Gathered together, the few who had braved the icy roads and come to the cemetery formed a narrow column behind the coffin. It was late Friday afternoon; the head of the Chevra Kaddisha, who had helped organize matters, had tirelessly worked to get the reluctant Boston gravediggers to come out in the storm and open the grave so close to closing time. "Wait for Sunday," they had urged him insistently. But these locals did not know or care about the Jewish law, which required an expeditious burial. They did not know or care that no mourning could begin until after burial and that the bereaved would be in a kind of limbo, no less than our dead, until we had laid the body into the ground.

Now, as we carried him up the path, as I saw the four men who had dug the grave—bundled up against the cold, stamping their feet, and looking ready to get things over with quickly—I knew that they should not take the body from us and complete the funeral. Instead, those who had cared for my father, who had shared his faith and worshiped with him in the synagogue, who had shared his life, who had loved him—they and they alone would place him in the grave. And, following in the custom of our people, they would bury him.

As the gravediggers watched, the men of the Chevra, experienced in putting coffins into the ground with the ropes and straps that the cemetery workers had prepared, slowly lowered the box past the piles of snow and laid my father into the earth. Now I wished we had buried him in Israel, where he would have been handed from the living to the living and placed by hand into the grave. But we were in America, in New England. The bleached pine stood out sharply against the brown mud around the hole, this wound in the mantle of fresh snow. "A grave dug in the snow," the New Englander Emerson once wrote in his journal, was "a ghastly fact abhorrent to nature." But the Talmud, in the tractate *Sanhedrin* (48b), proclaimed that such precipitation from heaven upon the coffin was a sign that the sins of the deceased had been fully atoned.

Already the mound of soil that waited to be returned to the hole from

whence it came was covered with a thin layer of white flakes. No one spoke as
my father's casket went in feet first, facing east toward Jerusalem. When it was
down, the ropes with which it had been lowered were gently withdrawn. Word-
lessly and swiftly so that we could finish before the onset of Sabbath, the men
of the Chevra were the first to take up the spades that like daggers were stuck in
the mound of dirt. We would not leave the body unburied, nor would we leave
any part of the task to the stranger gravediggers. They might open the pit, but
once the body was inside it, the responsibility for covering it belonged to us, we
from among whom he came. No one would depart this place until the entire
grave was filled up, until the wound in the earth had been healed and the healing of mourning could begin.

The grave must not be left open. Just as the face of the dead is kept from the
staring eyes of the living, so the body is covered rather than left bare in an exposed breach. While the Jewish community is expected to bury its own, the
mourners themselves are not. On the contrary, as with the pallbearing, so here,
too, they must depend on others, reminding themselves yet again that they are
wounded by bereavement and cannot get through this alone, even if the pain
of death moves them toward social withdrawal. Everything in Jewish custom
struggles against this desire and presses one toward the community of fellow
Jews. Indeed, the custom in which everyone—except the immediate mourners—shares in the burial may also be explained as one more symbolic expression of the conviction that the death of a Jew is not simply a private sorrow
but one shared by the community. It demonstrates as well that the community, no less than the mourners, has an interest in burying the dead and returning equilibrium to their world.

The burial itself remains impressively simple. The scraping of shovels in the
earth, the thud of the dirt and stones striking the coffin or falling upon the enshrouded body reverberate with mortality. The sight of the dead buried by a
blanket of earth offers a sense of closure. Symbolically, it completes the promise given to mankind in Genesis and so recently repeated: "For dust you are,
and to dust shall you return" (3:19).[96]

In the process of the burial one can see once again how the "dead inspire
a host of intense but mixed emotions."[97] The burial is carried out in such
a way that no one hands a shovel to the other—so as not to hand misery
around, as one observer explained. Instead, each person takes the shovel from
the ground and returns it thence for the next person to pick up on his or
her own. In some places, the custom is to use the back of the shovel for

filling the grave. This practice, which makes the actual interment take longer, serves, like so many of the other rituals of burial, to capture much of the ambivalence of the funeral, of the desire to be rid of the dreaded dead body but also to hold on to the life it contained. By shoveling in this way, the mourners symbolically display their reluctance to close the ground over the loved one who has died even as they continue to do so in line with the Jewish law that requires an expeditious burial.[98] The grave is filled—beginning with the head and then proceeding down to the feet—until the body or casket can no longer be seen.

One by one, people took shovels and began to throw earth into the grave. As I stood witness, the din of the spades and the sound of earth falling on the coffin sent a chill down my spine, while the words called out by the Chevra Kaddisha— "He, the merciful one, is forgiving of iniquity and does not destroy"—seemed to offer consolation.

Then came the continuation of the verse: "Repeatedly, He withdraws His anger, nor does He stir His entire rage." But of course it was not God but we the living who might feel angry and stirred to rage over the loss we had suffered. In reply, these thrice-repeated verses called out a warning to all the survivors that our anger and rage might once again stir heaven to anger and rage. Hence, so that God might not dispatch the angel of death against us, we were meant to invert our passions, to turn wrath into faith, the despair of death into the promise of life—"as God is merciful and forgiving so must you too be merciful and forgiving," as the rabbinic sages put it.

Each person took a few shovels full of the earth and threw it into the hole. The sound of the stones and frozen clumps of soil striking the casket thundered in my ears, punctuating with profound finality this last encounter with my father's earthly remains. When each person had finished his turn at shoveling, he placed the spade back into what remained of the mound. Then, whoever was moved to continue took it in hand and turned the earth into the hole. In line with the tradition, no one handed a shovel to another, a custom that seemed to express a mystical belief that death was contagious, passed via the living as they handed one another the burial spades. To me it seemed, however, that this custom had another meaning: it allowed each person to make the choice to bury the dead on his own; the shovel was taken not because of the social expectation that required one to accept what someone placed in his hand but because one felt an obligation toward the dead.

These men were not professionals; many—particularly those who were my father's contemporaries—struggled with the heavy shovels. Some simply pushed a few clumps of soil into the pit. Others—my sons among them—lifted heaping piles of mud, heavy with the wet snow, and hurled them into the cavity. The violence of their movements made them appear to be wrestling with the death of their grandfather, beating it down and covering it over, burying it deep in the ground. I do not remember how long all this lasted; for me, holding tightly to my mother, who was crushed by the burden of her loss, time lost its meaning. I only recall that when at last the hole was gone and the mound of soil leveled, all that was left was the memory of my father, of a man who lived and who loved us all. The corpse and the coffin were gone.

"Tzvi Kalonymus, son of Shmuel, who has been taken from this world by the will of the Lord who is Master of heaven and earth, may the spirit of God set him in the Garden of Eden," the rabbi began. Then, contrasting with the reality of what we had done, we all prayed that my father, now hidden in the ground, might instead be "hidden in the shelter of God," where he might "behold the pleasantness of the Lord and visit in His sanctuary, awaiting the end of days when he shall once again stand upright." This prayer for the benefit of my dead father was clearly meant no less to help lessen our guilt and any anxieties about what we had done by leaving him in the cold, cold ground. At last, as we concluded with the hope that my father would "rest in peace" along with all those among his people, it was time for me to recite the "great Kaddish."

By now, the Kaddish, its Aramaic words, rhythms, and cadences serving as a kind of obbligato throughout the funeral, had become a familiar companion, an incantation that punctuated each transition in the funeral. Yet this "great Kaddish" was unlike any other that I would ever recite, for it was filled with promises of resurrection and eternal life—not just for the one who has died but for all of Israel.

And what is the resurrection for which the nation can hope?[99] The rebuilding of Jerusalem, the erection of the Temple on high, the uprooting of alien worship from the earth, and the return of the service of heaven to its rightful place on earth, to which the Sephardic tradition adds its perpetual prayer to "cause salvation to sprout and the Messiah to come near"—this is the national resurrection, the moment of burial promises, a resurrection that provides for both individual and collective renewal.[100] It was a Kaddish for us all.

> When the grave was at last completely filled and someone had placed a tem-
> porary marker in the ground with my father's name on it, the rabbi called out,
> *"Yehi zichro baruch,"* may his memory be a blessing, and I through my frozen
> tears answered along with everyone present, "Amen."

As the living stand in the graveyard, they struggle against the fear and horror, the desire to abandon this place of corpses and run for their lives. Instead, they cling to one another and to the Kaddish. Of this moment, Joseph Dov Soloveitchik writes, "The ceremonial turning point at which aninut is transformed into avelut [mourning], despair into intelligent sadness, and self-negation into self-affirmation, is to be found in the recital of Kaddish at the grave."[101] This is because these first public words after burial uttered by the mourners, although mentioning nothing of the sadness of bereavement and affirming a faith in the continued existence of goodness in the world, also resonate with the echoes of generations of Jews who have mourned.

Once again inversion is the order of the day. In a striking reversal of the natural tendencies to flee, the slow recitation makes leaving difficult. Several customs associated with the departure from the cemetery and a funeral further slow down separation from the dead. As described in the Talmud, the procedure for departure originally required mourners to stand in a line while all their consolers passed before them from the left side, the side of the heart.[102] But because of a notorious incident in ancient Jerusalem during which two families argued and pushed past each other to be first in line to offer their condolences, the rabbis decreed that henceforth the consolers would stand in two columns and the mourners would pass between them and accept their consolations. The assumption was that, in their sorrow, mourners would not rush away in an unseemly fashion, and hence the dignity and solemnity of the moment would not be compromised. The passing between the columns is perhaps most dramatic, for it is a choreography in which the living shield and figuratively separate the mourners from the site of death.

But other customs also resonate with the contradictory feelings that accompany those who attend a funeral. Among the more interesting is the practice of pulling up a handful of grass or a clump of dirt and tossing it in the air. Folklorists attribute this custom—which does not appear in Jewish sources until the twelfth century—to be a Jewish version of the "common European practice of throwing things behind one in order to drive away pursuing demons—a motif which recurs time beyond number in folktales."[103]

Others have seen the throwing of the dirt as a repetition of an ancient custom, cited in the book of Job, in which his comforters "sprinkled dust above
their heads toward heaven" (2:12). Yet here, as in so many other adopted
customs, Jewish tradition has managed to laminate its own heritage, liturgy,
beliefs, and meaning onto a common practice with "foreign" origins. Hence
some sources, trying to make Jewish sense out of what the folk have done,
tried to distinguish between the tossing of dirt, which they believed sym-
bolized human mortality, and the grasping of the grass, which they saw as
standing for renewal and resurrection. To emphasize the Jewish character of
the practice, they suggested that when Jews, leaving the cemetery, threw
a clump of soil in the air, they should whisper the words "recall that we are
but dust of the earth," in order to strip the living of their false pride of
survival. Then, suitably chastened, they should uproot some grass and also
throw it to heaven, reminding themselves that, though they too would die,
they had a soul that was immortal. They would then recite the line from
Psalms: "Out of the city may men flourish like the grass of the earth."[104]
A contemporary American rabbi suggests: "Nothing more strikingly reminds us of our mortality and of the brevity of our existence than does
our participation in an interment. We symbolize this renewed awareness of
human transience by plucking grass from the ground and throwing it behind us. Truly, we can say with the Psalmist [103:15]: 'Man's days are like
the grass.'"[105] The Talmud itself drew that parallel, suggesting that "people
are like the grass of the field: they blossom and they wither."[106] Some explain
the grass practice as a symbolic allusion that is itself double: the uprooting is a
reference to the "tearing of the hearts of the bereaved," while the choice of
grass is a way of recalling the belief in resurrection, since grass takes root and
grows.

Still another twentieth-century commentator suggests that these practices
recall a purification ceremony in which ashes of the holy red heifer, water
from a spring, and hyssop—a grasslike plant—were combined and sprinkled
on those who had come into contact with death. The ceremony was meant
to demonstrate that the soul of the deceased had left his "animal-like" body
(the food for which is grass) and was now (hopefully) sustained by spiritual
nourishment.[107] Others attribute the custom to kabbalistic beliefs, arguing that it symbolizes the permission on the part of the bereaved for the deceased to abandon them and for the soul to abandon the body and ascend to
heaven.[108]

The funeral over, those members of the Chevra Kaddisha who are present
at the cemetery may whisper an appeal to the dead, asking him or her by name

once again (as they did at the conclusion of the *tahara*) to pardon them for any slights they may have committed during their sometimes too speedy and routinized labors. They, too, wish to leave the graveyard absolved of the nagging feelings of guilt and the fears of death that rumble just below the surface of consciousness. Then, wishing the deceased a renewed life to come in the end of days, they join the two columns through which the mourners, in the stockinged feet (if the weather allows) of Jewish mourning, pass to receive the consolation of those who have accompanied them to the grave.[109] It is a ceremony meant to touch not only those who pass between the lines but also those who form them: "the ritual despair, the obsequies, the acts of mourning, express the emotion of the bereaved and the loss of the whole group."[110] Death robs us all of life, mutilates our precious notions of being somehow exempt from eradication.

As I turned away at last from my father's fresh grave, I saw before me the somber faces of all those who had come for this final parting. They were lined up in two columns, their heads and shoulders covered by a light layer of snow so that they looked ghostlike to me through my tear-soaked eyes. How clearly they shared my sadness. Holding on to my mother, I made my path between them. We walked the several steps toward the road.

"May you be comforted among the mourners of Zion and Jerusalem," they all whispered in the traditional Jewish formula of consolation. Someone put a hand on my shoulder and squeezed it. Someone else grasped my hand. A few of my mother's old friends kissed her.

I felt at once indescribably lonely, bereft as never before in my life, and also deeply consoled by the nearness of the community that stood protectively around me. These people shielded me from the nearby graves and delivered me from what would have been my inclination not to move from the side of my father's grave.

"Go in peace and rest in peace and arise for your destiny in the end of days," I heard someone behind me saying. I turned around to see that it was one of the men of the Chevra, speaking as he backed away from the mound at my father's grave.

Had the ground not been frozen and blanketed with snow, I would have bent down to tear out some grass or grab some earth to throw over my shoulder as I had often seen done at the end of funerals. But that was impossible now. Instead, I let my thoughts wander until I could picture the face of my father, that smiling face I had been able to see all my life and would never see again. Already, it was hard to recall. I hoped it would return once again.

"Your memory will be my blessing," I silently told my father. Then I whispered, "May your soul have an easy ascent."

Shivah
Seven Days of Mourning

The funeral rites cannot entirely nullify the work of death.
Robert Hertz, *A Contribution to the Study of the Collective Representation of Death*

Dead and buried. One might assume from this cliché that with the end of the funeral comes a conclusion to all that death has wrought. But, of course, as anyone who has gone through the experience of such ultimate loss knows, no funeral, however elaborate or ritually complex, can complete the process of coming to terms with the end of life. For Jews, no less than for others, the dead, the bereaved, and the community all have more to do. *Life has been reversed by death, and now death will be reversed by life.*

As already noted, there is a mystical (some might say imagined) belief among traditional Jews that, particularly in the first days following the funeral, the spirit of the one who has died is unwilling immediately to leave its bodily form, to dissipate into the ether. This conviction is undoubtedly a projection of the lingering attachments that the living still feel to that same body, and even more so to the person of one who until now had been among them. Like the sensations that amputees feel in their phantom limbs, the presence of the dead that the bereaved feel may seem quite real. In great measure, then, there is a "transitional period of the living" that "is a counterpart of the transitional period of the deceased."[1] Indeed, the more deeply rooted the personal attachments to the deceased or the more sudden and unexpected the death, the more vigorously the living experience such an ongoing entanglement with the dead and the longer this transitional period can last. One might suggest that the particular alacrity of the traditional burial—so essential to Judaism—likely enhances this aftereffect and leads to an emotional inability to "distinguish temporary absence from permanent loss."[2] Is this loved one really gone forever? That is the question with which one comes away from the funeral.

In effect, many of the subsequent mourning rituals are an effort to compensate for the swift funeral and burial and to help rearrange the relationship between the dead and the living. They continue the effort to restore life's order that the funeral, and before it the *tahara,* tried to achieve in the face of death's chaos. They seek to answer the question of what precisely is the nature of the loss and what can be done about it. If they do their work, these actions will lead to an answer that is complex but ultimately satisfying. That grief work has "to do with entanglement and separation."[3] It includes repeated recollections and new ways of relating to the dead so that what was once a bond with a living person, an other, becomes transformed into a memory.[4] In the process, the grieving ultimately must conclude that even though for them the world is now, to paraphrase Freud, "poorer and emptier," diminished significantly by the death of their loved one, they will be able to hold on to its essentials, move beyond mourning and melancholia, and return fully to life.[5]

To move the mourners along this path, as we have seen, Jewish tradition demands the help of others and a concrete timetable of mourning. However personal the pain of the bereaved and however much the bereaved might want to withdraw into themselves and have their lamentation be private, for Jews it was necessary that their "mourning will be publicly known."[6] As a mourner, perhaps more than at any other time, "it is impossible to be a Jew alone."[7]

The process of mourning, moreover, begins even before the funeral is over—it is its final act. Hence, the drama of the exit of the bereaved at the cemetery, where, as we have seen, Jews traditionally conclude the funeral and begin their mourning by passing through the rows of those who console them. Accepting the formal words of condolence marks this transition to mourning. As these first steps must begin at the graveyard, in the company of the community, so the Jew will continue in a set series of stages that regulate a return from the abyss of grief.

But the symbolic consolations and kindnesses that conclude the funeral are insufficient for the task. Recognizing that all this cannot happen at once, Judaism divided the aftermath to the funeral into stages. Each of these stages has a name, and each name is identified in temporal terms. The first is shivah (seven days); the second, *shloshim* (thirty days); the third, *yud-beit chodesh* (twelve months); and the last, *yahrzeit* (yearly anniversary).[8] These days mark a gradual coming to terms with the undeniable reality of death, the development of a new kind of relationship both to the deceased and to the community, and ultimately an altered identity for the mourner and the dead.[9]

THE DAYS OF WEEPING AND LAMENTATION

In a sense, the existence of shivah not only demonstrates that the Jews recognize that, while a swift dispatch might have been right for the dead body, for the survivors the burial was too swift; it also reveals that the transitional period of being an *onen* was also too brief and unstructured for those left behind, and therefore something more extended is needed before the bereft can resume their lives. That is why shivah lasts longer than the funeral and is more structured than the *onen* period. With the dead body in its proper place, shivah is for the living a time of mourning governed by order and activity. And like everything else that happens when a Jew dies, it is time-bound and collective.

The first three days after burial are marked as a time when the sense of loss—the sentiment at the heart of mourning—is most intense.[10] These "days of weeping," as the Talmud called them, are recognized, in the words of the Midrash, as a time when "grief is at its strongest, since the facial features of the deceased are still recognizable."[11] The Talmud urged that these days—which overlap emotionally with much of the character of the funeral—be marked off in a variety of ways. For the mourners there is to be absolutely no return to work during this time, even for the poor whose labors consisted simply of begging. The community would provide for them as it did for all mourners. The bereaved simply had to sit down and learn to bear the burden of their loss. So paralyzing are these three days expected to be that even the normally overriding religious obligation to comfort other mourners or attend another funeral is suspended for those who themselves freshly mourn a loss.[12] In effect, the mourners are in a kind of holding pattern, a betwixt-and-between state of being, what one observer has called a "therapeutic holding environment."[13]

The following four days—the balance of the seven called shivah—and as many as thirty days are meant to be a period of lamentation, when feelings of deprivation still infuse mourners' consciousness but are expected to be increasingly offset by a growing recognition that life will go on and that the withdrawals and retreats of mourning must and will end. The seven days are a time when everyone visits the mourners, trying to occupy and sustain them both materially and spiritually. Words of consolation, help in the house, and material and spiritual support are the order of each day.

Jewish custom and tradition recognize that the dead and the immediately bereaved are not the only ones who suffer the aftereffects of death. The community does as well. No less than the bereaved need to find a way to ease the pain of their loss, the group needs to feel that it still has the capacity to heal, to provide order to those shaken by death. For neither is the funeral enough.

In its aftermath, both the bereaved and the community must find some way to mend more completely the tear in the fabric of life that death has wrought and to knit themselves together again. That is why the community is ready to co-operate in the shivah. By helping to repair and renew the bereaved, it also can repair and renew its collective self. For this to work, the inevitable expressions of hostility and conflict within a community, particularly those directed toward the dead or the bereft, must be inhibited, and cooperation is essential. This is how the community heals itself.

One cannot, however, regard this period of intense sociality and communion, of benevolent and compassionate cooperation, without also realizing how ephemeral it must be. The human community cannot long sustain this purely solicitous relationship. Thus, shivah lasts no more than seven days, and sometimes less. And why seven days? Seven days have always "played a prominent role in ancient Jewish liturgy and ritual."[14] Some trace it to the seven days that the biblical Joseph mourned his father Jacob; others argue that the tradition was affirmed by Moses; still others use a reference in the prophecy of Amos that God would turn all "festivals to mourning" as a prooftext, explaining that because all festivals last seven days, so, too, must mourning.[15] But of course seven days also represent the Jewish paradigm of creation, "and each person is a world, a world that never was before and that will never be again"; hence Jews mourn for seven days to re-create the world that they inhabit.[16] If the Creator could construct a world in that amount of time, we human beings can reconstruct our own in no less.

The seven days of shivah represent a kind of inversion of God's seven-day week. Unlike God's seven days, which begin with life and the creation of the world, the mourner's begins with death, as if to indicate that, at least for a week, the human response to death, the work of grief, reverses the divine order of creation.

There is a curious parallel in Jewish tradition between what follows a funeral and what follows a wedding. "In several places," Emanuel Feldman reminds us, "the rabbis connect certain mourning practices with those related to marriage."[17] No less than a fresh death, so does a new marriage create an incentive and an opportunity for those affected to withdraw from society. The bereaved would want to dwell only on the one they have lost, and the new husband and wife, so wrapped up in each other to the exclusion of everyone else, naturally seek to be alone—that, after all, is what the marriage is supposed to allow. Yet in the case of the newlyweds, Jewish tradition demands that these two who are naturally inclined to withdraw from society be forced back into it. Even their first solitary union (called *yichud*) must be monitored and is limited by community representatives. For seven days following their wedding (itself a ceremony that requires witnesses at every stage and crowds of others to offer blessings), the new couple is expected to share a series of meals with others, at least some of whom were not at the wedding, during which the seven blessings—the so-called *sheva brachot*—that were first recited under the wedding canopy are repeated. By the end of this week, the newly married will be reintegrated into the community as a couple, with a host of social obligations incurred, and the danger of their withdrawal from society will be significantly mitigated. No less is this the case for mourners at the conclusion of shivah.

Weddings and funerals, *sheva brachot* and shivah: both are collective experiences and both seek in seven days to reduce the natural inclination to withdraw into antisocial seclusion. Judaism recognizes when it must intensify collective consciousness and engagement. It remains an extraordinarily social religion, which, even at those moments in life when the social seems hard to sustain, creates the conditions that will nevertheless nourish it. The people that some have called "ever-dying" in fact is ever struggling against those forces, both within and without, that would sap its strength or undo its solidarity.

A full-time occupation, shivah seeks to absorb those who observe it. Filled with concretized expressions of grief, it serves even more extensively than the funeral to counteract "the centrifugal forces of fear, dismay, demoralization," and disorder that death engendered and that the funeral made manifest (even as it endeavored to assuage them).[18] In almost every aspect, the practices associated with shivah provide "the most powerful means of reintegration of the group's shaken solidarity and of the re-establishment of its morale" and the morale of the mourners.[19] In the "double-edged play of hope and fear which sets in always in the face of death," the ultimate message of shivah, with its collective consolations and gatherings in the home of the deceased or of the mourners, is that there is a "life after death," for both the dead and the living; that while one person has been lost, the rest of us still live and have one another.[20] In nearly everything that happens during shivah, the many and the one must interact.

If *tahara* prepared the corpse for the journey of death, shivah prepares the mourners for the return to life. Like the *tahara,* the shivah also begins with the laving of hands. This washing occurs after the conclusion of the funeral. Some rabbinic commentators saw in this ablution a desire for absolution, a way to wash away the implicit feelings of guilt that survivors have in the face of death. They recognized in this custom echoes of the ancient practice (described in Deuteronomy 21:1–8) that took place when an unclaimed body was found on the road and buried by the elders of the nearest city. These men poured water over their hands, announcing publicly that their hands had "not shed the blood" of the one they had just buried; they were not guilty in the face of this death.

Others saw the ablutions as a reminder of immersion in the "living waters" of the *mikveh,* the bath into which the impure or defiled dip themselves and out of which they rise back to life. The hand washing thus became a gesture by which the living indicated to the dead that "I do not wish to join you," but instead chose to once again embrace life, which has always been associated with water.[21] Still others saw the washing as a gesture of "purification" that must follow contact with the ultimate impurity of death. Some anthropologists have noted that this ancient custom stemmed "from the fact that death is always regarded in primitive thought as a contagion," and hence washing hands that have come in contact with the dead was one way to be "cleansed" of this communicable pollution. Today, long after such primitive beliefs about death's contagion presumably have been largely relegated to the realm of superstition, this custom retains its appeal perhaps because, in the most transparent manner, it allows survivors to demonstrate that they are ready to "wash their hands of death" and return from its domains to the world of the living.[22]

According to custom, most of those attending a funeral should perform these ablutions as soon as possible, even at the cemetery's gate, where a cup and tap often are made available. The "impure" lave their hands and then set down the empty cup for the next person to pick up (to hand it to another would only defile the newly purified). For those who will be sitting the shivah, however, this laving ritual is put off a bit—as if to say that they are not quite as prepared as the others to wash themselves of the dead. For mourners, the ablutions are commonly completed at the doorway of the home in which they will spend the shivah. Like so much else that in their days of lamentation will be provided for them by others, the cup and water often await their arrival. According to strict custom, no towel is provided. Resorting to the ever-present instrumental idiom of law, some have argued that this is simply because a towel itself may be ritually impure. Others, preferring symbolism, suggest that, like the droplets of water that remain on the mourner's hands, so the memory of death lingers even after one has washed his hands of it; as those drops evaporate, imperceptibly but inevitably, so, too, will the pain of their loss.[23] This of course mirrors a similar failure of those who completed the *tahara* to dry their hands following their final ablution.

IN THE SHIVAH HOUSE

While symbolically begun as the mourners depart the graveyard, the real work of shivah transpires mainly in the home, where the sequestered mourners tra-

ditionally spend the next seven days coming to terms with the death and accepting consolations meant to help them get past the sense of loss. Here they
may expect to undergo a metamorphosis, emerging from their confusion and
sometimes paralyzing grief.

Why sequestration? Some might see this practice as turning mourning into
a metaphorical and figurative drama. Thus, in this "imprisonment" there is a
symbolic reflection of the imprisonment of bereavement, or survivor guilt, and
of anxiety from which there is no easy escape. Others see in it a tacit empathy
with the deceased, who also have no easy escape. Some of the rabbis eschewed
metaphor and more concretely argued that by remaining indoors, the bereaved
would be less likely to be "diverted" from their mourning by the world's at-
tractions and concerns.[24] They wanted mourners to get past their sorrow and
return to life, but they also believed that a rushed return to this-worldly life
would rob them of their need to weep and come to terms with their spiritual
loss. They wanted to help the mourners avoid their most base and material
appetites.

The traditions of shivah also demand that mourners drop their front, let
go of their appearances: they must allow their hair to grow and remain un-
groomed, and they should not bathe. For all seven days they are expected to
wear the same garment they had ripped at the funeral. They patter about without their shoes (in some cases as they leave the cemetery, but most commonly
from the time they enter the shivah house) and walk about in stockinged feet.[25]
In a social milieu of traditional society, where these customs were formed and
where informality was not a way to encounter the world, all these were also
perceived as actions that would reinforce the sequestration of mourning. In
civilized society, as Jewish tradition conceived it, people who look this way did
not commonly set foot outside their door.

At first, this sequestration of shivah seems to fit a common pattern of lamentation found in the vast majority of recorded human societies where mourning requires a "formal withdrawal from society, a period of seclusion, and a
formal re-entry into society."[26] Yet while some features of this three-stage process are present in Jewish practice, shivah does not really offer complete separation or withdrawal from society. Even as the grieving individual endeavors
to remove him- or herself from the flow of life and remain confined for the
seven days of mourning, the community follows him or her into that confinement. With its endless condolence calls and gatherings for prayer in the home,
the particular confinement of shivah seems to create a perfect middle ground
between withdrawal and fellowship. On the one hand, by remaining inside,
mourners are granted the retreat and seclusion that they are inclined to seek
following death. At the same time, however, the fact that all sorts of others

from the world outside are expected to enter that private preserve, joining the mourners in their seclusion, obviously limits the extent and nature of the retreat. In effect, then, shivah takes one of the most private acts a person can perform—the first steps of mourning the loss of a loved one or a family member—and reconstructs it as a public event surrounded by ritual.

Jewish tradition prefers that mourning be carried on in the deceased's home, where the rabbis (and undoubtedly many of the laity too) believed the spirit of the newly dead still lingered and therefore more easily concentrated the grieving of the bereaved and focused the efforts of those who came to console them. This custom, of course, made powerful symbolic sense when people generally died at home. Today, more often than not, death takes place in the neutral domain of the modern hospital, often after an extended stay, or, in the case of the aged—today the largest population of the dying—at a nursing home.[27] Consequently, sitting shivah at the site of death is less and less possible. This effectively makes the decision of where to observe the mourning period more flexible, a matter of choice rather than fate—and hence also more revealing. This is complicated even further in complex modern societies where individuals are highly mobile and often do not live with or even near those for whom they are expected to mourn. Nevertheless, to mourn the dead in the home where they spent their lives still allows those present to more vividly recall the deceased and feel their lingering presence.

Mourning for my father in the same rooms from which only the day before he had left this world, in the house where I had spent so much of my youth, made the experience completely different from what it would have been had I sat shivah in my own house, where he was only an occasional visitor. Here, where I had always been able to find him, I could at once feel both his presence and the acute pain of his absence; he was everywhere, and everywhere missed.

Still dizzy from the events of the past twenty-four hours, in which I had learned of my father's death and seen him buried, I collapsed into the low chair prepared for me at home upon my return from the cemetery. At first I felt as if I might find him in the armchair where for the last five years, since his debilitating strokes, he had always sat. But he was not there and never would be again. The chair's emptiness was overwhelming. When I turned away from the sight to gaze out the windows, I could almost feel him standing nearby, meticulously closing the blinds as he did each evening before going to bed or quietly opening them in the morning when he got up—always the first one—ready to begin the day. If I turned toward the table in the dining room or the kitchen, my eyes were drawn first to his empty chair at the head of each. Even when I was surrounded by visitors, and we looked for chairs on which to seat them, those chairs remained untouched and in their place, silent witnesses to my father's lingering presence and absence.

At night, after the last visitors had left and before I went to sleep, the house still made me mourn his absence vividly. As I drifted into the bedroom he had shared with my mother to say good night, I found her huddled on her side of the now achingly empty bed, unable to move toward the center, as if expecting him to come in and lie down beside her as he had for over half a century. On the dark hardwood floor near his bed, his brown shoes still waited side by side for his feet to step into them. Lying inside the left one was the worn, pale, blue steel shoehorn that he had brought with him from Germany. I could see where his fingers had held it every day of his life for the last forty-six years.

In the closet, where I hung my own clothes, I met his suits neatly lined up, as he was always sure to leave them. I could almost feel him in the gabardine and wool. Holding on to a sleeve, I half expected to find his hand inside and clasp it in mine—but of course everything was empty. Even in the bathroom, when I went to wash up, I encountered his electric shaver, its green charger light blinking, signaling its readiness to ride over his cheeks. Looking at it, I recalled a dream I had when I was about eleven. In that dream I had suddenly learned of my father's death. So vivid and real was that dream that, when I awoke from it, I was in tears. But then, as I regained consciousness, I heard the buzz of his shaver. Running from my bed, I pushed open the bathroom door; there was my father shaving. He was startled to see me up so early, but before he could say a word, I grabbed and hugged him tightly, with a deeply felt joy I shall never forget. He was alive; it was only a bad dream. He hugged me back, smiled, and gave me a kiss, as if he knew the nature of the nightmare. Standing now in the bathroom, almost forty years later, I could still feel the warm softness of his freshly shaved cheeks. But now his death was no dream; the shaver light blinked silently, offering no consolation. Nearby was his toothbrush, still slightly moist.

I noticed the black skullcap that only yesterday had rested on his head and now lay on the hall table. Carefully, I lifted it up, and then, before putting it away in the drawer, I held it close to me. It was redolent with his smell, a distinctive odor that, from the time I was little, had always been an aroma of comfort, a familiar smell I sought out when I missed him and felt frighteningly alone, afraid that we would be separated forever—that fear that the only children of Shoah survivors like me often harbor. For now, the smell of his yarmulke—like the

> clothes that still hung in his closet—gave me the sense that he was near. But this
> time, although this last smell brought him somehow near, I knew that soon, like
> his lingering presence, it would dissipate forever.
>
> Yes, my father was dead and buried; but in this place that brought so much
> of the past back to me, I could mourn his absence as I could nowhere else.

The need to decide upon the location of shivah is a modern problem of a mobile society in which matters that were once beyond choosing now have become matters of preference. Among which "mourners of Zion and Jerusalem"
are they to be counted? Whose consolations matter most to them? Are yesterday's social connections more important than today's? The answers to these
and related questions, often revealing of deep-seated or even unconscious feelings, flow from the decision of where to mourn, a choice that must be made
early, at the very latest by the funeral's conclusion.

Thus, for example, adult children who choose to sit shivah for an aged parent at that parent's home, especially if this is far from where they themselves
now live, find that most of those who come to console them are people from
their own distant past, people from the parent's community and generation.
This no doubt focuses the days differently than if the mourners had spent the
period in their own home, where the visitors will principally be those whose
connections are to them and only indirectly to the deceased who were part of
another place.

Those who share their mourning with siblings—who in these days of high
mobility frequently live in different communities and locales—must also decide whether to spend the shivah together in one place (and, if so, which one),
or whether each will choose to be consoled in his or her own home and community. These decisions also have significance. A decision to mourn in one's
own home effectively emphasizes and fosters the individual mourner's desire
to be reintegrated into the community in which he or she lives. A resolve by
brothers and sisters to mourn together amplifies the family bond among the
bereaved. The chance to be together, to share common memories, is often a
most powerful way to recall and then mourn that person who served to connect them.

The consequences of the choices are not lost upon many contemporary
mourners. Consider the following report:

In my community, we frequently have two shivahs, one in the home of the
deceased parent (or sibling) and one in the home of the son or daughter. Many
of my friends' parents retired to Florida or live far away, so shivah is first done
in the parent's home for nearby friends and family and then is done in the

home of the son or daughter, for his or her friends. With this arrangement, there is a certain amount of alienation. If the parents moved to a retirement community, the children often do not know their parents' friends—perhaps only by name or just to say "hello." There is no shared history; these people are strangers. They will meet them during the shivah and never see them again. But the daughter or son will probably learn things about this part of the parent's life, the phase that was lived apart from the children (and grandchildren).

"On the other hand, sitting shivah in the home of the daughter or son brings together a community of friends, but these friends most likely did not know the parent who died or only met the parent (or sibling) briefly. How can one speak about a parent to someone who did not know him or her? Again, there is no shared history but only discontinuity between past and present."[28]

To be sure, often these mourning decisions are made impulsively, or even by someone other than the mourners themselves. Sometimes, even though they consider the implications of the decision, the mourners, like the one quoted previously, are torn, wanting to place themselves in more than one setting and community, wanting more than one effect from their seven days. Reflecting the fragmented existence and identities of contemporary life, many mourners have begun to divide the shivah so that some of its days are spent in one place and others in another—in a sense recognizing that they must connect to a variety of sites in the social web and accomplish a multiplicity of tasks during these few days.

Moreover, as a result of the growing propensity of some Diaspora Jews to bury their dead in Israel because of attachments to the Holy Land or because of spiritual associations (often inchoate) with its promised redemption or nationalistic ties to the Jewish homeland, the journey from the graveside to the house of mourning back in the Diaspora is often an extended ordeal. Not infrequently the turbulence and fatigue of jet lag have become inseparable from the initial bewilderment and exhaustion of contemporary Jewish bereavement. Yet this tribulation is not just the result of the journey; it is, rather, occasioned by the desire not to mourn alone—even in the land of Israel—but to do so in the context of a local, consoling community. Thus, while reminding mourners where their hearts are, shivah also reminds them of where their home and community are.

Nevertheless, even when mourners observe shivah inside what is to all appearances a familiar place, that place suddenly ceases to be familiar. Like their own lives, which they continue to inhabit but which somehow now feel unfamiliar, and even their bodies, which begin to feel strange, so the place in which they have lived before also seems unfamiliar. "What I remember most vividly about the shivah is my life was turned upside down, and so was my house," as one mourner put it. Inner changes are mirrored by outer ones. As the bereaved first enter the shivah house, they commonly feel disoriented and even somewhat estranged from themselves, as if they were not who they once thought they were. Reflecting this change in those who inhabit its rooms, the rooms themselves are changed. How?

To begin with, because everyone is allowed in to offer condolences, the house of mourning becomes a place of congregation for all people. Just as in mourning private feelings are made public and the family's personal loss becomes the community's as well, so now the private domain becomes a public one. As a consequence of their observance of shivah, those who mourn effectively lose control over what goes on in their home; they become passive residents, subject to the care and tending of others who now flood into their world on the tears of their bereavement. In many cases, mourners find almost no place in their home where they can be alone. Their living room is ordered and kitchen controlled by others; nothing seems private. The private is public; the familiar is strange.

Nothing so powerfully completes the transformation of the home into a public space as holding prayer services inside it, a common feature of shivah, especially where there are mourners who wish to recite the Kaddish prayer. Under these conditions, the home becomes a synagogue (literally a place of [religious] assembly), and its door can no longer be a barrier to intrusion or a portal that protects privacy. Instead, the door that was once commonly locked is now left open, a communal gateway through which people enter and depart as they please, and they do so from dawn until late at night.

While the rabbis argued about who would most properly lead these services—some maintaining that the mourner (particularly the orphan) should do so as a comfort to the deceased and others (particularly those attached to Sephardic custom) arguing that one who was distracted by mourning could not provide the necessary spiritual and moral leadership—all agreed that the convening of a *minyan* in the shivah house was desirable.[29] The sanctity of public worship and the presence of the congregation serve as spiritual counterforces to the disaster of death and the loneliness of bereavement; they can heal the house of mourning by guaranteeing that it is a place of communal life.[30] Congregation is the Jewish antidote to death's abandonment. The orderly schedule of prayer balances the disorderly schedule of dying.

Among those who encouraged the mourner to serve as prayer leader (*shliach tzibbur*, literally "emissary of the congregation"), there were mystics who argued that regardless of his own mental distractions, the mourner's leading the prayers was of spiritual benefit to the recently deceased. They believed that when the mourner intoned the liturgical invitation "*borchu et adonai hamevo-rach*," asking the congregation to "bless God who is the source of all blessed-ness," this freed the soul of the deceased beyond anything that even the reci-tation of mourner's Kaddish accomplished. For the mystics, acts on earth always had the capacity to mirror and hence influence the ethereal realm.

Thinking about this more sociologically, one might argue that the very act of the mourner summoning the congregation to "bless God" was a way of per-suading the living to inhibit not only their doubts about life's continuity but also their anger toward the all-powerful. If the mourner, who has so grievously been hurt, can summon such a blessing, surely we can all summon our hearts to bless God. To the religious, this both transforms the God of death into an ally rather than an adversary and confirms the mourner as a believer rather than one who has been turned away by grief. What *both* the repetition of Kaddish and the invitation by the mourner to the congregation to recite *borchu* do as well, of course, is to echo the sentiments first expressed when the living en-countered or were informed about the death: to bless and exalt God, and hence tacitly acknowledge not only his superior judgment but also their ac-ceptance of God's will. It was a sign of their having made their peace with the Almighty and with the reality of death. As such, then, the summons to "bless God" is a dramatic public statement that some order and spiritual healing have begun to fill the breach opened by death.

In some cases, this transformation of the place of shivah into a place where God may be blessed is facilitated by the rabbi or someone from the congrega-tion with whom the mourner is affiliated who comes with what may be called "a synagogue in a suitcase." This is a valise that can be used as a holy ark and that is filled with prayer books, a Torah scroll, some prayer shawls, and occa-sionally a candelabrum to be lit as part of the service. Then, as prayer begins, everything and everyone must be rearranged. Pictures on the wall that are appropriate for a home suddenly become inappropriate. Seats arranged to focus the gathering around the mourner must now be arranged for worship and turned toward Jerusalem. A dinner table may be transformed into a place for reading from the Torah scroll, while candlesticks become a synagogue menorah. Conversations are suddenly suspended, and the ambience of the room changes.

The presence of all these sacred items along with the recurrent assembly of worshipers, morning and evening, make the house connected to death and mourning into the most holy and pure public space the Jewish community can create. This constitutes a symbolic reversal of the highest order, a true conse-cration of the house.

Nothing was quite so jarring as the ubiquitous morning and evening *minyan*. Every afternoon at sunset and every morning at around six-thirty, people would walk into my house for services. The first morning I barely had time to jump out of bed before they came, so I learned to leave the front door unlocked. On a couple of mornings I sleepily walked into the dining room, where we had decided to pray, to find five or six men already in their prayer shawls and tefillin. There was no time to delay, for they would be off to work as soon as we were done, while I would retreat to the living room to continue my shivah. Or, just when the day seemed to be winding down, and when I might have expected a break for dinner, before the evening's stream of visitors, the afternoon *minyan* would come in and by their presence signal me that it was time to start *mincha*. Life in my house moved to the rhythms of prayer rather than to any personal tempo. Indeed, I lost my personal rhythms, and only those of shivah remained.

There was no chance to straighten up the place or prepare ourselves—we who mourned had the feeling of always being *on*. And because I needed this *minyan*, and was genuinely grateful that people had adjusted their own schedules to enable my fulfillment of this religious obligation, I could not even allow myself to feel put upon by this mass invasion. Hard as it was to jump out of bed in the morning or abandon my dinner, I did so without hesitation.

Moreover, because I was not simply reciting the Kaddish but also leading the service, a practice that offered a chance to recite the Kaddish a few extra times and was meant to provide the soul of my father, whom I was mourning, additional comfort and respite, I had to embrace the *minyan*, lead it, and make it my own. In both behavior and feeling, habitation and disposition, I had to allow myself to be taken over by those who came into my house to help me in my rituals of mourning.

Yet when I saw that those who had come to prayer here were themselves caught up in their devotions, I was deeply moved. This place somehow seemed to exude a holiness that was necessary to blot out the sadness that death had brought into it before the shivah. Each day, bit by bit, the residue of death seemed a bit weaker and the presence of worship and consolation a bit stronger.

According to one custom, the transformation of the house for shivah requires covering the mirrors. Some explain this common practice as stemming from the folk belief that there is a chance one will see, and therefore be drawn to, the lingering image of the dead person in the mirror. For that reason, anything that has a reflective surface and can serve as an entrance into the spirit world

needs to be blocked off at this time of transition. In a more contemporary explanation, psychologists report that at the moments of most acute mourning,
hallucinations and dreams in which the dead appear are not uncommon.[31]
Covering the mirrors is thus a way to protect the grieving from such disturbing sights. Others understand the custom as coming from the talmudic assumption that gazing at oneself in the mirror ultimately leads to or emerges
out of a desire to make one attractive; this, in turn, may arouse sexual passions,
which are prohibited during shivah.[32]

Yet one might also explain the custom more directly. Jewish mourners are
expected to ignore the aesthetics of their appearance, to neither comb nor cut
their hair, to wear their torn garments, to remain physically frozen in the grief
that struck them. Their unkempt appearance, as the Talmud explains, reflects
the disorder of life that death has brought about. A covered mirror allows them
to avoid seeing themselves in disarray. If mourners were to gaze at themselves
in their grief-driven decline, see their unshaved faces, their uncombed hair,
their torn clothing, their tear-soaked eyes, and their broken bearing—all mandated by the customs and rituals of mourning—this sight would make it far
harder for them to be sustained by these very same customs and rituals. Instead
they would see the face of death in their own, and vanity would perhaps con-
sume them, particularly at a time that so many guests have come to visit. Then,
presumably, it would be harder to nurture the feelings of renewal and rebirth
that must emerge from the end of mourning.

Moreover, mourners are marked persons, going through their changes in
public. It is better, the tradition demonstrates, for them to perceive this change
internally or in the faces and attitudes of those who come to console them
rather than in the distorted one-dimensional surface images that a mirror can
reflect.

The shivah house is also transformed and prepared by someone's bringing
in special low stools on which mourners are expected to sit during the next
seven days. The rabbis trace this custom to the scriptural description of those
who came to console Job in his mourning: "And they sat down with him towards the ground seven days and seven nights, and no one spoke a word to
him; for they saw that his suffering was very great" (Job 2:13). The commentators understood the reference "toward the ground" as indicating that the
mourner sat on chairs that were close to the ground. The low chair—as if the
mourner was caught halfway between the ground in which the dead lie and
the higher level of the living—is the position from which the bereaved see the
world. Whatever the reasons for this practice, its effect is that even in a room
crowded with people, those who mourn are easily identified, for they appear
to be "lower" than all the others. The double entendre works well; these are

people who *are* supposed to be feeling lower than everyone else around them. Moreover, because of their lowly situation, all those who come to console them must necessarily bend over and lower themselves to their level. As they are laid low by their grief, so they will be raised by their encounters with those who have come to console them and thereby help them resolve that grief and guide them to the community of the living.

LIVE AND DO NOT DIE

The reversal of the normal and the replacement of the private for the public are also implicit in the first ritual meal that, by tradition, must be eaten by mourners upon their return from the cemetery, the so-called *seudat havra'ah,* or repast of recovery. Jewish law mandates two key requirements here: first, that there must be such a meal eaten by mourners upon returning from a funeral—whether or not they are hungry; and second, that this meal must be prepared by people other than the immediate mourners themselves—that is, by members of their community.[33] The mourners are treated like children or walking wounded who need care and guidance. Some of those who have made the meal even join and help them to eat; commensalism leads to communion, and both transport one to life. And the guidance is so clearly Jewish: "Eat and be well, live and do not die."

The items that are customarily part of the meal include round cakes or beans (lentils, in some traditions) and hard-boiled eggs (in others), the latter peeled by someone other than the mourners.[34] Round foods, the heart of the meal, metaphorically recall the endless circle of life and death. "The world comes round," as Bahya ben Asher of Saragossa put it in the late thirteenth century, explaining some of these choices; death is not the last, but rather life follows death in an unending cycle.[35] And what could more vividly remind one of birth and new life than an egg?

Beyond these metaphors, the customs of the *seudat havra'ah* also reflect the natural reluctance or ambivalence mourners might feel about too hastily abandoning the province of grief and taking up the staff of life. Particularly in the case of those to whom one felt especially close, but to some extent in all bereavement, the psychological tendency is, as Freud once described, to believe that "our hopes, our pride, our happiness, lie in the grave with [the one we have buried], we will not be consoled, we will not fill the loved one's place." Such feelings lead naturally, Freud believed, to survivors behaving as if they "belonged to the tribe of Asra, who must die too when those die whom they love."[36] But eating a meal is a way of showing that one is not ready to die, "that behind all the vicissitudes of life we preserve our existence intact."[37] To be sure, the common habit in which those who have been at a funeral often gather for a meal—even when they are not mourners—suggests an intuitive understanding that eating is the best way to show one is getting over death.

Yet, in general, the grieving really do not feel like eating.[38] That is why others are expected to prepare and serve the meal, even peel the eggs, for even the slightest difficulty in actually taking in the food could lead to the mourners putting the meal aside—a choice that would symbolize the path to death and not life. Indeed, according to the code of Jewish law, during shivah, even on the Sabbath (when mourning is customarily offset by the otherworldly spiritual joy of the day of rest, the day when the dead no less than the living are given a taste of paradise), the bereaved are fed by others. While the *challot,* the two loaves of bread with which the Sabbath meal is begun, are commonly cut by the one who recites the benediction over them and the pieces placed on the table for all others to pick up, in the case of those sitting shivah, the sliced bread—the staff of life—must be placed directly into the mourner's hand.[39] The mourners' willingness to eat the food that others have prepared for them without delay at the very least demonstrates their tacit acceptance of the implicit nudge toward life and life-sustaining social obligations that comes with the proffered edibles.

Some, seeking to find in this meal some halfway point between the desire to join the dead and the affirmation of continued life, have interpreted the meal as a mystical bridge between death and life. In this kabbalistic belief, the dead eat a similar meal at the outset of their journey to eternal life.[40] Thus, this meal becomes a last communion with the dead or at least a reenactment of what the one being mourned is doing at the same moment. While the dead eat to go on to eternal life, the living eat simply to go on with temporal life.

The metaphor of eating and its message of continuity are woven into life throughout the shivah as people bring food to the mourners.[41] A table overflowing with edibles is a common sight at many a shivah. In some places the number of foods that have been delivered serve as a measure of the esteem of the bereaved. The well-connected mourners are inundated with comestibles; those more peripheral to the community may have little on the table.

Even before we left for the funeral, while we were still reeling from the blow of death, a call came from the synagogue's consolation committee. Susan, chair of these volunteers, wanted the key to our house so that she and some other committee members could get in before we returned from the cemetery. While we were burying our dead, they would cover all the mirrors in the house, set up the low chairs on which the mourners would sit when we came home, and place a bowl and pitcher near the door for washing hands. We were not to worry about anything, she assured us. The committee would coordinate matters with the rabbi to see that all the ritual items we needed for the shivah *minyan* would be brought over. Even the little ark that carried the tiny Torah scroll the congregation lent out to the bereaved would be set up. Which room should they put it in? she wanted to know. "Make sure," she explained, "that you put it someplace that faces east [toward Jerusalem]—and where you can fit in all the people." If we did not own enough prayer books for the ten or more people who would come morning and evening to help make the *minyan,* she would also arrange to have a box delivered.

All these were questions we were not ready to answer, staggered as we were by grief. But gently, Susan reminded us that many people would be coming into the house very soon and we needed to make some decisions. Even now we could not ignore the life and social obligations that would come after the funeral. Quickly, we determined that the dining room and adjoining study would be the best place to set up our temporary synagogue.

"Don't worry; it will all be ready by the time you get back," Susan assured me. But that was not all. Our meals for the entire seven days would also be provided, starting with the first one that, Susan informed us, would be on the table when we came home from the burial. She just needed to know how many people would actually be sitting shivah in the house so that she could prepare enough servings, especially for that first meal. She also needed to know how many people might come back from the cemetery to join them in the first meal. Insistent as these questions were, they were not the interrogation of a busybody. Susan simply articulated the inquiries of our community, which was priming itself to see to our ritual needs and assist us in our mourning. Here, in the fullness of the embrace of death, we were being pulled back into the web of life, forced to think beyond the funeral. What was at one level a concern with death and mourning was really a tether to life beyond it.

True to the promise, when we came home, everything went off without a hitch. There to greet us at our own door were Susan and Barbara with the water and meals. While we mourners tottered into the house and collapsed on the low chairs waiting to catch us, others solicitously surrounded us and placed plates holding the meal of recovery on our laps. Meanwhile, in the kitchen, someone posted a list on the refrigerator on which were noted the names of people in the community who had agreed to prepare and deliver a meal during the next seven days. Every breakfast, lunch, and dinner was accounted for—even the multicourse

Sabbath meals. Should anyone fail to arrive, there was a phone number of a substitute in parentheses. But no such calls had to be made. Like the people who arrived in the morning and evening to make the *minyan,* every meal turned up like clockwork. Ultimately, we found ourselves overwhelmed with food because many of those who visited during the shivah also brought edibles. All that we lacked was the opportunity to eat it, for the flow of consoling visitors was nearly unending during the next seven days. We were surrounded: from those who opened the front door at dawn's early light for the morning service to those who helped us close our eyes at night.

Upon entering the house, among the first things the mourner does is kindle a candle—commonly one large enough to last all seven days. There is a kind of symmetry in this act. As a candle was lit when the person died, so now one is lit as the mourning for that same person begins. The imagery is transparent: the body is gone, but the light lingers. Thus, some argue that the light is linked to the fate of the soul. As the soul migrated to the candle when it exited the body, when the candle has burned itself out at shivah's end, the soul will begin its journey in the darkness between corporeal life and spiritual eternity. At the end of the year of mourning, on the *yahrzeit,* a candle will again be kindled, a sign that the dead has returned on this anniversary for a brief call on those who mourn or, as other commentators see it, a sign that it has emerged out of the darkness and now is in the light of paradise.[42]

The mystics were drawn to the power of the candle, seeing in it a hint of man's union with God, an allusion to which they found in the Proverbial verse "The spirit of man is the candle of the Lord" (20:27).[43] The Zohar, the central text of the Kabbalah, considered the burning wick to represent the soul, while the candle that is consumed stood for the body.[44] The candlelight is therefore a visual allegory of the soul, which like the flame stays for a limited time connected to the candle but throughout its temporary bond "strives ever upward" toward the "supernal light" of paradise.[45] Yet it does not take a mystic to perceive the metaphorical capacity of flickering candlelight. Just as a flame is both real and yet not quite palpable, so, too, are the recently departed, whose presence at a shivah is real yet no longer corporeal. And just as the candle burns down to its end, so, too, does life.

Of course, in the most fundamental way, the candlelight is a physical object that offers the senses a way of imagining the otherwise completely ethereal and intangible spirit. That the candle should be such a vehicle is not out of keeping with the way candles are generally used by Jewish tradition on other occasions. Jews commonly kindle candles to mark the crossing of a temporal boundary. For example, the lighting of candles signals the onset of the Sabbath or a holy day, a time when the Jew's relationship to the universe must change. Now the candle indicates the start of a mourning period and a change in one's relationship to the world and to one who has been lost. It is almost as if the very act of kindling the light is a tacit admission by those who do so that for them, life in these next days will be different. The fact that this candle will annually be kindled on this same day—the *yahrzeit*—also indicates that life, as changed on this day (the day of burial and sometimes also of death), will never be quite the same for them.

Returning from the cemetery, my eyes were still filled with afterimages of the funeral, of lugubrious processions in the snow, of the blond pine casket containing my father's bodily remains gently lowered into the hard brown earth, of people hovering about a hole and then filling it up, of consolations murmured and warm tears on my cold cheeks. It was still hard to believe that the hands that had once held my own and the eyes that had once met mine with deep affection—that the body of my father whose life force had been the source of my own—was now lying in a grave underneath the mud and the snow. He still should have been here, in this house where I had always found him, sitting in his brown leather chair. Instead, I was here without him forever, beginning to mourn his eternal absence. I blew my warm breath onto my hands that were still stiff from the cold. The few droplets of water, still left from my ritual ablutions, rolled off with the blows. On the table in the dining room, a large platter of food awaited me: a round roll and a peeled hard-boiled egg on a circular dish brought round by the people of the synagogue who had seen to my every need and prepared the house in which I would spend the next seven days. But I was not ready to eat this food or anything else; my throat was dry and constricted. "At least eat the egg," someone importuned.

Those who had returned with me from the grave were gathering about me, seeking to offer me consolation and support. I needed some breathing space, to be able to quietly acknowledge the depth of my loss. But what to do? Then I saw the candle, in its long, thin glass, standing on the sideboard. I was drawn to it. Someone had placed it precariously close to a picture of my father, which I now gently moved aside, as if treating it too roughly would somehow bring harm to that man who was no longer.

Nearby were some matches. Striking one, I tried to light the wick. My hand began to tremble uncontrollably. Throughout my childhood, the grandparents, uncles, aunts, and cousins I never knew in life, all of whom had perished before I was born in the Nazi plague of hate, had for me been faceless; they were visible only in the candles that my parents lit when those dead were memorialized in prayer. Without pictures to look at, I had only those flickering lights that were the *yahrzeit* lamps with which my parents marked their relatives' dates of passing. Father was particularly scrupulous about these lamps because he had lost everyone. I remember watching him as he lit the candles silently and, with a wistful look and a slight pause, stood as the fire caught and then its flame grew steady.

But because my parents were living, I had never had to light such memorial candles. Now, however, with my father's death, the torch had been passed to me, and I was kindling my first memorial candle, while my father took his place among those who were flickering memories. Inside this house, where I could still feel, smell, sense his living presence, my tremulous hand was telling me that I was not quite ready to turn him into a candle. But the match was lit, and just as it began to singe my fingertips, I put its flame to the wick in the tall glass jar. As I watched the fire catch hold of the wick and stand its curly edge up, I consoled myself with the thought that this was not a light to illumine the physical darkness but rather to lighten the darkness of death.

Each morning, when I got up to lead the prayers, and each evening when I turned in to go to sleep, I checked the glass to see how much of my father's candle was left, as if believing that when this flame was gone even the living memory of my father would begin to fade. When, unexpectedly, on the morning of the sixth day of shivah the candle went out prematurely, I ran to the kitchen cabinet and dug out one of the reserve *yahrzeit* candles that my parents always saved for the other dead in our family. I lit it.

But when I saw this small, familiar flickering vision of the dead, the transition was complete. My father was now permanently joined with all the other dead in our family. His candle was indistinguishable from theirs.

While shivah offers an opportunity for the bereaved to return from the dead to the living, it also recognizes—indeed highlights—the difficulty of that return. One way this is accomplished is by creating certain symbolic parallels between the two. During shivah the mourner is allowed, even encouraged, to seem helpless, dependent on others, as if acting out the helplessness of the deceased who truly can do nothing for themselves. Additionally, just as the dead have given up the pleasures of life, so the mourner must in some way share in these deprivations, albeit symbolically. The mourners are forbidden to engage in lovemaking, to wash, to wear freshly cleaned clothes, to cut their hair, or to participate in any festivities—all behaviors that, when *not* prohibited, celebrate and give pleasure to the body. It is as if the mourners were thus subtly but undeniably trying to "establish an identification" with the dead even as they abandon them, thereby also trying to avoid the jealous wrath of the spirit of the dead whose own separation from bodily pleasure would be highlighted by anything the living to whom they remain attached might do. In other words, the physical hardships flow from a kind of psychological defense, a projection onto the dead of feelings that the living see as naturally human.

While this may seem anachronistic or even primitive in modern secular culture, Jewish tradition retains a powerful belief in the continued humanity of the newly dead; even though they have lost their human bodies, they retain their human emotions. And these emotions, no longer regulated by the constraints of civilization or the realities of face-to-face behavior, are now more difficult to control. Thus, the living are best off being particularly careful, even going to extremes to avoid incurring the dangerous envy and anger of the dead.

Yet it is not just the dead who are unhinged; the mourners can become so as well. Consequently, Jewish custom demands that those who approach them should do so with special care. During shivah, gregariousness, spontaneous conversation, even simple greetings and good-byes, are subject to circumspection and restriction. According to the strict letter of the law, those who come to console should wait for the mourner to speak first, and one source suggests that the visitor's first words should be "Blessed is the true judge." [46] In the home of a fresh mourner, as the Talmud put it, silence is rewarded. [47] The new mourners must not be jarred; they must be allowed their experience of deep sorrow; the principle here is, as Racine once put it, "the sorrow which keeps silence is more sad." [48] Such conversations as do take place are supposed to center around the subject of the one who is being mourned.

Yet while these dependencies and austerities seem aimed primarily to deprive the mourners of pleasure and keep them from emotionally crumbling, they also enable the sorts of intercourse that shivah demands. Thus, seeing persons in a disheveled and passive state tacitly gives license to and even invites others to approach and enter their physical and spiritual space. As the tide of consolers continues unabated from daybreak to long after the stars are out, the mourners, who seem to have been forced to withdraw from the normal flow of life, actually find themselves living in a house and according to a schedule that have been remade to accommodate the visits of everyone they ever knew or who had a relationship with the deceased. Never, it often seems to the mourner, has life been so full of social activity.[49] As Freud long ago discovered, "there are forces in mental life tending to bring about replacement by the opposite"; in place of silence or conversations about the deceased, visitors and mourners often talk endlessly about matters of their daily life and everything else.[50]

This becomes even more dramatically the case where relatively few consolers are present or where the shivah setting places the mourners in the physical focal point of a room. Under these circumstances, the mourners may discover that rather than being passive recipients of condolences, they must suddenly give a social performance, acting as hosts who entertain, introduce, or otherwise occupy the visitors who have come into this home.[51] In effect, in spite of the ritual and traditional constraints of shivah, the well-established rules of face-to-face social interaction take over. Mourners may find that rather than greeting callers with silence, they instead respond to them as if they were guests who elicit a whole array of customary social obligations.[52] Often they can accomplish this using few words but instead well-timed and revealing gestures—a surprised look, a knowing nod, a smile, a well of tears, a hand drawn hesitantly across one's cheek in a display of shock, a finger placed at the corner of the mouth, and so on, sometimes can display more than a spoken greeting. While this sort of hosting may contradict the religious goals of shivah, it nevertheless demonstrates the success of the social aim: to draw the mourners back to life and its sustaining web of affiliations and obligations.

I could barely catch my breath throughout the shivah. From morning to evening, people appeared before me. I felt as if I were "on" all the time: beginning in the morning, when I had to sit and make conversation with those few who remained with me after the conclusion of prayers, through the afternoon, when single visitors seemed to meander in in an endless stream, all of whom required my undivided attention, and into the evening, when the real crush of company came and I found myself repeating details of my father's life or my mother's capacity to cope or what was happening with my children. I learned how to accept with grace the many words of consolation or wisdom, as well as personal narratives aimed to provide some reference for my experience. Above all else, I was consumed by endless small talk. Even when I needed a rest or a bite to eat, I found myself forced to conform to the norms of the shivah call. I had to be available always for conversations of all sorts. How could I be absent, asleep, or eating, when so-and-so had come to pay a shivah call?

Beyond the visitors from the community in which my parents or I lived, other people reappeared out of the days of my distant childhood, as well as people who had known my parents but been out of touch with them for years. There were relatives whom I had not spoken to since my wedding or even my bar mitzvah, my father's cousins, whom I recalled as young and vigorous but who now, after more than thirty years, were aged versions of themselves. One had to search hard for things to say to these people, and I found myself digging deep into my store of small talk. Especially with those I had not seen for years, there were the inevitable conversations about what had happened to each of us in the interim that now required review. Sometimes I even ended up talking to myself as I tried desperately to retrieve the memories of who some of these people were or when I was confronted by a consoler who was at a painful loss for words. In some cases, I simply failed, but acting as a gracious mourner, I never let on my ignorance or my weariness and simply carried on as if we all knew one another and it was good that they had come. There were my own friends as well, some of whom had traveled great distances to pay a condolence call. Come to pay me respect, they of course required a return of special treatment and show of gratitude.

My mother, even more staggered by my father's death than me, was still in shock. Sitting near me, she was not always able to recognize these long-ago friends and relatives, to say nothing of those who came from my own social circle rather than hers. Although I knew that as a mourner I was not supposed to offer greetings or make introductions, from early in the shivah I found myself doing so. There was no remedy for it; I did not want to add to the pain of my bereavement the discomfort of social ineptitude. When my mother took a break because she was exhausted, I had to remain available, for there could not be consolers without someone in the room to console.

Before I knew it, the sorrowful undercurrent and religious dimensions of mourning were covered over by the social imperatives of these visits. Well, maybe not completely. I remained in the grip of grief, yet the presence of all these people pulled me out of the hole of despair and even recalled happier times when my father was with us. He would have loved the company, and so at the end of the day, in some way their presence made us miss him all the more, but now there was a sweetness in the sorrow.

Those who come to console can and often do share reminiscences of their own encounters with death and mourning. These personal revelations offer companionship, an antidote to the existential loneliness of mourning. Perhaps most fundamentally, they provide an achievable model of bereavement. You are not alone, these testimonies seem to suggest; as I once survived a loss like yours, so, too, will you.

Of course, just beneath the surface of this consoling message is another quite different one. As one listens to the tales of others' bereavement and loss, one also hears echoes of unresolved grief. That is, the report from the visitor is actually not really one of perfect survival. Instead, it says of the speaker: I may declare that I have survived my loss, but as you can see from the fact that I continue to repeat my story of bereavement, I still am not finished with my mourning. Now that I have an opportunity to speak to someone who, because of these circumstances, is attuned to such matters, I must repeat the story of my bereavement and again make the effort to come to terms with it.[53]

There were many who shared with me their memories of mourning, almost as if my experience brought back to them the trauma of their own. I remember one such recollection in particular. The source was unexpected: a rather standoffish woman from one of the founding families of my parents' synagogue, a person who had always seemed to me the closest our community had to a Jewish aristocrat, whose dignified bearing made her stand out from the crowd. This woman was fiercely protective of her privacy, of a life that every busybody in the synagogue community wondered about, but the emotional details of which no one really knew very much. When she walked into the house late in the afternoon, I could see all eyes in the room turn toward her, as if to say, "Look who has come." Even in the depths of my personal grief, I also felt a kind of electricity in the air.

Somehow a chair near my mother and me became vacant, and the woman sat down, while one of my sons took her coat and hung it in the closet. There may have been some social niceties offered at first—maybe not. Perhaps we just sat in silence, for I know I was unable to find something to say, and my mother was still reeling from the shock of the last few days. Recognizing that she would have to take charge and rather used to this, our visitor offered a few words about how fine a person she thought my father was, how she always admired his Old World courtliness and charm, loved his ever-present smile. But then, perhaps sensing this was not enough, she began to recall her own death vigil with her mother, and how devastated she felt when at last she, too, had had to watch someone so beloved fade away into death. Although this had happened more than fifteen years earlier, she still recalled the experience. Shivah, she continued, had for her been difficult, and comforts were not immediately to be found until a particular rabbi came by and presented her with what she now felt to be an enormous consolation.

"I found what he said to be much truer than I would have believed," she added. "He told me that when you lose someone very close to you to death, you discover that you somehow take on some of that person's best characteristics. That is, he explained to me, the one you have lost turns up inside of you, and you feel her presence. He said that the one you have lost actually inhabits you. And, you know, he was absolutely right. It happened to me; I found myself acting more and more like my mother, feeling her transforming the way I looked at the world and even at myself. In a way, she lives on in me, and I am now so much like her." She paused, we sat for a few moments in silence, and then she added, "I found that a particular comfort." After another silence, she concluded, "And I believe you will find in time that those special qualities that you associate with your father will become part of you as long as you live. You will find him living in yourself."

Later that evening someone told me about an ancient Jewish custom cited in the Talmud. According to this source, young sons who found it difficult to separate from their fathers would take a lace from their father's right shoe and tie it onto their own left shoe.[54] Commenting on this, Rabbenu Hananel reported that this practice, originally meant only for comforting little boys, had been adopted in some places as well as a way "to quiet the heart" of all sons who mourned their fathers.[55] I had no such lace, but I held on instead to my father's blue steel shoehorn. This relic of his life that he carried with him from Europe, with which, for as long as I could remember, he began and ended each day as he slipped on and off his shoes, offered me a special comfort. I guarded it now as among my most precious possessions, a sacred family relic.

Those mourners who, embracing the silence, reject or are unable to participate in any of these sociable encounters or consoling conversations are nevertheless pressed into the active engagement that inevitably comes with prayer and the mourners' Kaddish that punctuates it. For those who recite them—by strict tradition only the adult male mourners, but increasingly voiced by all those who mourn—the words of Kaddish become a ritual obbligato of shivah. The words are a rhythmic response to death, a mantra of mourning. To many of today's Jews, Kaddish is simply a reverberating echo of words that most of them have intoned for the first time at the funeral. Shunning wailing and swallowing tears, modern Jews have embraced this refrain as the paradigmatic voice of bereavement, even though a majority of them have difficulty with the Hebrew and Aramaic text and may even treat it like some mystical tongue-twisting incantation. Yet for those who persist, it becomes by the end of shivah their most concretely active and repeated response to bereavement and the true sound of Jewish loss. That is probably why many of those who mourn, however loosely, within the framework of Jewish tradition choose for some time to recite the Kaddish, and why it has for many become a kind of Jewish elegy. The mourner who can say nothing else in the presence of those come to offer consolation at the very least finds it possible to say Kaddish.

The rabbis demanded that Kaddish remain attached to "teaching and preaching."[56] Indeed, the power of Kaddish notwithstanding, according to Jewish tradition, the review of "Torah" and its associated texts has for thousands of years served as the preeminent life response of the Jew to all the vicissitudes of life. "The study of Torah supercedes all," as the rabbis put it and as the morning liturgy reiterates.[57] More than that, the Talmud refers frequently to Torah as a "life-potion" and to its review as providing "life renewal" and "hastening the day of redemption."[58] One might therefore assume that in the face of death, an occupation with Torah would be encouraged and that shivah might require a week of meditation on such texts. But this is not the case.

There are a number of reasons. For one, the rabbis—whose dictates guide many of the ritual details of Jewish mourning—perceived Torah study as a source of profound joy.[59] In its essence, however, mourning denies joy. Additionally, the rabbis reasoned, if, as the Psalmist declared, "the dead could not praise God" (Psalms 115:17), nor could they study, then in order not to arouse the envy of the dead, those in mourning ought not do so either. There was also the understanding that Torah study required undivided attention, a concentration that those in the shivah could not possibly maintain. Torah study that was not genuine but simply an empty iteration of words or a tool used for some ulterior motive—both of which a distracted mourner looking for comfort might conceivably do—would, the Talmud asserted, turn the very potion of life into a "drug of death."[60]

Scripture itself, the talmudic interpreters asserted, hinted that Torah study was to be discouraged during the most intense period of mourning. In the Babylonian Talmud, the rabbis reviewing the prophet Ezekiel's experience when his wife had died noted that "the mourner is forbidden to study Torah since the Merciful One said to Ezekiel, 'Sigh in silence.'"[61] The Jerusalem (Palestinian) Talmud derived a similar prohibition from a verse in which Scripture reports that in Job's grief over the death of his family, "no one spoke a word to him" (2:13).[62] For the rabbis of the Talmud there was no conversation that was not filled with Torah study. Silence could therefore only mean that Torah was not spoken. Finally, because the rabbis saw the paramount goal of mourning as a coming to terms with loss and a subsequent reintegration of the mourners into life and community, nothing that could compete with or eclipse those concerns was encouraged—even Torah study.

Yet because the rabbis for whom Torah study was the essence of living could not bring themselves altogether to prohibit mourners its comforts, which they believed contained remedies for everything, at least some of them suggested that certain portions of the Torah treasury could be utilized by those who mourn.[63] Hence they permitted the newly bereaved to review the books of Job and Lamentations and the jeremiads of Jeremiah. In Talmud, they recommended a review of the third chapter of the tractate *Moed Katan,* a text that dealt with the laws of mourning. Finally, the mystics—primarily Isaac Luria—suggested that during shivah a chapter of the Mishnah *Kaylim,* a tractate that deals ostensibly with the ritual purity of vessels and utensils, could be reviewed, since each of its utterances ends with the words "purest of all," a subtle reference to the purity of the soul of the deceased, in whose memory the Mishnah is recited.[64] Moreover, the Hebrew letters spelling "Mishnah" could be transposed to spell "neshamah," the Hebrew word for "soul," a fact the mystics considered of cosmic significance. Finally, and perhaps most important, the recitation of these Torah portions could serve as the pretext for yet another repetition of the Kaddish following them, serving thereby to abet the symbolic work of shivah. In this sense, the fact that such study led ultimately to Kaddish was simply an affirmation that even Torah study had been enlisted in an ideal blending of the immediate and the ultimate, in the service of the mourning and the spirits of the dead.

In effect caught between two imperatives—one that prohibited Torah and one that encouraged it as a lifelong and life-affirming activity—the rabbis ultimately found a way to endorse the latter. Insofar as the tradition embraced this option, it also indicated its bias toward the life affirming. Thus traditional Jews, so much shaped by rabbinic norm and attitude, in the end created a shivah in which it was inconceivable that no Torah would be reviewed. Even where the tradition was faded, someone would find that the gathering required a homily or other reference to the literature of Jewish life, called generally "Torah." If the lesson of shivah was that the mourners should embrace life, the community, and Judaism, then the study of Torah ultimately was an appropriate accompaniment to these three.

The sequestration of shivah is of course predicated on the mourners' success in attracting the ministrations and consolations of the community of the living. The decision to hold services at the place of shivah represents a confidence that sufficient numbers of people will arrive to facilitate them. But what happens when this expression of trust both in the community and in its sense of obligation to the dead and living is misplaced? What happens when insufficient consolers arrive?

The sense of abandonment, already part of the emotional landscape of mourning, necessarily becomes magnified. Even those mourners who want to be left alone cannot fail to be struck when, in fact, they are left alone. Perhaps these feelings are most acute when mourners who wish to recite Kaddish, which for its full effect cannot be recited in dead silence but requires the responses of others, find they must leave the protective membrane of the shivah house and seek out others. Just as the presence of others in the shivah house dramatizes the presence of a healing and assisting community, the journey in search of them magnifies its absence. The Jewish mourner who is too far away to find other Jews will at this time perhaps more powerfully than ever feel the tribal call. For some this will only be answered when at last they find a synagogue congregation. In those places where there were insufficient numbers of Jews to make a congregation in both a synagogue and the home of the mourner, Jewish law and custom demanded that the assembly for prayer take place in the synagogue; the needs of the community supersede those of the individual. The solace the mourner required would then be found at the synagogue.

It was the third day of my shivah for my father. The longer shadows of the afternoon had already made their appearance, but this day they were not accompanied by the arrival of the men I had grown accustomed to seeing when the time for the *mincha* prayers came due. Five minutes before sunset, the last possible moment to recite the prayers, and with only six others besides me, it was becoming apparent that there would not be a *minyan*. I felt devastated, as if I had somehow let down my father, as if his community had forgotten us both so soon.

"You'll just have to go to *shul,*" one of those who *had* come said to me. "I'll call ahead and tell them to wait until we get there," he added.

Although I had been sitting shivah for only three days and had already left the house for Sabbath services that first night, the thought of leaving the house now both angered and threw me into an inexplicable panic, as if by stepping outside I might break the bond that still held me to my father, that had gripped me so powerfully since the funeral. To leave before my time, to step out into the world a moment too soon, felt unbearable. But I dared not skip Kaddish either.

> So without changing out of my slippers or my torn garments, disheveled and
> disoriented, I allowed myself to be taken out. Someone—I no longer remember
> who—led me out and put me in the back seat of the car, where I almost never
> sat. I felt like an invalid. I was outside only for a moment, going from the house
> to the car and from the car to the synagogue door. Yet all the time I felt as if
> I were in some sort of cocoon, as if my mourning separated me from the air
> around me. When I walked into the synagogue, I sat neither at my usual place
> near my father's seat nor in the company of others but instead chose a place in
> the back row, near the door. The prayers passed quickly, and I intoned my Kad-
> dish, though its sound was deadened and lost among the chorus of others who
> were there to recite their own. As soon as *mincha* prayers were over, someone
> hustled me out and brought me back home, where the requisite ten had been
> gathered for the evening prayers that followed. Although it all passed in a flash,
> the bitter loneliness that this trip had engendered in me lasted well after I re-
> turned home.

If the trip out of the shivah house during the week arouses the anxieties of
abandonment and has the potential to make the mourner feel as if the world
beyond the protective walls of sequestration is suddenly uncaring or alien, the
same journey on Sabbath is somewhat different because the Sabbath is supposed to be time of another order, a respite, a piece of eternity. According to
Jewish tradition, on the Sabbath the burdens of shivah, while not truncated as
they are by the onset of other holy days, are nevertheless eased. In folk belief
not only the living but also the dead get a rest. "On all days of the week are
we judged," the dead report in a famous talmudic passage, "and on the Sabbath we rest." It is a respite that the celebrated Rabbi Akiva suggested is cher-
ished among the deceased: "On the Sabbath the sinners of Israel," and by
tradition all the newly dead are counted among their number, "are released
from Gehenna, and they find rest on the Sabbath until the Jews conclude their
evening prayers" on Saturday night.[65] As the dead rest from their travails, so
the bereaved rest from their mourning (and vice versa). On the Sabbath,
mourners throw off their ripped garments, for on this day the grief-torn must
be temporarily mended. While not required to abandon the insulation of the
shivah house, people are nevertheless given greater license to escape its bounds
to attend the Sabbath services at the synagogue.[66] The religious gathering and
collective life of the community, which on Sabbath reaches a spiritual inten-
sity, has the power to pull the mourners out of their sequestration.

Friday evening, with Sabbath's onset, the bereaved, having temporarily shed some aspect of their grief, are encouraged to leave the protective isolation of their mournful abode and come to the synagogue. To be sure, even though they are outside the common setting of their grieving, have changed clothes in "honor" of the Sabbath, and have muted what the Talmud calls the "public mourning practices," custom dictates that they are still to act and be recognized as mourners. [67] Thus in Ashkenazic practice, during the joyful songs that greet the Sabbath, mourners are unobtrusively escorted out of the sanctuary and wait just outside until these melodies conclude. Then, just before the call to *borchu,* the verse that ushers in the Sabbath and that the mystics regard as the liturgical incantation by the living that frees the soul of the dead from torment, someone comes to bring the mourners back inside to join the congregation. In one custom, a person from the congregation announces, "Let us go out to met the mourners"—in some places a clap of the hand against the pulpit is a sufficient summons—and the assembled stand and move or turn toward the door as the mourners enter.[68] Then, as one, the congregants repeat the words of condolence that punctuate encounters with those in mourning. With that, the mourners at last rejoin the congregation in its prayers.

> That afternoon my father had been buried, but now, just a few hours later, it was already Sabbath. Changing out of the slippers in which I had padded about since coming home from the cemetery and putting aside my torn garments, I had dressed in my Sabbath best so that I looked no different from everyone else who had come to the synagogue that night. Yet I felt an interior distance. The desolation of my fresh orphanhood—the utter and final separation from my father—still overwhelmed me. As I sat alone in the anteroom of this congregation in which my father had spent nearly half a century and where I had spent the formative days of my youth, I shivered—maybe from the cold or maybe from the thought of burying my father, with whom for years I had come to this place. At the beginning of the preliminaries to the Sabbath prayers, I had been ushered out of the sanctuary—these jubilant prayers were traditionally considered inappropriate for those in mourning. From where I sat waiting, huddled among the worshipers' hanging coats, the muffled sound of the familiar Sabbath melodies reached my ears. These were the tunes my father and I had so enjoyed singing together and with which we had for many years crossed the unmistakable divide between the rush of weekday existence and the special domains of the Sabbath, with its otherworldly charms and tempos. I knew, of course, just when the congregation stood and turned to welcome the "Sabbath Queen" and when it sat down again.

But this evening, while the members of the congregation raised their voices and did their turns and bows in unison, my father and I remained outside, both of us unable to share in all that. Death and burial left him in the grave and me remote and distant.

At last, when the congregation had completed the choreography of its Sabbath salutations with the closing words of Rabbi Shlomo Alkabetz's sixteenth-century song, "*Lecha Dodi*" (Come My Beloved), someone from inside came to fetch me from among the coats. As I stepped through the back door and slid silently into the sanctuary, someone else struck an open hand loudly against the pulpit while everyone turned back to face me and intoned the now-familiar formula of consolation: "May you be comforted among the mourners of Zion and Jerusalem."

Throughout the day that was what it was like: just when I felt myself settling into the Sabbath, some stroke of mourning would unsettle me, and my ambiguous and limited escape to the synagogue, with its bittersweet respite from the full force of shivah, would evaporate. When at last the twilight came on Saturday afternoon, beckoning me back to the shivah, I understood—perhaps for the first time in my life—my mother's admonitions on long-ago Sabbath afternoons when I was a young boy. Then, impatient for the end of Sabbath and its restrictions, itching for the rapid rhythms of Saturday night, I was ready to rush out with my friends to a movie or downtown. But my mother reminded me to slow down and let the Sabbath last just a bit longer so that the spirit of her parents, long since dead, might enjoy the day's rewards. I used to wonder what was she talking about. Now, I knew.

PARTING AND ENDING

While a shivah house is always open and people enter it at will, unannounced, blending into the circle of consolation, leaving is done with ceremony; it is not supposed to be easy to abandon the mourner, whose entire sadness comes from the abandonment that death represents. Therefore, Jewish tradition tried to shape the leave-taking into a recollection of collective consciousness, to allow the mourners to realize they are not alone, no matter how alone they feel when they are left.

A number of customs are followed as one leaves a house of mourning, but the main focus is on what one says in parting. There are no silent exits here. The Talmud simply suggests saying, "May you be comforted," but the most common phrase, particularly among Ashkenazic Jews, is "May you be com-

forted among the mourners of Zion and Jerusalem."[69] An echo of the consolations offered at the cemetery, it is the verse with which the mourner will be
bid farewell throughout the shivah. (Among Jews who trace their origins to
the communities bordering the Mediterranean, North Africa, and the Middle
East, the phrase "May you be comforted from heaven" is used.)

Rabbinic commentators have offered a variety of homiletic commentaries
and references to account for the origins of this expression. Some hear in it re-
verberations of earlier practices at the ancient Holy Temple in Jerusalem,
where mourners were expected to enter the holy places through a special gateway so that all those present could offer them their words of comfort. That
practice was repeated, albeit in somewhat different forms, after the Temple was
destroyed and synagogues became the primary locus of public worship. Now,
however, the personal grief of the mourner was coupled with a reference to
the loss of the Temple itself and the national mourning that followed. In so doing, the mourners were being reminded that, like so much else in Judaism,
even in the aftermath of death, the personal was wrapped up with the communal. Individual bereavement could not help but recall the great collective
sorrows that befell the Jewish people, epitomized in the Jewish mourning over
the exile from Zion and Jerusalem that, in theology and hagiography, was inextricably tied to the Temple's destruction. By doing this, custom made the
idiom of Jewish consolation, like Jewish prayer, collective.

According to the folklorist Theodor Gaster, this expression that dominates
Ashkenazic custom is not simply consolation but also a warning, a "symbolic
reminder of that wider mourning for Zion which the Jew must never allow to
be obscured by his own private sorrows." It is a hint to those who would put
their own losses above all others that the Jewish national losses must not be ignored even in the face of an individual's suffering.[70] The many trump the one.
But if this is a warning, how can it also provide consolation?

At the most rudimentary level, these (sometimes awkward) ritualized expressions of consolation and farewell serve as a compelling verbal reminder that
this meeting is not like any other social encounter. Beyond that, their repetition throughout the seven days slowly impresses the mourner with the realization that a great change has occurred and that others are aware of it. That
growing structure of understanding and rebuilt social connection may
strengthen the mourners' resistance to the chaos of bereavement. With each
offer and acceptance of consolation, sorrow becomes less inchoate, less an up-
heaval of the spirit, and more a practiced response to regret. The ritualized expressions of comfort and the gestures that the bereaved develop to accept them
gradually congeal the plasma of personal misery.

Perhaps the consolation is inherent in the declaration that implies that whereas the exile from Zion, the destruction of Jerusalem, and all subsequent Jewish catastrophes have made all Jews mourners, they have also made all Jews survivors. "*Vir zinen doh*" (we are still here), as the Yiddish lyrics of a Shoah partisans' survivor song puts it. The individual mourner, who may feel excruciatingly alone and bereft in the first moments after the funeral, is with these words made to recall links to the eternal Jewish people, a nation that by virtue of its experience of destruction and exile knows well such feelings of loss and bereavement. When that connection to an indestructible people is felt, the mourner is ready to understand that just as Jewry has survived the trauma of its desolation, so, too, will the individual Jew who shares in that collective memory and experience.

Some have seen the Ashkenazic expression of consolation simply as a general reminder that other Jews also have mourned: however alone bereavement makes one feel, the mourner is but one among many others who have shared this experience. If the pain people suffer seems peculiar to themselves, or if they perceive suffering as not fairly distributed in the world, they are "apt to have an angry feeling at its injustice."[71] The repeated message that others have also grieved over the pain of such a loss by death thus, at least in principle, aims to diminish the anger, if not always the sorrow.

Still others have seen the consolation connected to faith and the implicit reference to messianic redemption that this expression carries. As Zion and Jerusalem will be redeemed by the Messiah who will bring the Jewish people back from their exile and herald the resurrection of the dead, so, too, those Jews who share in the sorrow and hope over Zion and Jerusalem can expect that when those days come they will once again be reunited with their dead in life.[72]

To be sure, only mourners who share a deep attachment to the Jewish people's historical survival can partake in the full measure of this sort of consolation. Those who share no parochial ties, who feel unconnected to any particular groups—the paradigmatic cosmopolitans whose people are all people and whose home is simply the planet earth—are often also the ones who find it difficult or even impossible to express their grief and find consolation with these words. As they live alone, moving rootlessly through life, so they often will not allow death to stop their relentless existential rush; they choose instead to deny either death's sting or life's condolences and sympathies. For some of these ex-Jews, the Jewish customs of consolation may seem like a burden at best and a pain at worst.[73]

Yet even for those who know nothing of the collective trauma of Jewish destruction and exile, for whom the formulaic phrases of traditional mourning are unrooted slogans, empty and meaningless, or those for whom the Jewish people is but a distant heritage to which the feelings of connection are weak, there are still comforts to be found in these expressions of condolence. These stem primarily from their shared communal origins, from their connection to the presence of the consolers. Shivah is, after all, if nothing else, a time when mourners are not left alone, when they are reminded how much the life of one is bound up with the lives of many. The presence of all these caring others has benefit, for, as the psychoanalyst Melanie Klein once observed, "If the mourner has people whom he loves and who share his grief, and if he can accept their sympathy, the restoration of the harmony of his inner world is promoted, and his fears and distresses are more quickly reduced."[74] As Geoffrey Gorer discovered from his hundreds of interviews with the bereaved, "The grateful acceptance of spoken condolences is the most reliable single sign that the mourner is dealing adequately with his grief."[75]

Recognizing that shivah is an ordeal, and yet an experience that can swallow up those who allow themselves to surrender to it completely, the rabbis and Jewish tradition paid no less attention to its end than to its beginning. For starters, they used the Judeo-legal argument that when one counted days, "a part of a day" could be reckoned as equivalent to the whole.[76] Thus, one would not have to observe the entire seventh day in the shivah but could instead "arise" in the morning, commonly after the conclusion of prayers.[77] Yet because the experience of shivah is so much one of dependence upon others, they also dictated that this termination of the seven days of mourning could not be accomplished by the mourner alone. Rather, it required the urging of others, of those who were in the world beyond the shivah house. Thus, there evolved the custom in which on the seventh day the mourners, as during the previous six days, sit down on their low chairs at the conclusion of the morning prayers, mirroring their low emotional state and expecting the consolations that have become so much a part of their lives since the funeral. But on this day they are greeted instead with the life-affirming and resurrecting charge "Arise."

Some, setting this personal moment into the great chain of Jewish consolation, even add two verses from the spiritual reassurances of the book of Isaiah: "No more shall your sun set; nor shall your moon withdraw itself; for the Lord shall be your everlasting light, and the days of your mourning shall be ended" (60:20). These verses are followed by the words "As one whom his mother comforts, so will I comfort you; and you shall be comforted in Jerusalem" (66:13).

Among the Lubavitcher Hasidim the drama is extended. The consolers leave the room with the same words of consolation always offered upon departing

from a mourner. Then, however, they reenter the room in which the mourners have arisen from their shivah in order to greet them with the verse "May
the Almighty mend all that tears His people, Israel," and then to wish for long
years of life for those who have mourned.[78]

In both the short and the long drama, the final word is that the mourners
not only are offered a blessing but also are reminded that their loss was the Jewish people's loss as well. You are not alone in your mourning, nor shall you be
alone in its end.

Those who have come to offer comfort on this last day now physically raise
the mourners and help them to their feet. Replaying the moment during the
tahara when the dead were prepared by the living to leave behind their own
mortality, the mourners are then urged by the living to follow their spiritual
decree to "remove the filthy garments." With this charge, they immediately
change out of their torn garments and then, preparing for their passage out of
mourning, place shoes upon their feet. In the process they are undergoing their
own *tahara,* or purification from death, as their comforters escort them out of
the house and take them on their first steps back into the land of the living.
Some actually go out first and then change their clothes. But in either case, it
is as if they are expressing the sentiments of the medieval pietists of Ashkenaz
who urged the living to tell the dead: "In the name of God, I do not wish to
join you, or any other dead."[79] I do not need to die now; I choose to go on
living. In Freud's felicitous formulation, "choice stands in the place of necessity, of destiny. Thus man overcomes death,"[80] which in shivah "he has acknowledged."

As it was at the outset of the funeral, so it is at the end of shivah: the dead
go their way, and the living go back to life. Order is restored. The dark night
of mourning gives way to the new morning of life.

Shloshim and Kaddish
The First Month and After

To be a Kaddish is to be willing to suffer the grief of remembering.

Patricia Z. Barry, "On Being the Kaddish"

Stepping out of the restrictions and insularity of the intense period of mourning, commonly in the company of family, close friends, or rabbi, those who have completed shivah discover that "the continuity of the living is a more palpable reality than the continuity of the dead."[1] In spite of the occasion of a death and the grief it has engendered, for generation after generation, the bereaved choose to return to life; and we who have survived the loss of someone close to us are not alone; the order of life can be restored—these are the great lessons with which mourners emerge at the end of shivah.

Following the morning prayers on the seventh day, the rabbi came to the house and informed us that according to Jewish law our shivah was now complete. With that, he recited the words that urged my mother and me to arise from our low and downcast state. He led us, together with my wife and our children, out of the house in which we had been sequestered by our sadness. Cautiously, as if we had been ailing and were just taking the first steps away from our sickbed, we walked arm in arm out the door of the house and carefully, ever so slowly, took a few tentative steps down the stairs and then up the inclined street on which my parents had lived for almost thirty-seven years. Although we knew everything here very well—this was, after all, the route we had walked for so long that we could remember when the large linden trees that overhung the sidewalk were just saplings, and we could still recall the names of nearly every family that had

once lived in the two-family brick houses that lined the street—our slow prome-
nade seemed a journey into a strange, new world. It was almost as if the last
seven days, with extraordinary omnipotence and blinding speed, had transformed all that was once familiar into something utterly foreign. We were like
people who had spent a long time in a dark room and, having at last stepped
into the light, at first found it impossible to see things clearly. This was more
than metaphor; my vision actually seemed to blur, and my eyes, although not
filled with tears, felt unable to stay open so that I needed to tread cautiously, lest
I somehow take a wrong step. My mother who had once led me, whose hands
had once held me overprotectively, who had restricted my movements with the
sheer force of her will, now leaned on me and held on to me for dear life. Was
this really the same world in which we had always moved? Now, over four years
later, as I reflect on that day and those first steps, I believe that what was so
strange was not just the new relationship I had to the world and to my mother.
It was no less the eerie familiarity of everything. That is, at that moment it was
simply impossible for me to believe that with my life so unalterably changed by
my father's death, the world outside the door had not changed at all. Here were
the same houses and trees, the same blue sky, the same twittering birds, the
same neighbors going about their business—but where was my father who, too,
had once been part of this world, whose familiar form I expected to encounter
here, whose smiling face I expected to see over the horizon coming toward me
on his way back from the supermarket or the synagogue?

Yet just as the eyes from a darkened room quickly get used to the light, so
with each step up the empty early morning street, I felt increasingly confident
that I might somehow walk away from the sorrows of mourning and the imprisonment of grief. I could imagine my father just beyond my view, though not
sick and broken as we had seen him before his death but in some new way that
I would get to know. Perhaps the buds of my hopefulness were nurtured by
the fresh spring breezes that filled our nostrils, along with the fragrance of the
blooming lindens and the bright yellow of the forsythias that made it seem as if
nature itself was reminding us of the renewal of life that follows death. I recalled
how much joy my father always drew from the sight of those little yellow flowers that signaled the first days of spring. The tiniest sign of yellow in a forsythia
or the bud of a magnolia, and he would be awash in happiness that spring was
coming. He loved the rebirth of that season, as if it reminded him of his own capacity for rebirth after the many winters of life he had suffered.

Maybe my confidence was just the relief of knowing that the house out of which I stepped and the life I was leaving behind would no longer be filled with the flood of consolers and tears, that we had gotten through the ordeal of shivah. Whatever it was, by the time we reached the crest of the hill and slowly turned around and headed back toward the house, I was ready to believe that my intense mourning was at last at an end and that in a few more steps I would begin to rebuild the life that seemed all the more precious to me now.

Once inside again, while my mother lay down on her bed to rest, I quickly changed out of my torn clothes of mourning, garments I had worn for a week and that seemed to cling to my body. Then I jumped into the shower—something I had not done since the funeral. How revitalizing the water felt, as if washing away the melancholy and giving birth to a new day. I put on fresh clothes, casting aside forever the torn garments that, because I was mourning a parent, would never be mended or worn. The tradition demanded that I not wear brand-new clothes for the coming year, but the freshly washed clothes I put on now felt supremely new.

But of course my shower and change of clothes did not effect a complete break from mourning. Why hadn't I shaved, my mother wanted to know when I came out of the shower. She had forgotten that the newly orphaned must not cut their hair for at least thirty days, and some said up to three months—or until their acquaintances "reprimand" (that was the word the code of law used) them for their unkempt appearance.[2] My grizzled face was there to remind me each day and minute that I was still a mourner.

But an even more insistent reminder was my obligation to recite Kaddish, a responsibility that each day at prayer time would send me looking for a synagogue, where this public act of devotion could be carried out. The extent to which Kaddish would bind me to mourning my father and to the Jewish community that enabled it was something I did not then realize. The extent of its capacity to absorb me would be the most important lesson of *shloshim*, the first month of mourning, and the days that followed.

Jewish life, via its traditions of grieving, may seek to return the world to order and the grieving to life, but the completion of shivah does not end the chaos that death has wrought. Accordingly, shivah cannot finish the process of traditional mourning. In spite of the post-shivah exodus of mourners from the cocoon of the house of mourning to the domains of the living, the close encounter with death cannot magically or suddenly be forgotten or ignored. In fact, once outside, the mourners often experience the sudden loss of the structure of the previous seven days, which can make the next weeks more difficult to bear. After all, during shivah every moment of every day was filled with order and ritual—the details of traditional mourning. But afterward, as the consoling structures loosen, the grief returns, along with anxiety about what is going to happen next. Hence, the survivor may feel as if he or she is in free fall, not fully prepared for a return to the old order of life yet no longer able to be held in the framework of the full-time grief work of shivah.

Even as the tug of life's routines becomes more powerful, the emotional realization of life's broken connection—covered over by the intensive activities and obligations of the preceding week—becomes more imposing. The euphoric relief at shivah's completion, very real at first, is often short-lived. Many of its consolations turn out to be temporary in the extreme. One does not awaken from the suspension of normal life that shivah fostered with the discovery that it was all a bad dream. On the day after shivah, the dead are still dead, and those who mourn, no longer surrounded by the consoling presence of visitors, often feel particularly abandoned.

In a way, post-shivah mourners experience a double sense of abandonment: first from the one they have lost forever and second from the community of those who, in the immediate aftermath of that loss, had come to offer consolations but now return to their own lives, leaving the mourners to take care of themselves. The loneliness that follows and the effort to reconstruct life's routines and promise become an often excruciatingly solitary experience. Even as the mourners may seek to get on with their lives now that shivah is over, they are thus also often painfully aware how much the death and its aftermath still weigh upon them. In part, this is because the one who has died is not expunged completely from memory—quite the contrary, the survivors are enjoined to preserve that memory.[3]

The mourning continues because the separation from both the dead and an end of mourning can only occur, as Freud put it, "bit by bit."[4] In a sense, the thirty days of *shloshim* and, to a lesser extent, the next eleven months for those who have been orphaned reflect Judaism's recognition of this reality. Accordingly, after the intensive experience of shivah comes the less concentrated but still heightened mourning of the remaining twenty-three days that complete the period of the *shloshim,* the thirty days after the funeral that spell out the "bit-by-bit" approach of Jewish mourning. They offer some structure and detail, but also increasing freedom, leading the mourner to the next stage that will assist the transition back to life. For those who remain tied to traditional customs, the net of ritual obligation and social support, looser and not as visible, is still there to protect and guide them in the reconstruction of their new life's order. It defines a kind of "dialectic between 'holding firm' and 'moving on,'" between retaining practices of mourning and embracing the routines of quotidian life.[5] *Shloshim* is an important part of this.

As with so much else in Judaism, the rabbis looked for scriptural sources that supported the idea of a thirty-day extended mourning period, which they enacted. Maimonides, perhaps most famously, found support in the biblical reference to the thirty days following her capture in war that a captive woman would weep for her father and mother.[6] Different sages found other biblical parallels to mourning that used a month as a temporal measure.[7]

Affirming this "bit-by-bit" approach to healing the grief, the Talmud proposed to divide the *shloshim* into a four-week process of return, symbolically marking the transitions on each Sabbath. According to this design, on the first Sabbath (still within the frames of shivah), the bereaved neither can nor should be drawn out of their mourning in public. If they are in the synagogue, they are (as I have described) kept outside the congregation during its "joyous prayers." When at last they are brought back inside, the congregation must publicly offer expressions of condolence, reminding both mourners and everyone else that something is amiss. At the end of the service, mourners are expected to slip out of sight quietly, without any of the social niceties of leave-taking, and hurry back to the protective harbor of their shivah house. In short, during the first week, mourners might be in, but not at all part of, the synagogue and the outside world.

On the second Sabbath, in their immediate post-shivah situation, although mourners return to the house of worship, they do so as people still beset by grief, still recognizable by their unkempt, uncut hair and the special recitation of Kaddish. No longer expected to remove themselves during certain parts of the service, they share fully in collective prayer, but they are advised to sit in a place other than their normal one, as if to indicate that even on the Sabbath, with its respite from pain, they remain somehow communally unsettled.

On the third Sabbath, while at last allowed to return to their established seats in the community (something they could not yet do during their week-day synagogue visits), they are nevertheless expected to sit in silence, unable to participate in the social patter that is apparently always a part of congregational gathering.[8] They are to reflect their grief in the way they restrain their social intercourse.

Finally, and only on the fourth Sabbath, could mourners return publicly and fully to the community and act "like all people," as the Talmud put it.[9] In the end, no matter how an individual mourner might feel, the continuity with the living at last has to supersede the continuity with the dead. One, two, three, four, and the mourner has made it out the door; order should be fully restored.

In *shloshim,* Jewish custom and tradition evolved a series of measures that would slow the relentless return which the force of continuing life in the world outside the house of mourning inexorably abets. These measures were meant to remind those whose tone of life threatened to drown out the lingering echoes of their bereavement too quickly not to forget they were still mourners. Some were contained in the demands that during the extended thirty-day mourning period the bereaved desist from becoming married, preventing the seminal act of Jewish joy: building a new family. Tradition considered the mourners still too socially fragile for that. Others were articulated in simple outward signs: the grizzled appearance among men who remain unshaved; the failure to sit in one's customary place in the synagogue; the custom of not wearing brand-new clothing or—until the Middle Ages—the habit of wearing the *mitron,* or hood, the special garment of the thirty days; and the prohibition against responding to a greeting with *shalom* (all's well), for during these thirty days, all was not well or complete (*shalem*). During this extended period, mourners were also enjoined from listening to live music or dancing, activities that Jewish tradition associated with pure joy. All this was supposed to help both the mourners and other Jews recall that things were not yet quite right.

In the days when travel beyond the precincts of one's neighborhood or community was considered an exceptional experience, when life on the open road or high seas was fraught with both excitement and peril, and making a voyage was seen as a daring expedition into the unknown, Jewish mourners who were still in their *shloshim* were discouraged from such a bold step into the world, a lone adventure. They should not chance such a break from the comforting surroundings of the familiar. Yet, in keeping with the dialectical nature of this post-shivah period, Jewish law stipulated that should mourners' friends "reprimand" them and urge that they join *them* on a journey, the mourners might do so.[10]

Indeed, the demands of friendship—which stand behind this exemption— were quite important as an antidote to the restrictions of mourning after the end of shivah. *Simchat mere'ut,* the exchange of visits (and meals) between friends, which the interpreters of Jewish law understood to be part of a set of binding reciprocal social obligations (particularly when the friends "insist" one attend), was allowed—so much so that if mourners had incurred such an obligation just before bereavement, they would, in spite of the restrictions on joining happy assemblies during the extended period of mourning, nevertheless be obligated to reciprocate just after the end of shivah, while still within the thirty-day mourning period.[11] Similarly, social invitations on Sabbaths or holidays were permitted, as were some unplanned "drop-in" visits that were not expressly celebratory.[12] Long before anthropologist Marcel Mauss deciphered and documented the universal process of what he called "prestation," the threefold reciprocal obligations of giving, receiving, and repaying that he defined as an essential connective dynamic of society and one of the fundamentals of maintaining collective life, Jewish tradition understood the imperatives of communal reciprocity and recognized that they might even serve as the dynamic for undoing the social withdrawal associated with mourning.[13]

To be sure, given the essentials of mourning, there were restrictions even on the social demands of reciprocity. Hence, sharing in grand festive occasions where there would be large assemblies—weddings, parties, and the like—was to be shunned during the thirty days and, for those newly orphaned, for a full year.[14] This sort of plunge into what Judaism conceived of as supreme collective pleasures was simply considered impossible for those who, by virtue of their status as mourners, could still feel the aftershocks of their grief and therefore were insufficiently steady and secure to participate with the necessary exuberance.

Yet, in the fact that even for these gatherings some exceptions were allowed, the dialectic between "holding firm" in the grip if mourning and "moving on" in the flow of life is discernible. At weddings in one's immediate family or at gatherings for the sake of a circumcision or some other ritually marked Jewish rite of passage, the mourners, having to choose between alignment with life, with their family, or with death, would have to choose life and find some way to attend the religious and ritual component of the event, although often distancing themselves from the accompanying meal, which the rabbis viewed as purely celebratory.[15] Or, where mourners served as enablers of the events— if they were rabbis, accompanied the bride or bridegroom to the wedding canopy, assisted at a circumcision, or even were needed as the tenth in a *minyan,* in short, if their presence was crucial for the event to take place—they could participate in gatherings that would otherwise be off limits for them. Some sages even allowed mourners to attend testimonials organized for charitable causes, if by doing so they increased the amount of charity gathered.[16] In effect, all these exceptions had in common the fact that they added to the collective greater good and enabled Jewish life to go on.

For the mourner in *shloshim* this meant always having to weigh each foray into the world outside the domains of mourning, finding ways to weave between remaining apart from and a part of normal life. One might suggest that precisely that sort of hypersensitivity to the vicissitudes and demands of life was the balance that Judaism sought to engender in its returning mourners. In such hypersensitivity was embedded a recurrent awareness of the life change that the brush with death had caused. Furthermore, the person who must be on guard

against sharing in too much joy of course is constantly reminded of its ubiquitousness, a lesson appropriate for those who ultimately must be coaxed out
of the despair of mourning for good. Finally, persons who had to figure out
exactly how they are connected to a particular joy and to the community that
celebrates it, when their attendance is required and why, could not help but
also discover how implicated they were in life, and therefore how far from
death they truly were. They had to figure out the order of human existence
and how they fit into it, the exact border between the sad and the happy,
the ordinary and the extraordinary, the lingering demands of mourning and
the embrace of community. What better way to "bit by bit" return from the
despair of bereavement yet still not throw it off too lightly? How more appro-
priately to renounce death, choose life, and gradually make friends anew with
the necessity of living?

KADDISH

By far the most outstanding practice serving to remind the bereaved that they
are still in mourning, even as they are nudged back into the embrace of the
Jewish community, is what is commonly called the mourner's Kaddish.[17] In a
sense, this punctuation to daily life extends what mourners have begun doing
almost from their first public display of mourning, throughout their shivah,
and into the *shloshim*. As they increasingly discover that their mourning is not
a solitary experience of despair and anxiety but instead one that requires them
publicly to identify themselves and stand amid the community as they grieve,
they recite Kaddish—or perhaps the reverse is true. One might suggest that
the recitation of Kaddish, that paradigmatic traditional expression of bereavement, is a "rite of intensification," an occasion that brings both the mourners
and those who console them closer together and reaffirms the long-held
Jewish cultural value that "life is with people."[18]

In fact, both are true. As the mourners recite the Kaddish and the community witnesses and responds to it, they together both express the climate of
Jewish mourning and shape it. Both mourner and the community of consolers show one another how a Jew endures absolute loss and how to make "the
helpless contemplation of others' agony something bearable, supportable—
something, as we say, sufferable."[19] The recitation of Kaddish and the responses to it, of course, are only a little drama that symbolically points to the
far larger program of mourning and consolation that we have already seen
played out in the funeral and the events leading up to and away from it.

As it was in these ceremonies and their associated rituals, so it is in Kaddish
and the setting for its recitation that the community becomes witness to the

bereaved persons' continuing faith both in God (or, what is the same thing, an ultimate order to existence) and in continuity (or, what is the same thing, life over death). To be sure, all this works only where the symbolism of Kaddish is resonant and animating. Then, and only then, can "religious belief and ritual confront and mutually confirm one another."[20]

Unlike during the funeral and shivah, however, when the community always comes to the side of the bereaved, enfolding them and enabling their mourning, from the end of the seven days and throughout the remainder of the mourning period, it is the bereaved who must step out into the world, initiate the rites of intensification, and find their own ways back to the community. Wherever they find themselves, morning and evening, they must seek out a congregation at prayer whose presence offers the setting for the recitation of Kaddish and whose ritualized responses turn this prayer from a sterile mourner's monologue into a dialogue of praise of life and an engaging experience of community. If carried on according to the strict rules of religious custom, this return to the synagogue for Kaddish is not a quiet slipping in and out. The mourners do not sit anonymously and silently in the back. Standing up and saying the words of Kaddish aloud, they call attention to themselves—an experience that is particularly memorable when one is a solitary mourner in the room.

Actually, as already noted, for mourners, particularly during *shloshim* but also throughout the extended mourning period, Kaddish alone is not enough. By the strict rules of Jewish custom, the bereaved are expected to lead the entire prayer service, publicly to summon the congregation and themselves to bless God. That they often do not do so requires some explanation.

Perhaps it was too much to ask that the bereaved always lead the prayers—after all, that would create competition among mourners in a single congregation and lead not to continuity and order but to dissension and chaos, which threaten all group life, particularly that of the Jews, who as a minority were troubled by internal strife throughout their history. Indeed, to prevent such destructive disputes, Jewish custom evolved a hierarchy that indicated who among the bereaved has priority rights to lead the prayers. First in the pecking order is the mourner during shivah.[21] Second priority goes to one commemorating a *yahrzeit,* the annual anniversary of a death and bereavement (in some Sephardic traditions, those who are marking the anniversary of a death may claim the prerogative of leading the prayers during that entire week). This person is followed by one still in *shloshim,* and last comes any orphan who is still within the first year of mourning.

While the tradition worked out these rules to deal with potential conflicts among mourners (without, however, providing regulations that would order priorities where more than one person shared the same status), today, except for the Orthodox and the tradition-directed, most mourners have largely cast aside the role of prayer leader as a way of expressing their mourner status. Instead, those who still seek some religious and ritual expression of their mourning favor Kaddish. In part this came about as Jews moved into the mainstream of civilization and out of the world totally enclosed by the tradition. These "emancipated" Jews, and even more so their children, often lost their familiarity with liturgy and their capacity to read "holy writ." In short, they had neither the desire nor the ability to lead the congregation in prayer. Nor did they relish the thought of responding to bereavement by exposing themselves to an experience that publicized their incompetence. Instead, gradually, those who still held on to something from the Jewish tradition gravitated more and more to the shorter, albeit tongue-twisting, Kaddish.[22] Unlike leading the service, which some do better than others, every new mourner is a neophyte at Kaddish reciting it for the first time. Incompetence does not really mark any one more than any other.

Yet why Kaddish? The Kaddish is—as so many before me have pointed out—not obviously taken up with the subject of either death or bereavement. At first glance it appears, as already noted, to be essentially a Gloria, a hymn of praise to God, as well as a plea for the swift collective recognition of God's universal dominion and the blessings of peace and life upon all, especially the sages and people of Israel. How did this then become a universal prayer for the bereaved?

There are, of course, simple homiletic explanations. Thus, for example, Adin Steinsaltz, a contemporary commentator, focusing on the "glorious," suggests: "On the one level, when a dear one passes away, the natural reaction of the relatives is not only sorrow, but also anger. Saying Kaddish gives new proportions; for it says that even when someone dear to us passes away, we say words of praise."[23] Thus, the sting of bereavement is overcome with the acknowledgment of God—as it was from the first moment.

Yet to understand how Kaddish grew into its important role in mourning, a little history is needed. In one of its earliest appearances, the Kaddish is cited by the Talmud. One of the sages there asserts that no less than Elijah the Prophet, harbinger of the Messiah, himself informed him that whenever a Jew entered either a synagogue or a house of Torah study, he was to repeat the essential chorus of praise that is the centerpiece of Kaddish: "May His [God's] great name be blessed."[24] This was to resonate with affirmations of divine ultimacy and power; intimations of messianic redemption and "eschatological improvement," expressing the abiding Jewish hopes of better times to come, the essence of Kaddish. What could be a more appropriate way to enter a holy place that was an inferior version of the Holy Temple, which by then was a sad memory and in ruins? In fact, of course, this line from the Kaddish was also a subtle but unmistakably resolute rabbinic response to the anti-Jewish decrees of ancient Rome, which had destroyed that Temple and seemed bent on undoing Judaism.

Actually, the importation of Kaddish into the synagogue was itself a change from its original talmudic purpose, which seems to have been as a "liturgical corollary to a pedagogical activity." [25] At the completion of the recitation or study of some Torah text, be it scriptural or talmudic, the rabbis would intone Kaddish, this hymn of praise to God whose seminal gift of Torah they had just explored and interpreted. This, too, was a response to Rome and a way of distinguishing Jews from those around them. In fact, the extended version of the Kaddish, distilled from the Talmud itself and recited at the completion of the review of a tractate, was always preceded by a preliminary declaration in which the assembled thanked God "that you have put our portion with those who dwell in the house of study and not with those who sit on the street-corners," for "we arise to words of Torah, and they get up for vanity . . . we labor and receive reward, while they labor and receive no reward . . . we run to the world to come, and they run to the nethermost pit, the grave." The so-called great Kaddish that followed immediately was, then, the rabbis' way of both saying thanks for the Torah each time they "used" it and liturgically pointing to the distinctive continuity of the Jews.

Maimonides, the great medieval Jewish sage, codified the practice: if ten or more are engaged in the study of oral law (or any other sacred Torah text), they conclude their study with the recitation of the great Kaddish.[26] That great Kaddish came to be known as the "rabbis' Kaddish." As formulated by the rabbis, the text not only glorified God but also invoked (self-servingly) divine protection "upon Israel, upon the teachers, their disciples and all of *their* disciples and upon all those who engage in the study of Torah, who are here or anywhere else; may they have abundant peace, grace, kindness, and mercy, long life, ample nourishment, and salvation from their Father who is in Heaven." [27]

As scriptural and talmudic verses were gradually inserted into the developing Jewish liturgy, the rabbis' Kaddish that punctuated their recitation became part of the prayers themselves. It resonated with all its messages of continuity, cultural singularity (even superiority), and faith in God that were the hallmarks of the beleaguered Jews. Who better to give voice to all this and call for the affirmative "amen" than a child, the one on whom all the hopes of continuity were focused, whose very existence reminded the community that life goes on? There is ample evidence from medieval prayer books to suggest that at

least by the thirteenth century the Kaddish was commonly recited by young
lads, minors below the age of thirteen, as a kind of pedagogical lesson and
credal conclusion to the prayers.[28] This was a way of educating the young
and their parents to the idea that, no matter what, God was to be "magnified
and sanctified" and "praised, glorified, raised, exalted, honored and uplifted and
lauded." It served as a regular reminder that the Almighty was "above all
hymns and praises and consolations that are uttered in the world." It asserted
that Jews were different, special—nay, better—and finally repeated the wish
that God's messianic "kingdom was to come" not in its appointed time but
rather "in our days," or, as the Kaddish put it, "swiftly and soon." Upon that
arrival God would usher in a time of "peace upon us and all Israel."[29] No more
enemies at the gate of Jewish existence, no more fears of destruction and death.

By the Middle Ages, however, the recitation of Kaddish had also acquired
a more direct connection with mourning and the fears of death. In some prayer
books of the time, the youngster who was to recite this prayer was not just anyone but was "qualified as *mi she-ein lo av o em,* a father- or motherless lad."[30]
In other places he is called a *yatom* (orphan). Later manuscripts and even some
printed prayer books thus came to call this lad's recitation *Kaddish katan,* a
designation that could mean either the "Kaddish of the minor" or a "minor
Kaddish." If it was understood as the former, it could still be an educational
training tool for youngsters, which in time turned into a Kaddish for those minors who were orphans. But when it was understood as a "minor Kaddish"
(called by some "half-Kaddish"), it seemed to some a designation that described something about its often foreshortened text (which lacked certain
words and phrases that were part of the rabbis' great Kaddish or the one cited
in the Talmud). The minor Kaddish was, then, no longer just for minors; it
could serve as a recitation for anyone who was motherless or fatherless, a
mourner's Kaddish. In this form, this prayer was sometimes even treated as an
opening for personal entreaties.[31] But how was this evolution possible?

In fact, historically the Kaddish had associations with mourners. The minor talmudic tractate *Soferim* cites a practice in which the congregational
prayer leader would, following the *musaf* (additional) prayer on Sabbaths, go
outside the synagogue door where the mourners and their relatives had gathered in order to receive the attention and "kindness of the community." Here,
representing the community, he would bless them and then recite the rabbis'
Kaddish.[32] But this was a once-a-week practice. Moreover, it was not the
mourners who recited the rabbis' Kaddish but rather the *shliach tzibbur,* the
representative of the congregation who led the prayers, while everyone assembled simply uttered the liturgical responses.[33]

The connection of its recitation by the mourners themselves, however, appears rooted in a legend that emerged in the Middle Ages. According to these medieval texts, most prominently the *Machzor Vitry,* an early liturgical source, the recitation is linked by tradition to the legendary talmudic sage Rabbi Akiva. As the story goes, the rabbi was walking in a cemetery and happened upon a dark, naked man (in some versions the man is smudged with ashes from the fires of hell) who seemed alive but burdened by a heavy load and in a rush.[34] Startled by the sight and hoping to ease the man's burden, Akiva discovers from the man that he is in fact dead, that he has come from Sheol, the mysterious abode of the dead, and that the only relief possible for him and by implication all the dead is to have a son who would stand before the congregation and summon them to worship with the declaration that begins the morning and evening prayers, the *borchu*—Bless the Lord who is blessed—to which the people would respond, "Blessed is God, the blessed one for all eternity." In addition, the dead also benefited when the congregation's prayer leader (the mourning son) evoked from the assembled the words *Y'hai shmai raboh mevorach* (May his great name be blessed), the ritualized responsum to the rabbis' Kaddish and a variant of the same line cited in the *Soferim* text. In due course Rabbi Akiva—the same Akiva who informs us that the dead gain a respite from otherworldly punishments by virtue of the living observing the Sabbath—passes on the message of how the living may assuage the suffering of the dead liturgically. From this sketchy narrative, which on its face appears to urge the bereaved to faithfully summon and lead the congregation in prayers, from the very beginning of the services until their end (when the Kaddish punctuated the prayers), there evolved the practice that today is simply articulated as the requirement to recite the Kaddish. Among Jews, then, the voyage of the soul is dependent upon the actions of the one who is the reciter of Kaddish. As Leon Wieseltier sums it up: "The themes of the story? That the dead are in need of spiritual rescue; and that the agent of that spiritual rescue is the son; and that the instrument of spiritual rescue is prayer, notably Kaddish."[35] "Thus man overcomes death, which in thought he has acknowledged," but which in fact he never actually mentions, but reciting instead words of praise and hope.[36]

At first, Kaddish recitation during the public prayers was restricted to Sabbath (an echo of the practice cited in *Soferim*), and in particular Saturday night, that time when Rabbi Akiva's legend had it the souls of the dead were forced to end their paradisiacal Sabbath respite and the grieving go back to their shivah. As noted, that recitation was by either the prayer leader or a lad, an orphan perhaps. Only if the prayer leader was the mourner did the bereaved become active agents of the process. Nevertheless, a recitation that began as praise punctuating Torah study now became one that followed death as well, as if to say that not only Torah study but also the occasion of bereavement forced Jews to reiterate the praises of God, the singularity of his people Israel, and faith in the future.

But why were the words of the Kaddish Aramaic, the lingua franca of exile, rather than Hebrew, *lashon kodesh* (the holy tongue)? Some of the commentators argued that because the angels (who were always viewed by the mystics as competing with mankind for God's good graces) do not understand Aramaic but are limited to the holy tongue, the power of the Kaddish would not be degraded by their divine disapproval or slurs.[37] After all, it was the angel of death who summoned the souls of the living to their final reward, a summons that even the so-called guardian angels could not (or would not) deny. Other sources, most prominently the medieval French Tosafists, however, saw a more rational, pedagogical explanation, noting that when the text of Kaddish was set, the Jewish folk had lost their facility in Hebrew and could understand only the Aramaic vernacular of their Babylonian exile.[38] In the Judea of Roman times, moreover, Aramaic was the language that everyone spoke best.

Liturgy is, of course, driven by needs, and the need for the living to somehow continue mourning their dead, even in the aftermath of shivah, was powerful, especially in the wake of events of the First Crusades of 1096, the great Jewish tribulation of the Middle Ages, when Ashkenazic Jewry was decimated and feeling itself particularly vulnerable. Many families and communities found themselves grieving over the dead who had been slaughtered by the rampaging crusaders or in some cases murdered by the Jews themselves, sacrificed "in sanctification of God's name" so that those who loved them would not have to watch helplessly as they were ravaged by the attackers. By the twelfth century, those who remained among the living of Ashkenazic Jewry often perceived themselves as living insecurely in the shadow of death, seeing themselves as either survivors or mourners. The need to somehow restore Jewish confidence in order and continuity was felt in both the individual and the collective consciousness.

As Wieseltier puts it, "In the years before the Crusades, there was no mourner's kaddish. In the years after the Crusades, the mourner's kaddish makes its appearance. This cannot have been a coincidence."[39] Indeed, although we know that in fact there was Kaddish before the Crusades, it was not nearly as ubiquitous as afterward. "*Kaddish* is mentioned in the [medieval] *Sefer Hasidim* when Abba Saul ben Batnit asks a Jew who is dying to teach his son to recite it, but it seems to be codified in the mortuary liturgy only in the thirteenth century, at the time of the persecutions in the German lands."[40] By then Kaddish had become a consolation for mourning not just individuals but the entire people.

In the wake of this traumatic encounter with extermination and national destruction, the simple arrival for prayer as a way of assuring Jewish continuity or a way of mourning the dead seemed by itself insufficient. In that mass sorrow, who could claim personal precedence as prayer leader? Thus the actual recitation of Kaddish—not simply responding to it along with the rest of the congregation—became the special prerogative of the mourners, and in particular the orphans.

Of course there had always been a drama associated with death and mourning. At least as early as the eleventh century—and perhaps even earlier, beginning in Babylonia (as intimated in the tractate *Soferim*)—when the dead were mourned, the Kaddish played a part in that experience. At any assembly of prayer where the bereaved were present—and their presence was unmistakable, for they displayed the outward signs of mourning, most prominently a wrapped head and covered face but perhaps also the torn garments of grief—the one who led the prayers would turn to the congregation and urge it to "demand the reason" that these people were so marked. Here, perhaps, was the precursor to today's clap of the hand against the pulpit, a custom that commands the attention of the community to the presence of mourners among them and to the need to respond to their affliction. Thus where today we may offer the words "May you be comforted among the mourners of Zion and Jerusalem," in those days the appropriate public response was the same one that today the tradition demands Jews make when they first learn about the presence of death: to recite the words "Blessed is the true judge."[41] Yet it could surely not have been enough simply to say that God was blessed as a true judge in the public forum of the synagogue. The praises of the Kaddish would extend these sentiments, and perhaps thereby incur blessings instead of the curse of death. God is not just a true judge, the Kaddish asserted; he is magnified, glorified, and so on.

In perhaps one of the most powerful descriptions of its power, Joseph Dov Soloveitchik has argued:

> When the mourner recites: "Glorified and sanctified be the great name . . ." he declares: No matter how powerful death is, notwithstanding the ugly end of man, however terrifying the grave is, however nonsensical and absurd everything appears, no matter how black one's despair is and how nauseating an affair life is, we declare and profess publicly and solemnly that we are not giving up, that we are not surrendering, that we will carry on the work of our ancestors as though nothing has happened, that we will not be satisfied with less than full realization of the ultimate

goal—the establishment of God's kingdom, the resurrection of the dead, and eternal life for man.[42]

Still, by the Middle Ages and after the Crusade massacres, at least in the area served by the *Machzor Vitry*, it remained for a time the minors, whose faith remained sufficiently ingenuous, who could still ardently recite the words, mostly at the end of the Sabbath. Liturgy conflates, and history becomes a blur. The eleventh-century Crusades and the atmosphere of insecurity that lasted into the thirteenth century made all Jews feel like orphans in history. The power that Soloveitchik could describe in Kaddish in the mid-twentieth century—and that survivors of the First Crusades and those in the generations immediately afterward were beginning to feel—was ultimately more than the recitation of just any little children could carry. The minor's Kaddish became an orphan's and finally a mourner's Kaddish. By the fourteenth century it not only served as the punctuation to Torah or the conclusion to the service but also was firmly established as a theurgy for death, appropriated by adults. Carrying a special mystical power it seemed to have inherited from its role in delaying the end of the Sabbath, Kaddish became in the minds of many a liturgical vehicle by which the living extended the spiritual rest of the dead. For those who mourned the dead, this power to afford their departed loved ones with some comfort became an important compensation for maintaining the constancy of the Kaddish recitation.

Traditional custom associated Kaddish only with the males, who for most of Jewish history were the only, or at least the primary, congregants in the synagogue and the Torah study hall, the women being consigned dominion in the home. Indeed, in the slang of folklore, a son was often called "a Kaddish." Nevertheless, at least some traditionalist scholars suggested that where there were no surviving sons, even a minor daughter (i.e., one younger than twelve, the age at which Jewish girls reach legal majority) might recite the Kaddish (although not lead the services) in the synagogue.[43] Over time, as women and girls have begun to consider the synagogue and other Jewish domains outside the home no less their own, and as the recitation of Kaddish has become an increasingly important way to respond to loss and signal attachments to the dead, they, too, have begun to qualify as "a Kaddish," and are more and more found among the people reciting it.

At first, only one mourner in the congregation would say the Kaddish, while all other mourners present stood and responded. The rabbis explained this rule by noting that the "amen" response was, by Jewish law, restricted. One could answer "amen" only to the words of a single other, for by doing so one individual in effect shared in whatever blessing the other recited. The reciter was the respondent's messenger. Hence there was no need for more than one congregant to recite Kaddish, since anyone who listened to his words (only males could act as messengers) and responded with an "amen" had fulfilled whatever it was that Kaddish was meant to fulfill. If more than one recited, it would never be clear who was acting as the messenger for whom.

To satisfy the desire of all mourners to be the one to recite Kaddish, the tradition evolved a hierarchy of priority not unlike the one already mentioned for leading the prayers. This order, however was different. First for Kaddish came the mourner in shivah, next the one in *shloshim,* third in line was one in the first twelve months after bereavement, fourth was the mourner on the final day of reciting Kaddish in the year, and last was the *yahrzeit.* The logic here was that the closer one was to bereavement, the more spiritually necessary was the recitation, both for the mourner and for the deceased. Yet unlike the hierarchy for prayer leader, which still left Kaddish for the mourner to do, this set of priorities left all but one mourner in a congregation in the position of passive respondents. While this custom of one reciter and many respondents was maintained in many Sephardic communities and even in some communities in Germany, increasingly mourners were unsatisfied with the largely passive role of being respondents.[44]

Gradually, each mourner began to recite Kaddish, a practice that many of the rabbis found erroneous but that nevertheless gained in popularity. In some places, the mourners tried to make their recitations in succession, a practice that tried to hew to the demand that only one person recite the Kaddish, while also allowing every mourner to do so. This custom, however, not only intolerably extended the length of the service but also removed every repetition from its liturgical context. Moreover, in their eagerness to say the Kaddish themselves, mourners often jumped the gun and overlapped with one another, making the critical responses from the congregation difficult to execute properly.[45] In other places, mourners were careful to recite Kaddish in unison, in a compromise that seemed to maintain the fiction of a single collective voice. Such a practice, they believed, would allow the congregation legitimately to answer "amen." Where no consensus on a single reciter could be reached, this chorus became the practice to which the traditionalist rabbis grudgingly acceded.[46] In effect, it also made the Kaddish sound more like a chant, with each syllable and inflection dictated by custom. This is the special rising and falling cadence that is by now so familiar to anyone who has heard the prayer.

Yet why did Kaddish serve so well for mourners that they ran over one another in order to recite it? Some might see an answer in the Kaddish of Nachmanides,

the thirteenth-century sage from Gerona, Spain. In his version of the prayer
were added words that perhaps made explicit intentions and hopes that in
the other versions remained unspoken but understood: "May we and all our
brethren in Israel be spared destruction and captivity and death." These words
hinted at the underlying belief that recitation was not just a vehicle to offer the
dead repose but as well a way to deny death its dominion. Shaped by generations of Jewish experience in the Diaspora, where being a Jew usually meant
being part of an endangered and barely tolerated minority, Jewish liturgy required a constant reminder that whatever the vicissitudes of life, the God of
Israel watched over his people, Israel. Kaddish could so serve, and after the
Middle Ages it began to do so more and more. Everyone wanted to lead in this
charge against death's dominion. As generation after generation of Jews felt the
heavy hand of pogrom and persecution, the need to keep up the war of words
against death and destruction grew more deeply rooted in the Jewish collective consciousness. *Kaddish became inextricably bound up in the rhythm of Jewish life
and death.*

In its praises of God, moreover, the Kaddish did not allow despair and
bitterness to be the response to death. Not damnation but celebration, not the
curse but the praise of heaven. Jews always reversed the curse. After all, they
called the cemetery the "house of life." Such a reversal of fortune was what
Kaddish promised, and few mourners were willing to forgo that hope.

Around the time that Kaddish made itself imperative at the beginning of the
thirteenth century, the assertion that the God of Israel was not simply God *in*
Israel, but was indeed *the* God, one and only and everywhere, also became an
obligatory conclusion to prayer, an invocation that ultimately became articulated with the opening words "it is incumbent upon us to praise the Master of
all," the now famous "*aleinu l'shabeach.*" In this prayer, the Jews distinguished
themselves and their God from others with the words "for they prostrate
themselves to vanity and nothingness and pray to a god that cannot save them,
but we bow and prostrate ourselves and offer thanks before the Supreme King
of Kings." [47] These were sentiments that echoed Kaddish. However humble
and enfeebled the Jewish people might seem, especially after the Crusades,
they nevertheless survived. Therefore, their liturgical conclusion that "our
God is indeed God" (*adonai hu ha'elohim*), the essential and central declaration
of the *aleinu,* became the very words Jews wanted to hear ringing in their ears
as they concluded every gathering for prayer, along with the closing promise
that the day would soon come when their God would be recognized as the
universal, everlasting king. But all that was no less the message at the heart of
the Kaddish as well.

The credal conclusion of the *aleinu* and the acclaim embedded in the

Kaddish were thus two parallel punctuations to prayers, both of which praised God and promised the future. Both became merged in a kind of liturgical departure ritual, words with which one took leave from God and from one's fellow worshipers. Leave-taking from God recalled the leave-taking from one's ancestors, the dead. The enigma of death was, after all, "the starting point of all speculation." [48] According to kabbalistic belief, the dead were sparks returned to the great fire that was God, and in popular folk belief they were at the very least intercessors for the living before God. Departure from the congregation and the return to one's solitary existence likewise recalled the emotions the mourner might feel upon leaving behind the dead to whom one was once so firmly connected. So if the emotions had an affinity for one another, and the words and the circumstances of their recitation elicited this same feeling of affinity, then the liturgy worked as it was supposed to do. In brief, Kaddish became a prayer of leave-taking, a praise of God that carried the harmonics of mourning. In time, of course, it became not simply a prayer of leave-taking but *the* prayer of the ultimate leave-taking, the response of the living to the loss of the dead. Thus Jews left the synagogue, the realm of the numinous or spiritual, the purely Jewish domain, and returned to the mundane world. Kaddish and *aleinu,* with which each such departure was liturgically marked, made the transition easier. Mourners could appreciate that.

Yet as Kaddish became the single prayer most associated with mourning, its elements of praise of God became buried under the weight of its acquired symbolism. Missing in these Kaddish recitations were the expressively lively rising and falling inflections of talmudic discourse (some of which later animated Yiddish), the chanted melodies of Scripture, or even the conversational tones of spoken Hebrew. Instead, the near-monotonic cadences that Kaddish took on sounded more and more like dirge, whose melody was a threnody. Like an upset youngster forced to tell the parent from whom rebuke or punishment has just been received "how much you love him," mourners began to voice their Kaddish in tones that echoed the despair or even resentment they felt over being deprived of a loved one. Indeed, there is in this chant—so unlike any other of the "melodies" of Jewish life and life in general—all the evocative powers of music. This songspeak became so distinctive on its own that in time it could carry the harmonics of anger and pain, loneliness and awkwardness, innocence and ignorance, the anxiety about extinction and the willingness to oppose it—in short, all the mixed and often contradictory emotions that underlay bereavement and mourning. And thus the sound of Kaddish became and remains, like a bell tolling morning and evening, the reminder that life is changed and that one is in mourning. It was also a kind of ongoing deadened voice that could sound like the dead, even as it offered expiation from

the dead "for not having realized who they were until they were gone," for
not having understood what they meant to us until now.[49]

Shivah is over, and this evening I must find my way to the synagogue to recite
Kaddish for the first time as one of the mourners in the congregation. Although
I have had a week of these recitations during the prayers at my parents' house,
this evening in the community's house of prayer feels like a totally new experience, a kind of coming out in public. I have arrived early, even before the minimum ten worshipers. In his lifetime, my father, for whom I am in mourning,
always chided me for coming late to the service. But at least for the next eleven-
plus months, although he is in the hereafter, he shall get me to come on time,
for now I have to be here before things begin so I can say all the prayers that a
mourner must recite, from the first Kaddish, very near the start, to the last Kaddish with which the service closes. And while in my heart I fully believe that just
as my father always forgave me my synagogue tardiness and absences during his
lifetime, so he would surely be forgiving now. Yet though I can hear him and in
my mind's eye still see his beaming visage, he can say nothing. Death has closed
his mouth.

Besides, as demanding as the trips to the service may be, I don't really want
him to absolve me of this responsibility. I embrace it religiously. While on this
first day I know not what lies ahead in the coming year, my intentions are to
faithfully come to the synagogue and miss none of the obligatory recitations.
I will be my father's Kaddish. By my recitations, I will give evidence of how my
father raised me. "He taught me to be here, and here I am."[50]

I am now acutely aware that whatever commitments I am ready to make, I
cannot do this alone. I need, and will continue to need, the congregation to help
me fulfill this final filial duty. As I wish to remain constant to my father, I need
the community to be constant for me. It must make a *minyan* for me, and so for
this I now feel bound to the community in ways I never felt before. No one is
surprised at my uncharacteristic early arrival at the service. Knowing that I must
find a new place to call my own, I look for a seat in which to settle down, but before I do so, someone approaches and leads me to the pulpit.

"You're the man," I'm told. For the next days and into the days yet unknown,
I must lead the service and with my words help everyone to pray, even as they
help me mourn.

"Happy are those who dwell in your [God's] house," I begin the afternoon prayers. Later, I begin the Jewish evensong with "Bless the Lord who is blessed." No sooner do I start than can I hear behind me the members of the congregation respond to my call. I thought I was leading, but now I realize it is they who are carrying me with their prayers.

Day after day I head for the synagogue. At first I am so anxious not to be late that my day feels as if it is divided between two time zones: before and after going to the synagogue. My own life is what I can squeeze between the few hours before and after morning, afternoon, and evening services. I sleep restlessly those first nights after shivah, trusting neither my alarm nor my internal clock, and I find myself waking even before dawn, then lying restlessly in bed waiting for the ring to tell me when I planned to get up. All the rest of the day, when I am supposed to be back at work, I find myself stealing glances at my watch, trying to figure out precisely when I must leave for the synagogue to be there not just on time but early. I worry that I shall fall into old routines, forget that I am in mourning and then miss the time for the service. Even my grizzled beard, a lingering sign of mourning, is not as acute a reminder, since I am starting to get used to it, and besides the whiskers are getting soft enough so that the beard no longer feels like pinpricks against my skin, reminding me something is amiss.

Leading the service is not really a new experience for me. For years I have been called upon to chant it, my voice pleasant to many and my competence in the mechanics of prayer like second nature since my days as a yeshiva student. So in spite of the drama that some mourners might have felt in this role, I feel little of it after the first day back in the synagogue. Kaddish, however, is different. The monotonic incantation of the mourners is something to which I always listened and replied. Never was I part of that chorus of the bereaved. Day in and day out to be one of these rhythmic Kaddish voices is what gets to me. Every time I hear my deadened voice, I am reminded not only of my father's death and the new responsibility and status with which it has endowed me but also of my utter dependence on others, my not being able to go it alone.

On the first Sabbath after shivah, a day when mourners do not lead services but instead mark their status purely with the recitation of Kaddish from their seats in the congregation, I suddenly discern how those around me have found a way to signal their acceptance of my new dependence on them and acknowledge that they understand that this is a turning point for me. As I sing out the words, I notice out of the corner of my eye that a number of those in the congregation have turned to face me, their eyes riveted upon me in a subtle but unmistakable display of sharpened attentiveness. When the moment comes that I cry out for God's kingdom to come "swiftly and soon and all say 'amen,'" they and all the congregation do so with a loud and deliberately heartfelt "*Amen, Y'hai shmai raboh mevorach l'olam u'lolmayah*" (May his great name be blessed always and forever). This one's for you, they seem to say. Again and again they answer, and with each "amen" I feel myself pulled closer and more tightly to the community, reminded that I mourn not alone but in its midst.

As the days became weeks and the weeks months, Kaddish became my constant companion. I stopped having to look at my watch or suffer restless nights in order to be primed to get to the synagogue. The rhythms of my life shifted, and my visits to the services became its most consistent pulse. Except when I traveled and had to attune myself to the schedule of another congregation, mornings became easiest; I learned to start my day by tumbling out of bed and into the synagogue in time for the first Kaddish, the long one that came after the extended excerpts from Scripture with which the Ashkenazic rite service that I commonly attended began. (What a treat when, during an extended stay in Jerusalem, I found that the synagogue I attended customarily switched the order of the prayers, leading to the first Kaddish being recited near the conclusion of the service and giving me a few extra minutes leeway in the morning.) Because the times of afternoon and evening prayers, which began at sunset and concluded with nightfall, varied as daylight waxed and waned, the way I organized my day also had to shift. In the summer, I could plan on a long, uninterrupted day but found my evening activities strictly curtailed; in the winter, the sinking of the sun meant I had to find some way to break into whatever I was doing during the day to get to the *minyan* for my Kaddish.

Like others in my situation, I expected that there would be days and times when I just didn't make it; days I would be caught in transit or far from a Jewish congregation, times I would oversleep. But with each week that I managed to get to the services on time and each day that I succeeded in reciting Kaddish, my commitment hardened and I became more confident that I might achieve what at the outset seemed impossible: to recite a Kaddish in a congregation at every service, each day, during the eleven months that custom dictated that I do so.

To help me move around the New York area where I live and work, I acquired a copy of the Agudath Israel of America's "*Mincha* Map." This listing of places and times that groups gathered throughout the region for the afternoon service allowed me to find my way to a congregation when I was away from the familiar environs of home. I discovered the Millinery Synagogue in Manhattan's garment district, not far from where I worked, where from early to late afternoon Jews converged from all over the area every hour on the half hour for a *mincha* service. On other occasions, I discovered groups that gathered in law offices, in storefronts—even in study halls in the college library. At times I found myself racing through parts of the city to addresses totally foreign to me, only to discover there the familiar sights and sounds of Jews gathering for prayer. While the religious obligation to prayer in a *minyan* was incumbent upon all Jews, the profusion of those reciting Kaddish at every one of these congregations I joined convinced me that, at least in my day, it was the dead—or perhaps the sense of obligation to the dead on the part of the living—that helped promote communal prayer. If the community was servicing those who recite Kaddish by providing us with a *minyan*, it was the dead who were somehow the prime movers in all this, exerting their power upon the living to come together in their name.

There was an unspoken camaraderie in these congregations among the Kaddish people, a feeling that hovered in the harmonics of the chorus we created in our joint recitation. We all knew that we were brought to that room and that moment by the same needs. That commonality of purpose and motive made me feel that I was not just mourning my father when I recited Kaddish; I was also joining a fraternity of the bereaved. In the parlance of Jewish ritual, we were all recognized as *chiyuvim*, people who carried an obligation to the memory of the dead.

That recognition gave us a special status. too. Accordingly, wherever and whenever I made my way into a *minyan* that was new to me, when the time for Kaddish came and I stood to raise my voice, there was acknowledgment of my existential situation and standing—not just in the "amens" and other responses to my Kaddish but in the way that people took notice of my presence. If I returned to the same place for another service, someone would approach and offer me the pulpit so that I could more fully carry out my mourning obligations as prayer leader. Or else, if I came forward to ask if there were any other *chiyuvim*, the information that I was "saying Kaddish" or that I was an *avel*, a mourner (using the Hebrew terms was a subtle cue to the informed that I was Jewishly knowledgeable), was enough to bestow upon me the "honor" of leading the congregation, if no one else had an obligation of higher religious priority. In most places, no one asked me if I paid dues to the congregation (although often I left a charitable donation), or if I had always gone to the *minyan* before I became a mourner, or even how scrupulous I was in observing Judaism—they simply let me carry out my obligations as a mourner. To be sure, in those congregations where my appearance so obviously marked me as an outsider—places where long beards, black coats, and black hats were the common regalia—I satisfied myself with just saying Kaddish (although even in such places I was sometimes handed the helm). Or when I found myself a foreigner to the traditions of a particular synagogue—as, for example, I did in a synagogue in the marketplace in Tiberias, Israel, where the congregants were all Jews who followed the Kurdish customs of their fore-bears—I likewise recited only the mourner's Kaddish and was glad to do so.

I traveled. But everywhere I traveled as a mourner. About to get on an air-plane, when I was certain that I would not find an opportunity to say Kaddish with a congregation, I unexpectedly found a gathering at the airport gate, where another mourner like me had found enough Jews ready to make a *minyan*. On board, on yet another flight, I was summoned to the aft section, where a congre-gation had assembled in prayer; barely audible over the roar of the engines, I managed to say the Kaddish. When I returned to New York on a flight whose schedule seemed to leave me caught without a morning *minyan*, I found one on the way home with my Jewish synagogue map of Queens and slipped in in time to recite the first Kaddish of the service.

Wherever I went during my time of Kaddish, I needed to make certain that there was a place nearby where I could find a congregation at prayer, morning, afternoon, and evening. I was never far away from a community of fellow Jews. In Israel, where I spent much time, that was fairly easy. Elsewhere, when I trav-eled to cities, I made sure to plan my trip so as to find synagogues. A trip to Washington, D.C., landed me near the congregation in Georgetown; the journey back to New York required a detour to Philadelphia at evening time to reach a synagogue there in time for *mincha;* and so on. The communities of Jews into which I wandered were always ready to accept me; my recitation of Kaddish was the ticket of admission. In one case in Montreal, my quest to get to a synagogue was assisted by a cab driver who, inspired by my request to get to the morning services, spontaneously revealed himself to be a Jew. When he brought me to the front door, he decided to park his taxi and join me in prayer. My father was, it seemed, bringing more than his only child to the synagogue.

As the time of my Kaddish recitations wore on, I began to think that some unseen hand was reaching out to help me fulfill the obligation I had embraced. If I was willing to try to be steadfast in my Kaddish, the congregation would be there for me. Two such moments stand out powerfully in my memory.

Once I was on a brief summer vacation with my family. This annual excursion had been complicated this year by my need to find a place where the rustic pleasures my family and I craved could be braced by access to an active congregation where at the beginning and end of the day I could recite my Kaddish. I found such a place in Bangor, Maine, where the small Orthodox synagogue, about fifty miles from the majestic, unspoiled beauty of Acadia National Park, offered everything I needed. Both the rabbi and the congregation, used to the appearance of people like me during the long days of summer, accepted us with grace. Besides, along with my sons, I helped them to make up the daily *minyan*, which in their small community was not always easy to assemble. Mornings were easy, because the only hotel in town was a block from the synagogue, and we could easily start the day with the service, after which we headed off for the park and its this-worldly pleasures, the sorts of delights that the rabbis had not prohibited even from one in mourning. Getting back in time for the seven o'clock service was also easy, in principle, as long as we left the park by six, which would leave enough time for the journey on the country highway that led back to Bangor. For the first three days of our vacation, everything worked out well. We even managed to go out to sea for a whale-watching tour and make it back in time. But on the fourth day we got lost in the park, and by the time we found our way back to the highway to Bangor, only twenty-five minutes remained before seven o'clock—not nearly enough time to make it back for the service. Still, I pressed the accelerator and decided to see if somehow I could get back in time. Breaking the speed limit, passing whenever possible the inevitable line of cars that blocked my progress, I found that at seven o'clock I was still about twenty-five miles from the synagogue.

Inside the car, my family could sense the tension, knowing that until now I had somehow managed to not miss a single service at which to recite Kaddish since I began saying it at my father's funeral. Other than a few admonitions from my wife for me to be careful as I whizzed along—far fewer than I might have otherwise expected—everyone sat in silence. By five minutes after seven, one of my sons said what I already knew: "I'm sure Grandpa would have understood."

"Of course," I replied. But I still pressed forward, feeling guilty that a vacation rather than something more essential to life was going to end my unbroken series of Kaddish recitations. Rushing to beat the setting sun, I was hoping now at least to make it in time for the evening prayers, which followed directly, so that I could end the day with a Kaddish. To be sure, the day was long enough, and sunset was really quite a bit later. But the rabbis had decreed that if in a town it was difficult to assemble a congregation for prayer later in the evening, one could legitimately gather early and complete worship at dusk. In any event,

there was no other *minyan* for hundreds of miles that I could attend. Their time
was my time.

At last, at nearly seven-thirty, we pulled up in front of the synagogue, and
I rushed in. Seeing a few of the men whose faces had by now become familiar
just sitting there, I assumed they were in the brief break between the afternoon
and evening services. Breathlessly, I tried to confirm my suspicion. But instead,
one of them motioned to me to step up to the pulpit. Certain that my sons and
I would come, they had not called anyone else to help make up the *minyan*.
They needed me as much as I needed them; the congregation was there for me,
and I for them.

"*Ashrei yoshvei veitecha,*" I began, leading the opening words of *mincha*. There
might be other days when I would miss a Kaddish, but tonight was not going to
be the first one.

My next brush with disappointment came once again in the late afternoon of
a crisp fall day. I was on my way by car to a *mincha minyan* on the Upper West
Side of Manhattan, somewhere around Lincoln Center for the Performing Arts.
Having lived in New York long enough to understand the drawbacks of this plan,
I should have known better than taking a car to a place where parking spaces
were scarce. My foolish hope was that I might somehow find a place to leave my
car and make it in time for the service—or at least for the recitation of Kaddish
with which it ended. Given the imminence of sunset, if I failed to connect with
this *minyan*, there would be no time to make it to another service. As it was, I
had selected this place because by all my calculations—these are the sorts of
reckonings that the sayers of Kaddish learn to make—there was no other place
I could be certain to find the requisite congregation. *Mincha* times and gatherings—even those on the famous map—were notoriously subject to "change without notice," as the people of Agudath Israel noted. But the Lincoln Center Synagogue where I was headed was a known quantity; there would surely be a
service there into which I could count myself.

The traffic through midtown, from whence I began, was horrendous, but I
weaved in and out of it like a seasoned cabby, finding shortcuts that I retrieved
from somewhere deep in my memory bank of the arcana of New York street maps.
At last I found myself with six minutes to spare and the synagogue in sight. But
the parking space I hoped for—even the illegal one I was ready to chance—was
filled. Around the block I sped, up and down adjacent streets, frantically looking
for a place to leave the car and get to the service. But there was nothing. Even
the garage in Lincoln Center was out of the question. By the time I could check

in the car and run to the synagogue, it would be too late. The attendant in the nearby lot for residents of the apartment complex beside the synagogue was unrelenting. Neither the promise of a generous tip nor my word that I would be out in a few minutes availed; my car could not stay. Manhattan and its unrelenting hostility to parking stood between me and my fulfillment of a mourner's obligation. Frantic, or at least frustrated, as I realized that there was nearly no time left to make it to the Kaddish, I threw myself imaginatively into another time. Like the biblical Joshua who also needed more time and who had once commanded the "sun to stand still" (Joshua 10:12), I looked for help from on high. While I was not ready to demand such cosmic assistance from heaven, I found myself suddenly calling aloud. "*Ribono shel ha'olam*" (Master of the universe), I cried like a madman in my car or like some Hasidic master in the countless stories I had read, "you know I have tried to say Kaddish faithfully for my father and have done so without fail each day. I have not missed a single service. If you want me to continue to do this, if this matters, then"—and now with a faint echo of the one-line plea to God that Moses had used in his frantic prayer for his sister immediately to be healed from her leprosy—"please get me a parking space, *now!*"

Those who believe in a God who created the world but then left it to its own devices will not want to read further. Those who see such pleas to heaven as infantile and theologically demeaning will likewise want to turn away. And those who doubt the very existence of domains beyond the human will find nothing to interest them here. But the fact is that at that moment a car pulled out of a space in front of me, no more than fifty feet from the door to the synagogue. I swooped in and made it in time to say my Kaddish.

With help from the community and some from places I do not quite understand to this day, I went through the days of my mourning. Bit by bit, I found my way back to life, to the order of my life, Kaddish after Kaddish.

The Twelve Months and Yahrzeit
Anniversary

> For twelve months, the body of the dead endures, and its soul
> ascends and descends between this world and the next. After
> twelve months, the body becomes nothingness, and the soul
> ascends never to descend again.
>
> Babylonian Talmud *Shabbat* 152b

Death "is not completed in one instantaneous act," nor, as already noted, is mourning completed in a trice.[1] We have seen how through *tahara* and the funeral Jews, although expeditious in handling the corpse, recognize that death has a long aftermath. We have discovered as well that Jewish mourning has its own evolving rhythm.

Yet while the direction in which the events and traditional practices that occur when a Jew dies lead us toward life and a renewed order, those who have been through it testify that "grieving is not a straight-line progression. It's up and down as well as forward and back."[2] Jewish custom, recognizing that there are emotional stops and starts, that there are forces that can pull us all back into the chaos of anxiety and irredeemable loss, stresses that for *all* mourners and mourning there is and must always be an end.

For those who have lost siblings, a spouse, or a child, thirty days is supposed to be a sufficient period for life and order to reassert themselves (although this was presumably truer in traditional societies, where members of one's nuclear family were part of the web of extended familial and communal affiliations with which one was bound up and by which one was sustained—in our contemporary world these losses loom larger). For the loss of one's parents, however, thirty days of mourning was considered insufficient.

Does this mean that Jewish tradition assumed that after a month every mourner was healed or that orphans were more grief-stricken than those who had lost other loved ones—spouses, children, or siblings? Not necessarily, for the Talmud asserted that all "the dead are not forgotten by the heart until twelve months have passed."[3] Ancient Jewish practice also held that the "bones were not gathered up," the body of the dead not fully worn away, until a year's time, when, as the rabbis added, the spirit was at last set free.[4] In the natural order of life and death, however, children were expected to be affected most by the loss of their parents, and that was to be the paradigmatic experience of death, and therefore the one that took longest to get over.[5] Reflecting this assumption, the formalized practices of mourning, in particular the Kaddish and the public restrictions in the flow of normal life, were structured by the orphan experience, which the framers of the codes that define traditional Judaism considered the most common pattern of loss. Yet even here, a year was commonly viewed as the absolute limit of formal displays of grief.

Perhaps the extended formal mourning for parents emerged in addition from the deeply held belief in Jewish tradition that one shared a unique and eternal relationship with those from whom one's own life was drawn. The biblical injunction to honor one's father and mother—the premier familial relationship highlighted in the Ten Commandments and elsewhere in Scripture—remained in effect throughout the parents' lifetime, but, as mourning customs made clear, that requirement did not stop at their demise. "One should honor parents during their lifetime and one should honor parents after their death," as the Talmud put it.[6] Paradoxically, then, what seems at first glance to be an extension of a preoccupation with death—the extended formal mourning for parents—may be understood instead as a way for the living to assert that some elements of this primary relationship transcend death. Or, put differently, for Jews it takes longer to disengage from parents than from any other relationship, a situation that the customs of Jewish mourning reflect.

Is this not implicit in the common assertion that only when the parent dies does the child fully become an adult (and that in mourning for them one also mourns for the end of one's own childhood or youth)?[7] Jewish mourning traditions appear to suggest that this new order cannot be established right away, that when the parent dies, at least for one more year, the child must fully remain a child and recall the duties of that position. Emotionally, then, the orphan often oscillates between the desire to get past the pain of loss and the equally powerful desire not to forget that loss during the year of mourning.[8] For a year, those who have lost parents recite the "mourner's Kaddish," which is actually more commonly referred to in the liturgy as the "orphan's Kaddish." That is also why, as we have seen, from its outset the recitation of Kaddish was associated with children. So powerful was this connection that even children under the age of thirteen, who in the terms of Jewish law were still legal minors, were allowed to make such recitations upon the loss of a parent; and the congregation was required liturgically to respond to them no less sincerely than to anyone else.[9]

We have seen that as in the contemporary period of Jewish history, or- phaned daughters, no less than sons, have sought to honor their parents in the public manner that we call Kaddish, they have been forced to penetrate a tradition that always regarded them as dependent on males as their religious guardians and described a feminine ideal as eschewing public displays, ex- pressed in the words of the Psalmist who wrote that "the daughter of the king is all glorious within" (Psalms 45:14). In the inclination of that tradition, the idea that bereaved daughters would appear "without," beyond the boundaries of the Jewish home, giving glory to God and honor to their dead parents as *public* mourners, much less lead the congregation in prayerful praise, was unimaginable. But more and more daughters could imagine it, especially after they found their places in many public domains of the world outside the Jewish home. Once outside, these Jewish "daughters of the king," like the orphaned sons before them, began to find their way into the public space of synagogues. They came out not as sheltered princesses but instead prepared with a greater Jewish knowledge than that possessed by their mothers and grandmothers, a result of their enhanced Jewish education. They came, too, after they had already found a place as weekly Sabbath worshipers in the pews. Now, on the occasion of their bereavement, they were ready to step into the final fraternal preserve of synagogue life: the daily service. But they came not to usurp the authority or leadership of the men—even if some men insisted on framing their presence in those terms. Rather, they came to honor their parents and offer public testimony to their bereavement. So much has this as- piration surfaced among daughters that even the most traditionalist of rabbinic authorities have shown a growing recognition of these longings. Thus, for ex- ample, a contemporary Hasidic guide, unable to endorse a daughter's Kaddish, nevertheless suggests that a daughter who wishes to perform public acts of mourning like Kaddish in order to "credit her father should take care to at- tend all the services in the synagogue and [be there] on time in order to incline her ear to the recitation of *kaddish,* to which she must answer 'amen' with sincere devotion, and in so far as she does this 'the One-Who-Fathoms-All- Intentions' will consider it as if she had [personally] recited *kaddish.*"[10]

Those who wanted more than this began, first in whispers but ultimately with a voice raised in prayer no less than their brothers, to make Kaddish their own. As they have done so, they have embraced other obligations of mourn- ing, demanding as well the public consolations that come with it. In this long transitional process, they, like all others who recite Kaddish, have been transformed. In those congregations that have found a place for them, whatever that place may be, the end of the mourning period arouses in an orphaned daughter many of the same complex responses that well up in an orphaned son.

While the orphan's mourning during the full twelve months entails a variety of practices, including abstaining from participating in festive meals and joyful assemblies, eschewing new clothes, and avoiding musical performances, by far the most prominent ritual obbligato of life and reminder of mourning becomes, as we have seen, the recitation of the Kaddish. It is a kind of double-sided clamp linking the reciter with the abiding sense of loss, as well as with the Jewish congregation and its consoling embrace. Kaddish becomes the sound of mourning. As one mourner put it, "If you follow the Jewish way, mourning becomes the organizing principle of your existence." [11] More than that, the one for whom the Kaddish is recited becomes, no less than the recitation itself, part of this year's life.

"The enduring remembrance of the dead," Freud has argued, "became the basis for assuming other modes of existence"; it fostered the conviction that "life continued after apparent death." [12] Among Jews, the recitation of Kaddish may serve implicitly to give voice to that conviction and foster a continuing relationship between the living and the dead who, although in some "other mode of existence," are remembered. "Over time," explained a mourner reciting Kaddish for his father, "the sense of loss was replaced by a sense of closeness, of companionship with my father." The relationship that once existed in life now expressed itself "in the reality of Kaddish." [13]

Gradually, however, this clamp of Kaddish is loosened as the mourning period draws to a close and a final reintegration into some sort of normal life draws near. Among most Jews of Ashkenazic origins who hold to tradition, daily recitations are carried out only through the eleventh month, although some extend it through the first day and others through the first three weeks of the twelfth, stopping only during the final week. Among many of those who follow Sephardic traditions, Kaddish is suspended during the first week of the twelfth month and then resumed during the rest of this last month until the first anniversary of burial. In rare cases, the custom is to continue recitation for the entire twelve months. [14] Why these customs?

A simple explanation might suggest that this is merely another expression of the "bit-by-bit," start-and-stop approach that characterizes all the stages of mourning. The complex nature of grieving is therefore reflected in a Kaddish that, although ultimately taking the mourner a bit nearer to closure, is withheld near the end of the year so that the mourner can test the waters of a life without it for a bit; then, at the last stage of mourning, on the first anniversary, the *yahrzeit,* it is brought back one more time with feeling, with all the power and the emotional freshness of a new recitation.

Other explanations have been offered as well. Recall that at its outset, the commemoration of the dead that ultimately evolved (some might say "de-volved") into Kaddish was essentially an exercise in intercession by the living on their behalf. Rooted, as we have seen, in the Rabbi Akiva story, the original impetus behind Kaddish was the conviction that words spoken and deeds accomplished by a son while standing amid the congregation, a summons to prayer and praise of God, could alleviate the suffering experienced by the spirit of his dead forebear. But the rabbinic interpreters of the custom never forgot that the father in that aboriginal tale had been wicked, and that the actions of his son had served as his *kappara,* redemption from the punishment of his im-mortal soul. While they derived practices of mourning in all cases from this one case, and believed that "there is not a just man upon earth that doeth good and sinneth not," in the famous and oft-quoted formula of Ecclesiastes, and that in fact "the sins of a person are engraved on his bones" the guardians of custom nevertheless sought some way to preserve the distinction between the truly wicked and everyone else.[15] The customs that emerged with regard to when mourners cease reciting Kaddish daily were the way they found to do that.

Jewish tradition considered children's actions as a projection of their par-ents. Nothing did this more clearly than the orphan's steadfast recitations of Kaddish. "For months and months, the child goes to shul to say—no, to show—who his or her parent was," as Wieseltier puts it.[16] An orphan who re-cited Kaddish for twelve full months would, the rabbis asserted, thereby give evidence of a parent so wicked that the maximum number of recitations were needed to redeem him from punishment. But if the orphan concluded the Kaddish a month, a week, or even a few days early, surely this would demon-strate the child's moral confidence in the fundamental goodness of the parent, a parent who was more than protected by the eleven months of praises to God. Now this need to protect the parent's reputation in public, as some rabbis noted, was not theologically sound but instead was the result of popular su-perstitions and the assumptions they fostered.[17] Nevertheless, since one of the primary aims of the Kaddish had become to give honor to one's parents even after their death, anything that diminished that honor in the public mind (and that was where honor was projected), even when based on popular miscon-ceptions, was to be avoided. That included saying Kaddish for the full twelve months. So the eleven-month rule or variations on it in effect were in har-mony with at least one of the essential spiritual goals of extended mourning, to honor the parent.

Yet this eleven-month custom also demonstrated something else. It confirmed that, although dead for nearly a year, the parent still had a reputation to protect among the living. It remained the child's duty to see to it that that good name was protected, something the twelfth-month Kaddish suspension could accomplish subtly but unmistakably, at least among those conversant with Jewish custom (who when these customs were instituted were far more numerous than they are today). In a sense, this custom revealed that in the calculus of community life, the dead still figured and the activities of the living on their behalf were consequential. What better way to show that death did not have the power to cut the social bond?

To some mourners, this twelfth-month loosening of the ties to a daily Kaddish recitation is experienced as a sudden release. These people—including even some who have until then unfailingly come to the synagogue for their Kaddish—often reveal these feelings by disappearing from the synagogue after their last Kaddish, or within a day or two of it. At last able to close the book on their filial Kaddish duties, they run away from their mourning routine and its funereal associations.

Some might see this hasty departure as an expression of their feeling so completely healed of their grief by virtue of their quotidian rituals that, like the patient who after a long convalescence cannot wait to leave the sickroom, they cannot bear to delay their return from the world of mourning. Or perhaps they seek to test their recovery, hoping to discover whether they can recapture the old tempo of their lives and a renewed sense of normalcy. Maybe they have just had enough of doing for another and now hunger to do for themselves. Although, like any Jew, they retain the same religious responsibilities to pray daily with a congregation, the synagogue has become for them so associated with mourning that they seek to escape it as they try to slip from the confinement of mourning.

But others find parting from the routines of mourning far more difficult and continue to linger in the synagogue as if they were still saying Kaddish. "Now that my eleven months are up," writes one orphan, "I find I do not want to get out of the habit" of coming to the synagogue for Kaddish.[18] Another explained, "By the time I got to the 11th month I started to panic: I was scared of coming back. I was scared of letting go of my father."[19]

> Today is the first day of the eleventh month, the final month of kaddish. I thought this would bring me cheer. When I left shul this morning, however, I was anxious. Suddenly the kaddish felt like a farewell, and I did not want it to end. For as long as I have been organizing my life around the kaddish, I have been organizing my life around my father. When kaddish is over, he will be gone. My strict observance of the year of mourning has had the consequence of delaying the return to normal life.

I have lived in a state of suspension, shielded from a fatherless world by a fatherful practice. The Jewish way of mourning has turned an absence into a presence.[20]

Who are these reluctant runaways from the Kaddish obligation? Perhaps they are mourners for whom the experience accompanying Kaddish has been one of such lasting personal transformation that they do not really know how to make the transition to the next stage. These are people whose presence in the synagogue, no less than their steadfastness in Kaddish, allowed them to demonstrate to themselves, no less than to all others in the community, the depth of the impact that their parent's death or their parent's life, or both, has had upon them. To rush away at the first opportunity seems perhaps to diminish the sincerity of their loyalty to Kaddish or even to deny the depth of that impact. It suggests that the months of sharing in collective prayer, of ritualized devotion to memory, of constancy, were not the projections of a deeply felt emotion and sense of responsibility but the externally imposed requirements of custom and social or religious expectations. To such lingering mourners, the premature departure vitiates the connections so transparently created over the year.

Recognizing and even trying to abet this attitude, some of the same rabbis who had cautioned against too swift a departure from the graveyard at the funeral suggested an alternative to a complete stoppage of Kaddish. They ruled that simply by devotedly answering "amen" to someone else's Kaddish, these twelfth-month mourners could still provide spiritual support for their parents, while at the same time clearly signaling their confidence in the parents' essential righteousness.[21]

Some will, of course, object that because the religious obligation to worship daily with the congregation is not limited to mourners—in fact their obligation is simply to be there, summoning others to praise God—therefore this rabbinic "solution" is really connected more to intention than to activity, a camouflaged way of getting the mourners to stay in the synagogue and remain counted as part of the congregation. There is, after all, nothing about the end of mourning that should lead to a sudden departure from the synagogue. Yet the rabbis understood the extra dimension that the rituals of mourning added to the synagogue religious experience. They realized that the reluctance of some mourners to end what we now bundle into the notion of Kaddish was a way of expressing a desire to nurture mourning's life-transforming Jewish experiences. For these Jews the rabbis had something more than just a devoted "amen." For them they also offered Jewish study.[22] Study was to these rabbis the ideal occupation. After all, that was what they, who never wanted to get away from their binding relationship to Judaism, did.

Prayer and Kaddish might assist the dead and the grieving over the long haul, but "the study of Torah profits sevenfold more than all prayer, and by means of it the dead may be admitted to Eden." The rabbis had in mind not just any sort of study; they wanted learning that was creative at the same time that it was rooted in time-honored, sacred texts. "If the son breaks new ground in the study of Torah, there is no measure to the credit that accrues to his father in the session [literally, the yeshiva] above," and accordingly, "every mourner for a father or a mother should strive to make the utmost effort to study as much as possible according to his capacity."[23] Surely, a superabundance of study would break all barriers. Presumably in a world where daughters study Torah no less than sons, they, too, could share in this extra practice.

The motive here was to use the occasion of bereavement not just to inaugurate mourners into quotidian and timely Jewish religious synagogue service or to bring them back to a dependence upon and feeling of closeness to the community but ultimately to usher them into the domains of Torah and tradition, to create a new order in their Jewish lives. This would be supremely achieved by tying them to the order of study, to thereby transform them even more than might be possible by the far more restricted conditions of Kaddish and public prayer. The death of the father or mother would lead to a new life for the child, one that far more firmly held him or her to Judaism and the Jewish people. Mourners who began such study, who broke "new ground," would be included in the great chain of those who added to the Jewish treasury that was Torah.[24] They would become groundbreakers in the field of sacred scholarship, allies in the struggle against Jewish illiteracy, guarantors of what the rabbi/scholars considered the only way to assure Jewish continuity. If death led to enhanced Torah study, it meant that death led to life, but not just for the people as a whole. Those who devotedly pursued such study could use it as a "security deposit" in the heavenly savings account that awaited each Jew in the world to come. It was a way of ensuring the student's own eternal life.

In the world the rabbis imagined, Jews did not want to go to their graves loaded with gold; they wanted to be accompanied by the credits of *mitzvah*.[25] Those who did *mitzvahs* (and the study of Torah, the Talmud asserted, was the "greatest of these") on behalf of and in honor of those they mourned shared those benefits with the dead as well. The rabbis even imagined a kind of joint contract between the living and the dead. Thus, for example, the son who studied the Mishnah in honor of his deceased father thereby protected the soul of that father, who in return acted as an advocate on his behalf in the court on high. Even more so than the Kaddish or worship in the congregation, the study of Torah joined the accounts of living and dead, this world and the next, child and parent. From Jewish loss would come Jewish gain.

I have reached the end of my mandatory recitations of Kaddish and, like so many before me, am surprised at how reluctant I am to stop. Not that my eleven months of daily experiences in the synagogue have always been spiritually uplifting. On the contrary, I have often been frustrated by the recurrently mundane character of what goes on, the way in which for so many "worshipers" what might be their most precious moments of reflection and soul-searching prayer are turned into mechanistic mumblings hurriedly squeezed into the interstices of their lives. I have even found myself rushing through Kaddish or my mind wandering as I now recite each syllable from memory. Perhaps it is too much to expect the regular to also rise to the level of the extraordinary—even if that is what in principle the guardians of Jewish tradition claim their way of life offers.

Yet, for all my spiritual disappointments, I have also received genuine consolation from many of these encounters. The idea that, wherever I go, I must and can find a congregation ready to help me fulfill my orphan's obligation—people who accept my need, even if they know nothing about me or even who I am— has been comforting. During this year, wherever I have found myself, the familiarity of what happens in a synagogue service and the familiar responses to my Kaddish have helped me compensate for the unfamiliarity of mourning. I have been moved, sometimes even when I did not expect to be, by my standing up and calling out Kaddish. I have felt this even in the congregations whose customs are distant from mine; the collection of Kurdish Jews in Tiberias with whom I happened to pray one evening, the Syrian Jews I encountered in a tiny one-room chapel behind the Jerusalem market, the Jewish aristocrats in a Montreal temple, the garment workers in the Millinery Synagogue, the small-town Jews in a Down East congregation on the Maine coast, the transplanted German Jews of Washington Heights in New York, the anonymous clutch of Jews who gather in the nameless synagogue of Tel Aviv's Central Bus Station, or even the urban professionals of a Manhattan synagogue.

In one place, where I listened in at a breakfast for the "Kaddish crowd," a rabbi explained what he believed was the essence of the contribution the congregation made. I think he got it right. It provided, he believed, a place where people came "for comfort, for strength, for solace, for the encouragement the community is able to offer. We offer it to people sometimes by words we say. There also is a beautiful verse in Psalms, 'to you, O God, silence is praise.'" (I think he meant the line in Psalms 62:2, "My soul waits in silence only for God; from him comes my salvation.") Then he added, "Sometimes, I've learned in my profession—a profession that is often associated with talking but also recognizes the simple power of our presence—that in certain occasions, and I've been humbled by that, I've found that the greatest gift we can give to another human being is simply our presence, simply being there."

That was the special gift that every congregation within which I recited Kaddish throughout my year of mourning provided for me. They were an abiding, enabling presence. They reminded me I was not alone.

With all its human failings and spiritually leveling forces of this-worldliness, the experience of being part of a Jewish congregation and sharing what it has to offer has become an important presence in my life. I am no longer sure whether I am attending because of my obligations to my father or those I have made to myself. Like my father and me, these motives have somehow become conflated. As much as I worried at the outset that I would never manage consistently and faithfully to complete my term, day in and day out, now that I have come to the end, it feels hard to go back to where I was before I began all this. I am not the Jew I was at the outset. But, I suppose, that was a tacit goal of the process.

Watching a neighbor who, having come to the daily *minyan*, is just beginning his year of recitations, I long to tell him what he is about to go through, about the lows and highs, the day-in and the day-out—but only his own experiences can inform him. At best I can tell him that, if he allows himself steadfastly to stay the course, he will be comforted.

Throughout the year, I have gradually taken on new religious practices, as if to reflect or perhaps to magnify the change I feel in myself. This was something my father used to do. As he gradually moved from his assimilated Jewish upbringing to the quiet piety that characterized his later years, he would absorb some new Jewish practice. When his wife was saved from the terrible swift sword of the ghetto's liquidation, he took up some new recitations in his prayers. When his son was born after the war, he added another religious practice. Whenever some change occurred in his life that he saw as significant, he marked it with a new small Jewish obligation that he made his own. Now, I was doing this too, as if I were him.

About six weeks after the funeral, I began each morning, after the close of services, to recite the psalm whose number was equivalent to my father's age—a practice a Hasid I met around that time informed me provides special consolations. This added recitation became part of my own ritual of mourning. Although at my mother's earnest urging not long after the end of *shloshim*, I reluctantly shaved my mourning beard, I tried to hold on to some external changes in my appearance—as if they would mirror the changes inside—at least while I was in the synagogue. Although I did not wear the *mitron,* the hood that mourners once wore throughout the twelve months as a sign of their isolation from the joys of life—since the Middle Ages this practice has fallen into disuse, and I have never even seen such a hood—nevertheless, I took to throwing my tallit over my head during the morning services, as my father had done in the later years of his life. Each day I made time to study a chapter of Mishnah in my father's memory, a practice I learned during shivah was "a greater remedy than leading the prayer service."[26] To remain connected with my father, I have gradually but undeniably become more traditionally Jewish. At long last, I am putting aside the rebellions of my youth.

These many months of my mourning, the practices I have taken on have in some way that I cannot quite articulate dissolved the emotional distance between my father and me. Although I have always thought of myself (and my father) as steeped in rationality, I see that many of this year's changes drag us toward the mystical, which has always stressed the dissolution of the relationship between subject and object. Underneath my tallit I am not a rational man. Here I keenly feel my father's presence beside—inside—me. In the whispered words of the Psalms, I hear his voice more than the Psalmist's. To stop all this and leave, to abolish these routines, is somehow to leave my dead father behind, to forget him and hence lose a part of myself that has become powerfully attached to this new incarnation of his spirit. How can I do that?

Somewhere I have read that in line with the principle that emissaries who carry out a *mitzvah* for someone else are an extension of the one on whose behalf they act, parents during their lifetimes may command their children to commit themselves to the fulfillment of a particular commandment or practice on their behalf, make them messengers of a *mitzvah.* The effect of this parental directive, the rabbis argue, extends beyond the parents' lifetime, no less than does the requirement to honor them. When children fulfill these commitments, they in effect keep alive the Jewish engagement of their parents, who from beyond the grave may draw the spiritual benefits that such activity is meant to engender. Of course, at the same time the emissaries remain inextricably bonded to the ones who have sent them on this mission. I have learned that, in the ethereal realms of the spirit, this sort of service is valued more highly than even the recitation of Kaddish. So, even if I no longer recite the Kaddish, I can still carry out any number of *mitzvahs* for my father. I can contribute what was his money to charities on his behalf; I can care for my mother (whom he loved more than his life); I can teach his grandchildren to carry out the Jewish customs and practices that he made our family's own. As long as I continue to do all this and come to the synagogue, study the Mishnah, as he would have had me do, I dissolve the distance between us. We pray together; we study; we go on together as one. When he was alive, I could detach myself from him, go away from where he was. Now he is always with me. We have conquered the breach of death.

When the eleven months are over, I keep coming to the synagogue, repeat my father's practices, throw the tallit over my head, recite Psalms, go on studying the Mishnah. I latch myself to the great chain of Jewish being, not just to Kaddish. And my father, precisely now that he is dead, is the linchpin of this all.

"Until the age of scientific progress," the historian Philippe Ariès tells us, "human beings accepted the idea of a continued existence after death."[27] Until this year, I thought I was firmly anchored in that age of scientific progress. But during these eleven months of mourning, I seem to have become loosened from its shackles and gradually embraced the totally unscientific idea of a continued existence after death. I cannot and do not perceive my father's death as a simple end and bodily decomposition. That is what this year of Kaddish has wrought, and why I cannot and will not stop all I have begun doing simply because eleven months have passed since we buried my father's bones.

Perhaps that is why the Zohar, repository of Jewish mystical traditions, avers: "A righteous man even when he departs from this world, does not [truly] rise above or vanish from any world. For he is to be found in all worlds more than in his lifetime. In his lifetime, he is found only in this [material] world, but afterwards, he is found in three worlds, and accessible therein."[28]

YAHRZEIT

We will grieve not, rather find
Strength in what remains behind;
In the primal sympathy
Which having been must ever be;
In the soothing thoughts that spring
Out of human suffering;
In the faith that looks through death . . .
                    William Wordsworth,
        "Ode: Intimations of Immortality"

For all of the attachments to Jewish routines and extended practices that the newly orphaned establish during this year, the formal end of mourning cannot be deferred. As each of its stages draws to its definite end and nudges mourners back into the world and society that await their return, so, too, these last vestiges of mourning ritual must, the rabbis assert, end precisely a year to the day, actually twelve Hebrew (lunar) months, from the burial.[29] Affirming the absoluteness of such closure, the Talmud offers instruction from the venerable sage Rabbi Meir, himself forced to mourn two children whom he lost to death on a single day.[30] The rabbi discourages anyone seeking to lengthen the twelve months with even the seemingly minor solicitude of a word of consolation after the year has passed. One who does this to another who has completed twelve months of mourning is, Rabbi Meir asserts, like a doctor who, encountering a person who had fractured a foot that has already healed, says to him, "come to me and I shall break your foot again and heal it so that you may see how well I can heal the wounded."[31] Here was a most stringent application of the famous dictum from Ecclesiastes that "to every thing there is a season, and a time to every purpose under the heaven. . . . A time to weep, and a time to laugh; a time to mourn, and a time to dance" (3 : 1–4). Consolations that go on past their time do not ease the return to life; they impede it. Worse still, those who mourn longer than is permissible for their dead, who remain stubbornly and endlessly in the framework of grief, not only will fail to regain life but also, according to folk wisdom, will tempt fate and find themselves all too soon forced to weep and to mourn some new death. Mourning must not become melancholia, with its endless despondency.[32]

In the established order of Jewish custom, the deceased must ultimately rise from the grip of death and find a new way to associate themselves with their existence and the living, while, for their part, the bereaved must also return, in one form or another, to full human association and find a new way to live. The living must ultimately "turn back to everyday pursuits with a sense of having done the right and proper things about the social loss."[33] According to Robert Hertz, moreover, this is not just a matter of concern for mourners. Rather, "this release and reintegration constitute . . . one of the most solemn actions of collective life."[34] Yet all this cannot happen without some clear marker of the end. That marker is called *yahrzeit*.[35]

In principle, as already noted, *yahrzeit* is the anniversary of death and burial. But in fact, the word means simply "a year's time." This term thus allows us to speculate that it is not the dead alone for whom this "year's time" is marked; it is no less for the living and in particular the bereaved. After all, this first commemoration is also the day on which mourning ends, and as such, perhaps more than any subsequent one, it is characterized by ambiguity and paradox. It is for the dead and the living, a recollection of sadness and loss but also a time of joy and liberation, the end of a term of mourning and the beginning of a new lease on life, a "phase of triumph" after grief has run its course.[36]

This first occasion of what will become an annual observance cannot help but recall and hence arouse again much of the sense of loss and many of the anxieties of the original day of death. Contemporary grief research speaks of "anniversary reactions" that are often flashbacks to the trauma of the original loss. The Jewish mystics, using their own imagery, asserted that on this day no less than at the time of the funeral there are parallels between what happens in the domains of the dead and those who mourn them. Once again both the living and the dead are judged on high. Once again the dead and the living come together in time and yet must separate from each other and orient themselves to new attachments. Once again the mourners must make their way to the grave to visit the dead and to the Jewish community to recite Kaddish and be comforted. Once again the dead must try to ascend from death to eternal life. Once again both the living and the dead must conclude this was a good day to die. Much of the day is therefore a symbolic reenactment and a distant echo of the passages that began on the day of death and burial.

Early on, perhaps when Judaism, like many primitive religions, was more powerfully affected by the popular tendencies of ancestor worship, mourners were encouraged to fast on the *yahrzeit*.[37] Since only the living eat, fasting was of course a way to symbolize solidarity with the dead. Moreover, because Judaism also identified fasting with acts of penitence, mourners who fasted could thereby display contrition, an attitude that would engender God's protection from the evil angel of death who, exquisitely attuned to coincidences, otherwise might choose this day to physically unite the mourners with their dead. Finally, because mourners were always assumed to act on behalf of their beloved dead, fasting and the penitentiary activity associated with it could also expiate any remaining sins that might prevent the soul of the deceased from completing its yearlong journey and at last reaching the realm of pure spirit or, as the Bible puts it, being "gathered up by its ancestors."[38] This would be the last display of piety that the mourner does for the one who has died, hoping by this deed to serve as a proxy for the deceased and to assure that God's good graces are aroused by this act of self-abnegation. Such fasting, however, has largely fallen into disuse because of, as one recent codifier put it, the "weakness of recent generations."[39] In its place, the practice of giving money to the poor is suggested by some, for according to Jewish belief, charity, like fasting, "can spare one from death."[40] Charity, moreover, is a kind of economic self-denial that endows the poor with new life.

Fasting or charity, however, was not all there was for the living to do as part of what came to be called *tikkun*, restoration and repair.[41] Given new life by

the mystical and sometimes pietistic practices that Hasidism inserted into popular Judaism during the last two hundred years, and augmented by the practices
that were maintained by North African and Middle Eastern Jews even after
their arrival in the modern State of Israel and the precincts of Westernized
Jewry, *tikkun* practices might include immersion in a *mikveh*, a purification
ceremony recalling the *tahara*. This time, however, the living who are about
to conclude mourning are the ones who are made pure by the dip into water.
Tikkun practices also dictated a recollection of the burial, namely, a visit to
the grave (which by this date needed to be clearly marked with some sort of
monument). Mourners were encouraged not to go alone to the graveyard but
to assemble at least the ten-minimum congregation—an echo of the need
to mourn amid the community that played such a large part in the funeral and
the entire period of mourning—so that they may recite Kaddish as well as
the *El Moleh Rachamim* prayer with its special personalized petitions, to which
there could be the necessary responsive "amens."[42] Of course, the mourner
was to use this last occasion in the period of mourning to summon the congregation to prayer, in a kind of reprise of the entire year.

On the *yahrzeit,* mourners also rekindle the memorial candle, recalling the
flame lit the year before.[43] The symbolism here is transparent. Like the flame,
the memory of the dead still burns brightly. This, too, is the light that comes
after the dark year of mourning, the light of new life both for the soul of the
departed and for the life of the mourner, which is now restored. But this
yahrzeit candle is not the long seven-day shivah one but a smaller version, one
that would burn for twenty-five hours only. In some variants of this custom,
candles were lit both at home and at the synagogue.

Among those who hold to Sephardic customs, a variation on this was practiced. Instead of lighting a single candle, on the anniversary date the mourner
would supply all the oil needed for lighting the synagogue lamps; when he was
called for his annual *aliyah* to the Torah, the epithet "he who kindles candles"
would be added to his name. In this way, the commemoration of a personal
loss was combined with an act of kindness for the community. While recalling
the deceased, the mourner could at the same time symbolically requite the
community's support.[44] You helped me in my darkest hour; now I shall help
put a light to illumine your darkness.

Following a medieval custom established by the kabbalist Rabbi Isaac Luria
(1534–72), Sephardim also recited a litany of verses from the mystical Zohar
on this occasion, reviewed a series of Mishnahs acrostically related to the name
of the one whose death is being recalled, recited a requiem called a *Hashkavah*
(there are separate texts in memory of men and women), and followed all this
with a festive meal, an echo of the *seudat havra'ah* (meal of recovery) that was

eaten after the funeral.[45] But while that first meal was generally taken alone by the mourners, this one is eaten with at least nine others; and while that meal was unpretentious and limited, this one is effulgent with sweets and drinks. While that one marked the beginning of mourning, this one marks the limits of mourning and celebrates the eternal life of the soul and the human spirit.

The day of burial was a day of descent, and in Judaism descent has always been associated with death.[46] The day of its commemoration, however, becomes a time of *aliyah,* or ascent. Whereas the living mourner rises to stand at the Torah, the soul of the dead is supposed to rise from the depth and stand in paradise. To be sure, each day, as we have already seen, the actions of the mourners are seen as a vehicle for the ascent of the soul of those whom they mourn. However, on this day, as the mystic Luria argued, the ascent was to the highest heavenly plane. In mystical tradition, "throughout the twelve months one's body (still) remains intact and the soul ascends [to heaven] and descends [to the body], but after twelve months, one's body is nothingness and the soul ascends, never again to descend."[47] Death turns out to have been *"yerida l'tsorech aliya,"* a descent for the purpose of an ultimate ascent.

In many places, mourners begin the commemoration of the *yahrzeit* and *tikkun* on the preceding Sabbath. This is related to the kabbalistic belief that on every Sabbath each Jew becomes endowed with a *neshama yetaira,* a supplementary soul. This spiritual endowment is part of what, according to rabbinic lore, makes the Sabbath *"maiain olam habah,"* a taste of the world to come. In keeping with these notions, one mystic tradition maintained that even after death that supplementary soul continued to exist. Following that reasoning, guardians of this doctrine concluded that while the *yahrzeit* marked the day that the soul of the deceased made an ascent to a higher plane, the preceding Sabbath was the time that the *neshama yetaira* made its parallel ascent. On this day, therefore, mourners should, on behalf of the one whose *yahrzeit* occurs in the upcoming week, be given an *aliyah,* the call to "rise to the Torah," in a kind of sympathetic magic that would allow the *neshama yetaira* of the one they mourned to likewise have an *aliyah.*

On the Sabbath, the *yahrzeit* celebrant is also asked to recite a selection of the *haftarah,* the additional readings from Scripture that follow the weekly Torah reading in the congregation. The explanation for this is to be found in wordplay. The common etymological root פטר that united the word *haftarah* and the Hebrew word for death, *petira,* was seen as mystically significant. Moreover, the blessings with which the reader of the *haftarah* concluded echoed some of the same themes and words as the famous *tzidduk ha'din* (justification of the judgment), which was commonly recited at the funeral.[48]

All this makes clear that the *yahrzeit* does not simply recall sadness and loss or reenact death and transfiguration, but rather becomes the setting for celebration. But this is not simply a personal celebration; if it were, it would have little, if any, significance for others in the community. The mystics and their Hasidic counterparts therefore understood a *yahrzeit* (in particular the *yahrzeit* of a *zaddik* or saint—commonly a great rabbi) as a day that could promise not just the anniversary of an end to a particular period of mourning but an end to all mourning, not just *aliyah* for one Jewish soul but for all of them. That is, it would hold out the promise that *tikkun*, the repair of the world by humanity, might indeed succeed. The *yahrzeit* thus intermingled utopian, messianic hopes with the conclusion of personal sorrow.

Hasidim excelled in this sort of mixing of personal and collective, symbolic and mystical. For these Jews who (at least originally) located themselves at the intersection of popular folk and esoteric kabbalistic practices, the best way to demonstrate faith in that restoration and repair was to turn mourning into joy, to banish all sadness precisely on the *yahrzeit*. Food and drink were their ideal vehicles. Turning the *yahrzeit* into a "day of *hilulah*—a 'feast' with *schnapps* and cake"—became the common Hasidic practice, mostly for their own rabbis, but in principle for everyone.[49] That is, the mourner might be fasting, but the congregation of consolers was offered an opportunity to recite the blessings over food and make the traditional *l'chayim,* a toast to and embrace of eternal life. This was appropriate at the very least on the first *yahrzeit* because, as already noted, that was the day the soul of the deceased was expected to break free of its last ties to the mundane reality of corporeal existence and find its own repaired eternal life. There is also the kabbalistic belief that at the end of the year the soul is at last reunited with its divine source—one the mystics called the return of the sparks to the great fire—and this "marriage" needs to be celebrated no less than a wedding of two human spirits. *L'chayim* is toasted at both. As they partake in the collation, members of the congregation wish the mourner that the "soul might have an easy ascent," that the "soul should at last find a true rest" or "its true home"—phrases that resonate with many of these mystical beliefs. Here was a crystallization of the essential attitude toward death: recognizing it as the sad termination of corporeal existence while denying its dominance by transforming its occasion into an affirmation of life.

In time, the toast to life and the celebration supplanted the identification with death and grieving, while the custom of offering toasts of *l'chayim* in memory of the dead to mark the end of mourning supplanted the practice of recalling the day of burial with fasting. If one was genuinely ready to put aside the sorrow that had marked the period of mourning, a toast to life, the intoxicating feeling of joy, and a gathering with others were the best ways to do that. Collective rejoicing displaces individual mourning. What was celebrated was the messianic hope that was kindled and the fact that we Jews do not mourn interminably. Death is reversible; sadness can be replaced by merriment. In the end, Kaddish can be paired with a *l'chayim*. In time, this folk practice became, in popular Jewish tradition, an apodictic truth, establishing as absolutely true this notion of *yahrzeit* marking the soul's ascent.

Unable to bring the *yahrzeit* celebrants back to fasting, the scholar opponents of the Hasidim, the rabbis of the Lithuanian yeshivas, leaped on the idea of joy by redefining it in their classical scholarly terms. What greater joy was there for a Jew than Torah study? Thus, for example, Rabbi Hayim Soloveitchik, the famous scholar of Brisk (Brest-Litovsk), made it a practice to study Mishnah the entire day of his father's *yahrzeit*.[50] A common choice was to pick chapters of Mishnah that spell out the deceased person's name. Some tried to time their study of texts so they would complete a section or volume in time for the an- niversary and thus combine the two events, marking both with an especially well-endowed festive meal. The latter was also seen to have kabbalistic signifi- cance, grounded on another mystical anagram and gloss—this one based on Genesis 49:20—which transposed the Hebrew word for "well-endowed" or "well-to-do" (שמנה) in order to spell out the word *Mishnah* (משנה), sug- gesting that one who rescues the dead from Gehenna by studying Mishnah thereby makes both the living and the dead "well-endowed" or "well-to-do."

Others used the *yahrzeit* occasion to recite a selected series of Psalms, some doing so while encircling the grave, others while standing within a few yards of it.[51] This sort of propinquity to the dead body of course made it harder to experience the occasion as one of celebration, and it reflects the difficulties that the scholarly tradition—in contrast to Hasidism—had with joy.

For the most part, as one reflects on the character of *yahrzeit,* one discovers that it became for all those who commemorate it a kind of "sacred time." "*By its very nature,*" Mircea Eliade tells us, "*sacred time is reversible.*"[52] At their core *yahrzeits* can and do reverse the emotional charge of the day, making what was a sad occasion into one that is treated as if it were happy. At first, of course, this inversion is more the product of the rites and customs that become asso- ciated with the day. However, with each subsequent *yahrzeit,* as the pain of the loss recedes further into the past, this anniversary becomes an opportunity to actualize the powerful myth of spiritual ascent and allows those who were once mourners to celebrate their conviction that the one whom they recall on this day has been "saved from nothingness and death."[53] Of course, for those for whom the anniversary lacks religious content in which this myth is anchored, the anniversary loses its transfigurative power; instead of being a sacred time, it can continue to remind them that there is no remedy for death.

For those who religiously continue to mark them, however, *yahrzeits* can serve as private family festivals on which the family's dead are turned into objects of veneration and remembrance. With the passing of time, their lives more than their deaths become the subject of those recollections. These are framed by religious significance and rituals tinged less with melancholy and more with bittersweet nostalgia, making this a day when the living turn back their thoughts to yesterday and try to reverse time and its relentless march to mortality.

My father's *yahrzeit* had now replaced his birthday as that day in the year when, whatever else I was doing, my thoughts turned to him. Unlike his birthday, March 3, which we always celebrated according to the solar calendar, his *yahrzeit*, the sixteenth of Adar, like all other Hebrew dates, was based on the lunar calendar, and it moved around, rarely falling on March 7, the day on which he died. So because I was largely anchored in the solar calendar, I had to take special care to be certain I did not miss it. Although the rabbis had proclaimed the month of Adar, the eve of spring when the holiday of Purim is celebrated, as a happy time—"when Adar comes, we abound in joy"—for me the onset of Adar had become quite the opposite. On the *yahrzeit* itself, I made sure that I would be near a synagogue with sufficient worshipers to make a *minyan* in which I could recite Kaddish (or which would even allow me to lead the services, as I had during the year of my mourning). At first it was difficult for me to lift a glass and drink a *l'chayim*, as I was told was the custom on this day. I was, after all, missing my father more than ever on this day. Fasting seemed rather more appropriate— though I was certain Dad would have urged me against it, not wanting his son to suffer at all on his behalf. But a toast?

Nevertheless, the imperatives of Jewish custom weighed heavily upon me. As I completed the final Kaddish of the service with which I marked my father's *yahrzeit*, and even before its closing words, "He who makes peace on high, may he make peace upon us and all of Israel," had stopped echoing in my head, I found myself clumsily hustling back to my pew in the synagogue to fetch the bottle of scotch whiskey and cookies I had packed that morning to mark the end of my mourning. I needed to set out the little collation, which I would invite everyone present to join before they left for work or whatever they did on a weekday after the end of prayers. I felt awkward as I beckoned the assembled to join me for a toast of *l'chayim* in memory of my father and in honor of this new anniversary of his. That awkward feeling only intensified as I tried to balance the drinks, shot glasses, and snacks that I carried to a table outside the sanctuary.

Even as I listened to myself tender the call, I was baffled at my actions. How could I be doing this? How could I take a drink in celebration? How could I ask for this at a time that I should have felt the melancholy of memory?

But my fellow worshipers were pleased to join me, and they held off their normal rush out the door. One by one, as congregant after congregant lifted the little glass of golden liquid and toasted my father's soul, wishing him a gentle ascent from the oblivion of death to the supernal heights, offering me their hopes that "his *neshoma* should have an easy *aliyah*," as they put it, I felt the awkwardness slip away. The cumulative effects of a collective spirit of joy and grace meant to lift my father's spirit was lifting my spirits as well—and away the vapor of sadness flew. We were free, all of us, my father from his body and the fresh weight of death, I from my grief and the long wait of mourning, and the community from its need to support and sustain me each day of the year. We had survived even death, and as long as I used this day to recall that, all of us would persevere against the pain of its sadness.

I raised my own glass and drank it down in one gulp. "*L'chayim*," I cried.

During the years that followed, the toasts to life became easier. The pain of loss was replaced by the delights of memories of my father. In time, even the joy of Adar that his death had erased returned. I would of course always miss the man, but on his *yahrzeit* I would learn to feel his presence and what was his vitality more acutely, and that provided a sense of intense gladness unmatched during the year.

Beit Olam and Yizkor
Forever

Memory is a living thing and makes alive.
Theodor Gaster,
Customs and Folkways of Jewish Life

While in these days of cultural homogenization and blurring of group identities, historian Philippe Ariès' argument that "the cemetery has been and may
still be the identifying sign of a culture" may be difficult to document, lingering aspects of the place of burial still reflect cultural elements.[1] In large measure because dead bodies were objects of dread, danger, and defilement, the
Jews generally placed them outside of the city limits, where contact with them
could be limited. Yet they did not abandon them there. On the contrary, while
these "necropolises" represented a kind of counterpoint to the city of living,
each living community, no less than each family, had its own neighborhood in
the city of the dead, with its family plots or caves. Today we no longer speak
of the city of the dead but instead refer to the cemetery. Yet, as we shall see, in
many ways Jews still treat the cemetery as if it were the city of the dead in
which each grave site is someone's house, a *Beit Olam,* a home everlasting.

This term deserves more attention, for it reflects a degree of ambiguity. For
Jews the idea of resurrection, although traced by the sages to scriptural sources,
became active relatively late. They preferred instead to think of their dead as
"living" eternally in *olam ha-ba* (the world to come).[2] Hence, when they referred to the graveyard in their indigenous Hebrew they called it a *"Beit
Olam."* The word *beit* is easy to translate; it means "house" or "home." *Olam,*
however, is more ambiguous, for it means both "everlasting" and "world." In
other words, to the Jews, the place where the dead are buried was not a temporary resting place but rather a house or home, a world, to which they have
gone not to sleep but to dwell for eternity.

In the classic Jewish folk practice of inverting the negative so that only the positive is spoken, cemeteries have also, as previously noted, often been called "*Beit HaChayim,*" the house of life (or the living), hinting also at the idea of a place where there is an eternal life in death.[3] While probably motivated in part by deep-seated superstitious fears of the dead, this designation also references the spiritual revival of the soul as articulated by the mystics, as well as resurrection. In a sense, calling the cemetery by these two names seems to capture the complicated and sometimes contradictory attitudes toward death that we have already discovered in Judaism, which at once affirms the corpse's decay and end (though prohibiting any postmortem "damage" to it), as well as the idea of the soul's immortality and the promise of some sort of life after death. Others may perceive in these two graveyard designations a projection of anxiety or alternatively hope rather than despair and a representation of the pervading theme of Jewish attitudes toward death: a denial of its destructive power and a transformation of its reality into something life-affirming.

The first sorts of graves that we find Jews choosing for the dead are those mentioned in Scripture, primary among them being the tomb of the patriarchs and matriarchs in the Cave of Machpelah in the Hebron hills. Indeed, the connection that those who view themselves as heirs of these ancients and the children of Abraham and Sarah have to the land of Israel is in some measure traced to the location of that tomb. Until at least the beginning of the common era, Jews (particularly those who lived in the land of Israel) followed this example and deposited their dead in family burial caves. There the bodies would be laid on a stone platform, the family bier, left to decay; then, commonly after a year, the remaining dry bones would be gathered up and placed in the family ossuary at the back of the cave. This last step, when the dead were joined with their forebears, became conflated in the popular imagination with the idea of the end of mourning and the spiritual rebirth of the soul. Such practices were by no means unique to the Jews, although, as with so many other practices, the Jewish religious and cultural associations that became laminated onto them transformed what was a general custom into a Jewish one.

For more than a thousand years, however, caves have ceased to be the Jews' final resting place of choice. Instead, Jews began to bury their dead. For this practice, they also found ample precedents in Scripture (see, for example, Genesis 35:20). Burial, unlike placement in a cave, necessitated a monument, or *matzevah,* as it was called in Hebrew. These grave markers were probably put in place to serve as a means of warning the living against digging or sowing crops where a cadaver had been buried. In time, as concern with purity and danger increasingly became religiously important to Jews, these markers took on ritual meaning and were used as well to help the living avoid the spiritual defilement they might encounter by stepping on or near the place where a corpse lay.[4] But these utilitarian and ritual motives, however important they once were, have over time been superseded by more symbolic and social ones. Among these is the fact that the monument concretizes the place of burial and provides a physical representation of the deceased. The body is gone, and its capacity to move through space has ended as well, but the gravestone, this physical marker of where the bodily remains can be found, gives a kind of territorial reality to what has otherwise moved to the realm of memory and spirit. Indeed, some Jews refer to the marker as the *nefesh* (soul), presumably because they believe that the soul hovers above the grave just where the monument stands. The *matzevah* became its palpable representation.

In Jewish tradition, the monument itself may take a variety of forms and may be put up any time after the end of shivah. Discussing the matter in the Jerusalem Talmud, the rabbis decreed that any money that remained after the funeral and the purchase of a burial plot was to be reserved for the erection of the monument, whose completion and engraving were to be accomplished by the fifteenth of the Hebrew month of Adar, the joyful month of the year.[5] The raising of the monument was considered a sign that grieving was coming to an end and would be replaced by joy.

Although some graves are marked simply with foot stones, more commonly throughout Jewish history, monuments to the dead have been some form of vertical structure: a pile of stones, pillar, stele, obelisk, cenotaph, sepulchre— in short, an upright form that points upward rather than down to the abyss, a column linking earth to heaven. Indeed, in both biblical texts and other Jewish sources, "raised locations" have been long identified as sacred places.[6] To mark the place of burial as a raised place is in harmony with the transformations that are part of the Jewish encounter with mortality, stressing sanctification, ascent, and rebirth. It is a movement from low to high, the physical representing the emotional.

The practice, popular at various times in this century outside of Israel, of erecting symbolic figures and statues of guardian angels, stone tree trunks, mausoleums in the shape of Greek temples, weeping Niobes, and the like as tomb markers—a custom also seen in Jewish graves of the Greco-Roman periods—while evidence of Jewish acculturation and often discouraged by unreconstructed upholders of Jewish tradition, nevertheless serves likewise to turn aside the visitor's attention from the abyss of the grave. The artifice of sculpture, even in its crassest popular form, is, after all, an effort to capture life, lift the spirit, and as such is a means of taking the dead out of the decay of the grave and installing them instead in some sort of living art, even if its aesthetic is banal.

Of course this practice is also freighted with issues of social status. The well-to-do often erect ornate, ostentatious monumental mausoleums. The more important (however importance is measured) the one who is buried was in the life of those who recall him or her, the more the survivors put into the grave site. These distinctions run counter to the talmudic ones that sought in death to remove all differences between the rich and poor—recall Rabbi Gamaliel's famous dictum that all Jews be buried in the same simple way. Nevertheless, the impulse to draw social distinctions apparently has remained powerful, among Jews no less than among others, as evidenced in the fact that these or-nate grave markers can be found as early as the Hasmonean period and as late as today. Some critics have charged that these structures come dangerously close to idolatry and death worship, and at least one, Rabbi Gamaliel's son, Rabbi Simon, sought to counteract this tendency by asserting that one should not erect a *nefesh* for the truly righteous, "for their words would be their me-morial."[7] Was that not the case for Moses, whose burial place no one knew and whose everlasting monument was his five books?

To be sure, mourners sometimes erect impressive monuments even at the graves of the less notable and well-to-do in order to compensate for their own feelings of guilt for a lifetime of neglect or when the deceased was victimized. Like other physical relics that come to stand for the dead, but perhaps more powerfully because it marks the spot where the body lies, the monument at these and other sorts of burial places is often endowed with a powerful emo-tional charge that no amount of disdain from the rabbis can discourage.[8]

The objections of Rabbi Simon ben Gamaliel and others notwithstanding, these days, no less than in the Hellenistic period of Jewish history, the need to have a place to pray for the soul of the deceased and the desire to mark the place of death have led at times to the construction of little houses of prayer, particularly at the grave of a *zaddik*. Sometimes those whose importance emerged after the monument was erected—the "concealed *zaddik*" or "hid-den righteous"—might find that whatever marks their grave might take on iconic importance or, failing that, be enhanced with something more "monu-mental."[9] Graves where the saintly or the otherwise prominent were buried frequently were marked by a tent, in part to create a shelter for the many who visited them. The term *ohel,* meaning tent, is often used today when referring to such graves. Commonly, mausoleums or small buildings are constructed to-day at such sites instead of actual tents. Where this is the case, however, the grave and the visit to it have become conflated with pilgrimage and take on a life and character of their own.[10] In some cases, for example, at the Galilee tomb of Rabbi Shimon bar Yochai (in Jewish mythology thought to be the author of the kabbalistic Zohar text); the Cracow, Poland, grave of the great Jewish codifier Rabbi Moses Isserles; or the New York site of Rabbi Menachem Mendel Schneerson, the man whom some followers consider a Jewish messiah, synagogues have become attached to the grave site, in spite of the ritual problems of defilement that a corpse creates and the resonances of idolatry that such places produce.[11] Such sites hold particular importance for Jews with Hasidic enthusiasms or those associated with Middle Eastern and North African Sephardic traditions—all of whom have elevated the *zaddik* to a kind of *axis mundi* and his grave to a place of special religious significance.[12] As such, the trip to the grave of a loved one or a *zaddik* became like a pilgrimage to other sacred places. Family graves constituted a sort of personal center of the world, a place where those who were related to the one buried there could more easily have "communication with the *other world,* the transcendental world," the realm of the spirit.[13] This, too, was in tune with the Jewish theme of reversing the baleful, injurious, and defiling properties of death into their antithesis. The grave site became a place to go for blessings, grace, and healing; the visit became a time of *hillulah,* religious celebration.

In choosing their graves, many Jews tried to select "final resting places" in locations that could more easily fit into the Jewish religious ideal of where the world was centered. Hence, Israel in general and Jerusalem in particular became idealized burial places, supported by a folk belief that in the end of days the resurrection would begin there a full forty years before anywhere else in the world (everyone buried elsewhere would have to repeat the forty-year earthly journey of that first ascent of the Jewish people to their holy land from Egypt). The visit to the grave, moreover, would more easily parallel Jewish pilgrimages, which generally went to the Land of the Bible. Absent such a grave site in the holy land, Jews chose to be buried among other Jews, reasoning that a place where Jews congregate (even in death) would be holy ground.[14] As a sign of their ultimate intention, they traditionally inserted some of the soil of the holy land into their shrouds and caskets.

Of course, precisely because the grave was a kind of personal *axis mundi,* many Jews had thereby implicitly replaced the Jewish center of the world in Jerusalem with their own personal center. The Jew who had spent his or her life in Boston or Paris, for example, whose loved ones were also buried in that place, would want *it* to be the location of his grave. A sense of place was clearly connected to the idea of the cemetery. Yet wherever it might be, the Jew's grave was meant to be a narrow gateway for the spirit, a temporary home, and the *yahrzeit* commemoration at it an opportunity to pass through it.[15] "This is the gate of the Lord, into which the righteous shall enter," as the Psalmist put it (Psalms 118:20) and as the Jews had written at the entrance to many a graveyard.

Although the book of Genesis is replete with accounts of grave monuments, a number of traditional commentators pointed to the book of Deuteronomy (16:22) as a source for proscribing their erection. Apparently it was not the monument itself that was bad but the fact that it was also part of the idolatrous worship practices of the "other nations" that the Deuteronomist suggested would surround the Israelites when they entered into the promised land.[16] In other words, when the erection of monuments obfuscated the religious distinction between the Jewish people and others, or when it threatened to become the object of devotions that rivaled the accepted ones, its construction was discouraged. That was how Rabbi Simon ben Gamaliel's proscription came to be understood. Nevertheless, graves continued to be marked. There has, however, remained a tension surrounding the nature of these markers, with those who hew closely to Jewish tradition seeking constantly to find ways of making their monuments distinctively Jewish and those who became assimilated into the larger surrounding culture choosing to mark the place of their dead in ways that conform to the general norm.

This need to mark Jewish graves distinctively became essential when, following their departure from their homeland, and especially prior to the Middle Ages, Jews in the Diaspora were frequently buried among Gentiles.[17] Here the monument became not simply something that had spiritual and ritual meaning but also something used as a way to mark Jews off from those around them. Among the most common ways of distinguishing the Jewish graves, of course, was by inscribing the *matzevah* with the names, epitaphs, and pertinent dates of the deceased in Hebrew. In fact, several codifiers went so far as to suggest that Jews were prohibited from marking their gravestones with a "date according to the birth of the Christians' Messiah," arguing that to do so would "shame" the "House of Israel."[18] Even those who, rather than using Hebrew, inscribed names and dates in the local vernacular often added some markings that designated the Jewishness of the deceased. These could range from putting on Hebrew epitaphs and scriptural quotations to etching the stone with the Hebrew acronym תנצב"ה, meaning, "may his (her) soul be bound up in the bond of life," a common closing to Jewish memorial prayers (derived from Samuel 25:29), or to marking the monument with widely recognizable Jewish symbols like a six-pointed Star of David, a Menorah, or a Torah scroll. In effect, in every case the monument became a Jewish text engraved in stone.[19]

Today while in areas where Jews are concentrated, they have their own cemeteries, the practice of burying them among non-Jews is still carried on, particularly where the Jewish community is small. Moreover, in Diaspora communities of all sorts, Jewish burial grounds are often separated from those of other groups in only the most minimal way, reflecting the increasing links between Jews and non-Jews in life. For most Jews of the Diaspora, visiting a Jewish grave in today's world outside of Israel often means taking a trip in the same direction as everyone else who goes to the cemetery.

When I first began to visit my father's grave, located in a section of town that some wags dubbed "cemetery row," I was always confused about where to go. My first trip there had been in the back of a limousine, in a snowstorm, with my eyes blurred by tears. Now, as I tried to come back on my own, it was harder to find my way. All of the graveyards seemed to look alike. Their names were not very helpful either because although they had formal names, no one really knew what they were—or at least no one whom I found in the neighborhood or asked for help in finding the Young Israel of Brookline Cemetery had any idea where that particular plot of land was. In fact, most locals simply referred to the different burial grounds by the names of the streets they were on, or where their gateways were. So there was the Baker Street cemetery or the Grove Street cemetery and so on. Those names helped me get to the general vicinity, but I needed more.

The Young Israel section, I knew, was a tiny field in the complex of graveyards on Grove Street. It was hidden behind a variety of other Jewish sections, each of which had its own name and association. The dead were ordered by group no less than the living, except that this belonging would last for an eternity. In time, I learned that to get to the Young Israel section, and its adjacent other Jewish burial grounds, I needed to watch for Jeschurun Street, a little lane, distinguished by its Hebrew name (it meant "the righteous"), which led to the Jewish sections in the Grove Street complex. Jeschurun, however, was not a street that would appear on any city map, and the small sign that the Jews had probably put up was in the warm months partially hidden by overgrown trees. The truth was that, to find my father's grave, I learned first to look for the prominent statue of the dying Jesus on the cross that marked the entrance to the large Holy Name Cemetery, and there I would find the tiny Jeschurun lane. As the relatively few Jews of Boston had lived surrounded by their Catholic neighbors, now those who chose to be buried here would rest eternally near to them.

Those for whom or for whose surviving relatives, the ones who arrange the funeral, Jewish identity is secondary in importance have often chosen to have their lives marked in ways that emphasize their primary identity. Thus, celebrities are buried in celebrity graveyards; fallen soldiers may be entombed in military cemeteries; or those whose association with the nation at large is most prominent may be laid to rest in a national shrine.[20]

The custom that some have adopted of not erecting or "unveiling" the monument until a year has passed after death probably comes not only from the ancient practice of gathering the bones but also from the rabbinical pronouncement that discouraged excessive visiting of the grave during the first year, a practice in harmony with the goal of encouraging the mourner to reenter normal life bit by bit during that year.[21] Visits to the fresh grave may, after all, arouse feelings of despair. "Better . . . the day of death than the day of one's birth," as Ecclesiastes put it, and as Sephardic Jews repeat when they visit such a grave, perhaps in an implicit desire to mute survivor guilt or to expiate the anger of hovering spirits.[22]

To be sure, a countertradition (more commonly practiced today in Israel than elsewhere) of visiting the fresh grave at the end of shivah and then at the end of *shloshim,* when Israelis erect the monument, is meant not to reanimate feelings of gloom that the preceding seven days were supposed to mitigate but to remind the mourner that while the most intensive mourning is over, the memory of the dead is not to be easily abandoned.[23] The recently bereaved therefore come to the grave because they feel, as one mourner once put it, "My days of mourning have run, and my heart still sighs."[24] Perhaps the fact that there is no universal and formal ritual associated with this erection of the monument (whenever that monument is raised) points most vividly to the essential lesson that is to be learned: the monument must be erected, the death must be marked again, and the deceased should be recalled, but above all else the mourners need to turn their attention to mending themselves spiritually and get back to where they belong—among the living.

The best way to ensure this was to de-emphasize visits to the graveyard. Judaism's ancient priestly elite, the guardians of ritual life and purity—the *cohens*—could not even set foot in it except to bury an immediate family member. Other kinds of Jews simply were supposed to limit their trips. The guardians of the tradition wanted to move Jews away from ancestor worship, and they recalled the Deuteronomic warning that had associated the *matzevah* with idolatry. Prayer at a grave could shade dangerously close to praying to the dead. Perhaps because both pagans and Christians concentrated so much of their attention on the dead, the rabbis were particularly insistent that Jews not repeat this pattern and not become mistaken in any way as either a cult of the dead or Christian. Indeed, the rabbis stipulated that "one should not pray *to* the dead but only to the Holy One Blessed be He."[25] One had to take care that any petitions, the rabbis were quick to point out, were not actually directed to the dead, for to do that would come perilously close to the sin of ancestor worship—*doresh el hamaytim*—the idolatry the Deuteronomist condemned. Rather, the dead were to be the emissaries of the living petitioners whose requests were directed to God.[26] According to some of the death manuals that tried to manage this practice, the living might directly address the dead but only to urge them to "serve as a worthy advocate and importune God on our behalf"; the *yahrzeit* was considered a particularly auspicious occasion for this, but any visit offered a chance for such communication.[27]

In general, those who championed such visits tried to shape them so they benefited both the dead and the living. According to the mystics, that was the only spiritual incentive for the living to make such visits. It was why the custom of visiting the graves of one's parents during the prepenitential month of Ellul, on the eve of the Days of Awe and Atonement, became an established practice. For on these days, the living could pray to God on behalf of the dead, and the dead could return the favor. Some of these sentiments are implicit in the custom of the visitors' placing their left hands—those on the side of the heart—on the monument (almost as if they were touching the dead person) while reciting the following words:

> God will guide you always, sating your soul in thirsty places, and rescuing your bones; and you shall be like a watered garden, and like a never failing spring of water. From you the ancient ruins will be rebuilt; you will re-establish the structures of generations. They will call you, "the one who repairs the breach and resettles the ways of civilization" (*Isaiah* 58:12). Lie in peace until the coming of the Consoler Who Will Announce Peace.[28]

Although in many ways intoned like a prayer, these words imply the hope of the living that as I pray for your safekeeping, so may you do so on my behalf. Hence the visits were a way not only to link dead and living with God but also to re-create the mutuality that is at the heart of truly loving relationships.

If the dead remain alive to the needs and concerns of those who visit their graves and care about them, they can be turned to in times of particular need. The Talmud cites a practice, projected backward into the time of the Bible, of visiting the graves of relatives, "in order that [the deceased] should ask mercy for us."[29] Hence, in times of sickness or distress and adversity, visits to the graves of one's own dead or the especially prominent dead were seen as appropriate. To pray at the grave of the one whose *yahrzeit* was observed was (like stopping Kaddish after the eleventh month) a way of suggesting that the one mourned was among the righteous, who were the ideal go-betweens between the worshipers and God. While the prominent and the righteous were considered powerful intermediaries with God in their lifetimes, all the dead thus became endowed with this powerful capacity. Enduring remembrance of them by the living could protect against the annihilation of life.

"Eternal Master of All Worlds," begins a prayer that Sephardic Jews recite while standing at the grave of a father, "hearken to the voice of my entreaty and accept my prayer with your many mercies and kindness so that my own soul may be worthy to rest with the soul of the *zaddik* who is buried here and with all the other righteous ones . . . and grant me a share of his merit and some of the reward for the many good deeds done in his lifetime, for I have come here in his honor and to prostrate myself on his grave and to pray for his soul."[30] The prayer ends with the wish that the visitor may have children and grandchildren, that is, that death may not triumph over life. Where better to invoke all this than at the grave site of a parent?

So great could this power be that even the most traditionally religious Jews were willing to make contact with the ritual impurity of death in order to engage in such prayer. The Hasidim went so far as to assert that the grave of the righteous was not capable of defiling anyone and even a *cohen* could visit it. There is a practice recorded (probably traceable to the Gur Hasidic dynasty of Rabbi Moses Alter) of the bereaved requesting aloud that their arrival for a visit to a particular grave be announced to the dead by one of those buried nearby, with the promise that whichever soul complies will have charity given on its behalf.[31] Presumably, one's mourned loved one would be the "best advocate" to those who can control the world of the living. Thus Jews reformulated what might have been foreign customs and made them their own, or at least sufficiently their own so that they could feel comfortable performing them.

Other psychological elements are inherent in Jews' graveyard visits. These come from pietistic tendencies, including what some viewed as the need to control and diminish the natural hubris of life. Thus, many mystics viewed the visit to the graves of one's forebears, and even more so to those of the great and mighty, as a means of "humbling" the evil inclination, from which all hubris comes, and consequently also as a means of arousing in the visitor feelings of reflection and penance.[32] Others imagined that the visit to a grave of one over whose death one had mourned—such as a parent or a child—would "arouse grieving and lament, opening one's heart entirely, just as when one's dead is actually lying before one, at which time one's heart is truly broken."[33] That was another reason to visit on the eve of the Atonement.

For many among the bereaved, the *matzevah* became endowed with a kind of charisma, often becoming the physical incarnation of the memory of the one whose grave it marked. Mourners thus embrace, kiss, caress, and even support themselves on it, as if it were the body of the one they mourn. It is not uncommon to find that the bereaved choose the grave site as the place at which they commune with the dead, as if there, in the presence of the physical remains, the channel to them is most direct. One man described to me a funeral of his mother in which one of his grieving aunts (in a practice reminiscent of Gur Hasidic custom) threw herself on the nearby grave of the dead woman's mother, telling her that her daughter was coming to join her and tearfully urging her to pass the word to all the rest of the members of the family who were already among the dead.[34] More common is the custom of coming to a grave and sharing a private thought with the one who is buried there. People who would otherwise never communicate aloud with the dead find that such conversation is possible at the grave site.

Many mourners try to beautify the grave site by planting trees or flowers there. It is as if by doing so they are beautifying the corpse, replacing or covering the ugliness of decay with the beauty of nature that renews itself. Others choose spots that they believe would offer pleasure to the dead because they offer solace to the living. In all this the grave provides a way of relating to the dead as if they were still somehow among the living.

The well-known and increasingly popular custom of placing a stone or pebble on the grave (commonly, atop the monument) may be seen in this framework. The stone is not only a means of enhancing the tomb with evidence of a visit but also a gift to the dead. The nature of this gift is twofold. First, it offers a way for the visitor to heighten the monument. This ancient custom may perhaps repeat the original practice of creating a monument by means of piling stones on one another. The additional stone left by the visitor simply enlarged the pile, so that those dead visited most frequently would also have the tallest and most impressive monuments. The eye that beheld them would look up higher.[35] Alternatively, when the monuments were only piles of stones and the "elements or roving vandals dispersed them," leaving a stone after a visit assured that a monument would remain in place and warned vandals that the living had visited and would be back.[36]

Second, leaving the stone offers all others who come to the cemetery evidence that the person buried there is still remembered and important in the life of the living. The more stones, the more visits, the greater the evidence of this importance. As in all gift giving, credit accrues not just to those who receive the gift but also to those who give, who can because of their offering expect some sort of return.[37] In return for the attention that the living show to the dead, the dead, now so much more powerful, can be assumed to go on caring for the living. Hence, in the graveyard visit, a prayer or private thought is offered, the stone deposited, and the relationship between the living and the dead affirmed.

While the visit to the graveyard at the time of burial is of course part of the organization of the funeral and is carefully choreographed, notwithstanding the three-step visit I have just described, subsequent visits are far less structured. Both rabbinic dicta and customs were far more concerned with *when* such visits should occur than *how* they should be carried out. Accordingly, the literature is filled with discussions of the most auspicious times for a visit—the anniversary of day of burial, the conclusion of shivah, before various holy days, during the Hebrew month of Ellul, on the eve of the New Year or Day of Atonement, and, of course, the day of the monument dedication. But precisely what should be done during these visits remains vague. In some cases—for example, at the dedication of the *matzevah*—the custom seems to be to create a very abbreviated version of the funeral, leaving out the core element of the actual funeral: burial. Essentially, this consists of gathering a congregation (among the traditionalists this means at least ten), offering words of eulogy, and reciting some of the prayers originally used at the funeral. Yet these utterances are shortened; the Kaddish is not the special long version recited at the funeral but the regular mourner's Kaddish, nor are the words of eulogy extended. Psalms are repeated, as on the day of the funeral (in some traditions the verses from Psalm 119, the "Grand Alpha Beta," whose opening letters spell out the word *neshamah* (soul) and then the name of the dead person are selected for recitation), and commonly someone intones the *El Moleh Rachamim* prayer. Although some Hasidim and those under the influence of mystical motivations have taken to immersing themselves in a purifying ritual bath prior to the visit, spending many hours in meditation, prayer, and even celebration at the graves of the saints, these practices are not viewed as models either *of* or *for* most visits.

Yet what is perhaps the essential symbolism of the return of the living to a grave site of one they mourn is that it underlines the Jewish assumption that, as I have already emphasized, a relationship is not ended by death. These visitations give evidence of the Jewish belief in "an eternal timeless community in which the living and the dead are alike embraced."[38] This is reflected not simply in these practices that make up the religious etiquette of the visitation. It may be seen as well in the code that asserts that one who has not visited the grave of a parent for ten years (some say seven) may no longer return, for, according to this opinion, it is not death but neglect that ends a relationship and destroys communion.[39]

The rain fell like an endless set of curtains barring my way, but I was determined to penetrate it on the way to my father's grave. This was the last day of Ellul, the eve of Rosh Hashanah, and I was resolute in my desire to pay this visit on a day that the rabbis had asserted was among the most appropriate days of the year for such a rendezvous. Perhaps they believed that when one was about to enter the season of reflection and judgment, the Days of Awe, nothing focused the mind more than a trip to the *Beit Olam*. Perhaps so, but I was going because I could not bear the thought of going to the synagogue to sing the melodies and recite the prayers that in my mind so powerfully recalled my father without him. For years, since I had overcome my youthful rebellions against him, his presence near me was the key to my own meager efforts at penitence and reflection. When he became solemn and pensive, I felt my own capacities in that direction vitalized. When tears came into his eyes with the melancholy melody of the opening Kaddish of the service, my own eyes began to tear. Now that his bones were in the ground, I still felt the need to be near them to sense the awe of the occasion.

The rain was horrendous, and I told myself that my father would surely forgive my decision to turn back. He was always ready to countenance all sorts of lapses on my part for the simple reason that he loved me unreservedly, a love he could always demonstrate by the way his face lit up when we met after some time apart. Even a day apart was enough. When I was about ten or eleven and on lazy summer days would sit on a road marker a few blocks from where we lived, awaiting his return from work at around six thirty in the evening, he would always turn on his luminous smile when he saw me as his car turned the corner and we became visible to each other. But though he would absolve me of this responsibility to visit, and I could hear him do so in my mind, something in me refused to listen. Something told me that I must make my way to the graveyard this last day before the Jewish New Year.

By the time I reached the cemetery, the rain had slowed a bit, making me think that the sheets of falling water had simply been part of death's stinging rebuke, a test of my loyalty to my father's spirit. I was pleased to have gotten past these. Opening the door to the car, which now stood on the rocky path just beyond the row of tombstones, I gathered myself together and tried to prepare the liturgy that I knew was the traditional accompaniment for such encounters between the living and the dead. Yet as I stumbled along the cracked concrete path between the freshly doused headstones and then headed toward the little back section of the graveyard where my father lay, most of what I had learned about these traditions flew out of my mind, and all I could think about was finding a pebble with which to mark my visit. Half expecting to see my father, whose face I now saw before me and whose voice still echoed within me, I instead stood face-to-face with the black granite marker engraved with his name, the dates of his birth and death, and the simple epitaph that summed up what we who survived him believed was most important to know about him: that he was beloved as a husband, father, and grandfather.

This was not him. I walked carefully around the grave site, the outline of which was still distinctly visible after three years. The wild grass and clover that grew atop his coffin were so clearly different from the surrounding turf. I tried to imagine him, knowing that he lay inside the shrouds with which the Chevra Kaddisha had swaddled him. But that was not him either. Nor could I bring myself to think of him as a corpse. Instead, I leaned over and kissed the cold, wet granite. But this was stone, not my father.

I began to pray, to recite the Psalms I knew, the Twenty-third with its references to "fearing no evil" even though I walked in the "shadow of death." I repeated Psalm Ninety-one, the one that corresponded to what my father's age would have been had he still been among the living. Then I stood in silence, the rain turning my face into a stream of tears. It was as if the same heaven that had stood between me and this visit was now at last helping me complete my task. I placed my pebble on top of the tombstone alongside ones that others had left, then turned to go before the next cloudburst.

When I was halfway back along the broken path, however, I felt an irrepressible urge to turn around and rush back through the now recurring rain to my father's grave. I could not leave without a word from him, I blurted out, my voice piercing the awful silence of this place. But there was, of course, no reply, only the silent gray stone with his name etched on it. The stone said nothing except perhaps to remind me that if I wanted an answer, the graveyard was not the place to go. I turned again and went home.

That night, when I went to the synagogue and began to pray, listening to the familiar Rosh Hashanah tune of the *borchu*, the summons to all to pray, at last I heard my father answer. I heard him in my own voice and the voices of my sons who sat near me. I heard him in the continuity of generations. "Be for me," I whispered to him while the cantor prayed, a *meilitz yosher*, my defender on high, my worthy emissary. Then I looked down in my prayer book, and the line that met my eyes could have been my father's reply: "Restore me back to life, and bring me back from the depths of the earth." In my refusal to forget him, that was what I could and would do.

Where the grave is missing, as, for example, for the millions of victims of the Shoah, or where the place of burial is too distant to visit, something palpable is often felt to be lost. Those who mourn such a death may feel as if they have no place on which to focus their attachments and to share communications with the dead. The desire to set up alternative sites, memorials, and the like can be understood as an effort to create a place that will serve as the personal *axis mundi*. The near obsession to create memorials to the victims of Shoah as the remaining survivors reach the end of their lives can be explained as an effort to create places where the bereaved Jewish people can offer their promise to "never forget" those who were lost. Lacking concrete memorials, the living may turn to a more spiritual way of locating their dead. Time becomes place; thoughts become visits; and prayers, of course, can be recited in the synagogue, which serves always as a stand-in for all Jewish sacred places.

The time had come for my planned visit to my father's grave. That place, in an undistinguished corner of West Roxbury, Massachusetts, had become a sacred place for our family, our personal site of pilgrimage. The first *yahrzeit*, of course, was overwhelmed by the year of mourning that had preceded it and which it now completed. But the second year in some ways felt like the first true *yahrzeit*, for it was that island in time in which the memory of my father was raised out of my sea of remembrances. The day of his death was now a holy day for me. Instead of his birthday candle, I was lighting his memorial lamp; instead of talking to him, I was talking to myself about him. In place of finding him at home, I would have to meet his remains in the graveyard, where all I would see was a gray granite monument. But as it happened, I could not go that day, for I found myself in Jerusalem, nearly six thousand miles away. Had my father been alive, I would surely have telephoned my wishes for a long and healthy life, as I had so often done after leaving home. Now, how would I share my feelings with him?

Suddenly, an idea occurred to me. No longer did I need to use the telephone or make an actual visit. Now that my father was dead and in the realm of spirit, as long as I thought about him, he was always where I was, always with me. We were one. With this consolation, I went to the synagogue and recited Kaddish. And then closing my eyes, I saw not the gray granite monument on which his name was engraved or the memorial candle that burned on the table at home; I saw instead his face and his incandescent smile.

YIZKOR

Tombstones crumble, words come and go, words are forgotten,
The lips that uttered them turned to dust,
Tongues die like people, other tongues come to life,
Gods in the sky change, gods come and go,
Prayers remain forever.

Yehuda Amichai,
"Gods Come and Go, Prayers Remain Forever"

If the visit to the grave and the celebration of *yahrzeit* are structured opportunities in which Jewish tradition provides a place and time for the *individual* to recall a relationship with those who have died, *Yizkor*, the synagogue memorial service, represents the *community's* establishment of a recurring opportunity to turn one's thoughts to the dead. This service, so-called because its prayers begin with the Hebrew word "*Yizkor*," meaning "may [the Lord] remember," is, among those who follow the Ashkenazic tradition and especially its Polish variant, regularly included just before the *musaf* (additional) prayers on the last day of Passover, Shavuot, and Shmini Azeret—the three major Jerusalem pilgrimage festivals—as well as on Yom Kippur, the Day of Atonement. Some Ashkenazic communities also recite *Yizkor* on the Sabbaths preceding Shavuot and the ninth day of the Hebrew month, Av, the day commemorating the Jewish national tragedy of exile and the destruction of the Holy Temple in Jerusalem. Sephardim, particularly those of Spanish and Portuguese origins, do not recite this prayer specifically but rather repeat the memorial recitation of the *El Moleh Rachamim* on the afternoon of Yom Kippur, following the Torah reading in which appears the verse "And the Lord spoke to Moses *after the death* of the two sons of Aaron" (Leviticus 16:1). But every Jewish group has marked occasions when everyone in the community turns their thoughts to the dead they have lost.

In substance, the *Yizkor* prayer, which appears to have its origins in twelfth-century western Germany in the aftermath of the martyrdoms of the First and Second Crusades, is a petition to God for the repose of the souls of the dead "under the wings of the Divine presence, in the exalted heights reserved for the holy and the pure." [40] At its outset, this prayer appears to have been dedicated to recalling only those who had died in the preceding year, but in time worshipers began to include all those dead they wished to remember.

The practice of recalling martyrs and praying for their souls' "repose and peace," as both *Yizkor* and the *El Moleh Rachamim* prayers do, had been a common feature of church services from at least the fourth century. During mass, the martyrs' names would be read from two boards folded together like pages of a book. When this was developed into a longer service, it became known as the "Memento," from its opening words, "Remember (memento) O Lord thy servants male and female who have preceded us."[41] The parallel with both the *El Moleh Rachamim* and the *Yizkor* is remarkable. Clearly the Jews, no less than their Christian neighbors, collectively wanted to remember their dead—especially after those very neighbors had added to the number of dead.

Unlike Kaddish in which no dead are mentioned, in the traditional version of the *Yizkor,* the petitioner, commonly but not necessarily a relative, enumerates the names of those whom God is being asked to remember "along with the souls of Abraham, Isaac, and Jacob" (or Sarah, Rebecca, Rachel, and Leah, in the case of women). A collective Jewish bond is being expressed here: my dead and all Jewish dead, my loved one and the patriarchs and matriarchs of all of us. My dead, I shall recall on the *yahrzeit;* all our dead, we shall all recall at *Yizkor.*

Along with the mention of names, the worshiper promises to give charity in their memory. There is a kind of covenant here: one good deed will lead to another, and when the charitable pledge is fulfilled, God will likewise grant the enhanced repose for the dead. As the text of *Yizkor* put it, "By virtue of this vow to charity, may his [or her] soul be bound up in the bond of life, together with the rest of the righteous who are in the Paradise of Eden." The institution of *Yizkor* provides the living a chance to act as this-worldly agents for their dead, effecting otherworldly improvement. Often, the synagogues within which these *Yizkor* "agreements" are pledged provide a concrete opportunity for giving by accompanying the prayers with formal appeals, during which worshipers are encouraged to make specific promises of donation to a particular charity. In other words, charity will save us all from deathly oblivion.

The vows to offer charity were apparently not part of the original versions of *Yizkor.* While there were customs, some going back to the ninth century or earlier, that associated charity with prayers for the dead, based as we have already seen on the conceptions (drawn from Proverbs 11:4) that the poor are like the dead and therefore "charity saves one from death" and its horrors, *Yizkor* was initially a separate service whose primary goal was remembrance rather than redemption. However, "the combination arose at a later date in consequence of the fact that the commemoration of the year's dead, *with the accompaniment of vows,* happened to coincide, on the Day of Atonement, with the *Yizkor* service proper."[42] To be sure, the connection to charity and the mutual obligation between the living and dead that it seals as part of the memorial occasion serves also to differentiate *Yizkor* from its Christian counterpart. Accordingly, the connection to charity became religiously and culturally essential. Without the giving or the pledge, *Yizkor* remained incomplete.

Yizkor remains among those traditions that even those who hold on to very few Jewish practices tend to maintain. As such, synagogues have built on it, and *Yizkor,* while strictly speaking a prayer that can be recited by the solitary individual in any place, has become the occasion (perhaps, more accurately, the excuse) for many Jews to return to the synagogue and the Jewish community. This power to attract and recall even the most distant individuals to the precincts of Judaism may be explained by the fact that *Yizkor* is located at the conjunction of aroused memories of the beloved dead, the obligations that the living still feel they owe them, the emphasis on community, anxieties about mortality, "the obscure sense of guilt which has been common to man since prehistoric times," and the power of collective attachments.[43] If nothing else, *Yizkor* provides an opportunity for everyone to assuage their feelings of guilt for continuing to live, as well as to express their connection to the dead, the community, and the Jewish people at the same time. The increasingly common practice of including a special *Yizkor* for all victims of the Shoah, along with other Jewish martyrs, has added to this emotional power and transformed the prayer, for some, into an occasion for expressing the desire to demonstrate Jewish solidarity as well as "never to forget," both of which have become important elements of assertive forms of contemporary Jewish identity. Additionally, the almost universal inclusion in today's synagogues of a special *Yizkor* for soldiers who have fallen in the "defense of the State of Israel" attracts Zionists, as well as Israeli expatriates in the Diaspora and many secular patriots in Israel, where the national desire to remember dead soldiers remains powerful. The coincidence of *Yizkor* with the *yahrzeits* of many soldiers who fell in the Yom Kippur war of 1973 has also added to the number or people who come.

Most compelling, however, are the personal attachments between the bereaved and the dead that *Yizkor* recalls. The association and coincidence of this recollection with holidays is also emotionally appropriate, for the Jewish celebration of holidays is closely tied to family gathering. Deaths are always breaches in the family, and those ruptures are always felt most keenly at holiday time. It is, after all, an ancient idea among many peoples that "at seasonal festivals the dead return and rejoin the living."[44] *Yizkor* gives expression to the longing that the living still harbor for sharing relationships and encounters with those who are dead. Moreover, *Yizkor* does all this in public so that the bereaved can witness the fact that they are not alone in the feelings of loss and rupture which they experience at this time. The common custom of all those who do not recite *Yizkor* leaving the sanctuary during its recitation reinforces this sense of a common experience among those who remain inside. They are all part of the congregation of those wounded by death.

Yet there is also something about this experience of recollection that is private. This element is also part of the *Yizkor* service, for although it is done in the synagogue and with the congregation, after the public repetition of the *Yizkor* for the martyrs and soldiers and the *El Moleh Rachamim,* the actual recitation of the *Yizkor* for one's own dead is spoken quietly, each mourner murmuring the prayer and the names of those being recalled in words the speaker alone can hear against the aural backdrop of others' quiet lamentation.

When Passover arrived, barely a month after my father had died, all of us who mourned for him missed him enormously. This holiday of the spring, this celebration of Jewish renewal and time of family gathering, had been inextricably tied to him. So many of the customs we repeated at the Seder—the melodies we sang, the memories we shared—were all associated with him. Although my father had been weakened and muted for the last five years by a series of strokes, he had always somehow marshaled sufficient strength to make it to the Passover Seder. Although he was dead now, we could not forget his presence. Therefore, we left his chair empty and at the head of the table, as if he were still with us; and when we repeated his songs and particular customs, we heard his voice and gave life to his memory. But for all our efforts to bring him somehow to life, we could not get past missing his presence.

The next day in the synagogue, some of that feeling of emptiness continued to hang over me, a cloud of melancholy that just would not lift. Although I tried to call up my father's spirit and make it present within me as I intoned the prayers that we had so often whispered together, sitting side by side, I heard only my own solitary voice. With each rhythmic repetition of my Kaddish, I felt the pounding beat of his loss knocked harder and harder into my consciousness. Not until the last day of the holiday, when the time for *Yizkor* came, did I find help in overcoming this existential loneliness and a way to bring my father close to me in the synagogue. It came with *Yizkor.*

Until that day, I had been one of those innocents in the congregation who, never having been orphaned or immediately bereaved, happily used the occasion of *Yizkor* to make my hasty exit from the congregation, taking the opportunity to chat with others outside or enjoy a breath of air and break from the commonly overlong holiday service. This custom that allowed—indeed encouraged—those exempt from *Yizkor* to remove themselves from the room when it was said was undoubtedly steeped in superstitious fears that the angel of death might pounce upon the unbereaved and decide to join them to the bereaved. For those safely separated from death, the mournful tones and tears of *Yizkor* were to be avoided. While the rabbi habitually tried to assure his congregation that there was no need for those who did not recite *Yizkor* to leave the room during its recitation—in fact, they should stay while we commemorate the dead of the Shoah and those who fell in Israel's wars—his message usually fell on deaf ears, as people often rushed to the doors.

Today, for the first time, I stayed behind as all those I had once joined now departed and left me with the orphaned and the bereaved. Some maintained that new mourners did not have to recite *Yizkor* but could wait until the second of the festivals after the funeral—some even said one waited until the year of mourning was over. They thought that the daily recitation of Kaddish was sufficient and that saying *Yizkor* was piling on too much. But I felt the need to stay, not to deny my loss and not to try to pass myself off as being among those untouched by death. I was right to do so, as I discovered when I recited that first *Yizkor.* As I stood there with others who also had been in the place of sadness I now inhabited, the melancholy miraculously began to lift. For while Kaddish made me remember my bereavement and enhanced my mourning, *Yizkor* allowed me to remember my father, the one I was mourning.

I am not certain now whether it was the company of others who were also recalling their dead, whose murmured list of their dead mingled with my own, or whether it was simply the act of reciting my father's name as part of the prayer that brought him suddenly near. But when I finished, I felt that at last he was close to me in the synagogue. More than that, now that I had found the key to retrieving people from the world of the dead, I began to recite the *Yizkor* for all those others who had died, souls my father had recalled during his own *Yizkor* recitations. These came now at my mention of their names. There were my grandparents, my aunts, uncles—all those in my family who had died. Now I was the one who had to remember them. No longer was I a child who could leave these memories to my parents. The death of my father had propelled me into a new position, and *Yizkor* affirmed it. These dead were now my responsibility; I would recall them and they would be there for me.

In time, as the years wore on, I would be asked to lead the *Yizkor* prayers for the congregation of the bereaved. It always worked its power on me. Yet no recitation ever touched me as powerfully as that first one, when I discovered how *Yizkor* could open the door to a world I never knew existed inside the synagogue.

Now at last I understood why even those who barely ever set foot in the house
of worship found that the time of *Yizkor* beckoned them in ways that could not
be denied.

Yizkor makes clear that as long as the dead are remembered, they are not truly
dead. The one who recites it faithfully for a parent or for a sibling, spouse,
child, other relative, or even a friend offers with that recitation evidence of a
relationship that still lives; death notwithstanding, the past has not been interred with the bones.

In the face of feelings of loneliness, elements of anxiety and guilt, as well as
love and attachment, *Yizkor,* especially but by no means exclusively, among
those who are lax in most or all other Jewish rituals, can be a way to feel better fast. The ancients might have called this appeasing the dead; the moderns
might call it easing anxiety. But there is more to it.

Yizkor is the sanctification of memory in a collective drama. As Theodor
Gaster notes, "*By the very act of remembrance,* oblivion and the limitations of the
present are defied, death is made irrelevant, and a plane is established on which
the dead do indeed meet and mingle with the living. The ceremony is transformed from a memorial of death into an affirmation of life." *Yizkor* makes no
reference to resurrection, "for what needs to be affirmed is not that the dead
will someday arise from their graves but that even now they are indeed alive." [45]
This, as both Maimonides and other Jewish thinkers argued, is what Judaism
truly meant when it referred to *techiyat ha'metim,* the Hebrew expression that
means "the bringing the dead to life." [46] Those who recite *Yizkor* recognize,
at some level of consciousness, that "it is not merely the lack of burial that ren-
ders a spirit unquiet"; instead it is neglect.[47] But while the ancients believed
the neglect disquieted the spirits of the dead, as must by now be clear, the spirits of the living are the ones truly agitated when the dead with whom they have
had an important relationship are neglected by them. *Yizkor* is the chance to
show this is not the case, either for the community or individuals. As such, it
is no less for the living than for the dead. The ancients may have thought and
taught that the recitation of *Yizkor* would make the dead feel better, but in fact
it is the living who emerge from it feeling stronger and at peace.

Final Thoughts

I have no pleasure in the death of him who dies, says the Lord
God; therefore turn, and live.   Ezekiel 18:32

The principle that everything that lives, lives not alone nor for itself is an idea
that the great Jewish sage Hillel framed in his famously Jewish question: "If I
am only for myself, what am I?" [1] In these pages I have tried to make clear that
for Jews in death no less than in life, solitariness is replaced by solidarity. Jewish life *and* death are with people, and hence in the face of death no less than
in life, the answer to Hillel's question is "You are not, cannot be only for yourself." In their traditions and customs, Jews reveal an understanding that for
them death is not and never can be a purely personal matter. It strikes at the
heart of collective existence, for the death of one can portend the death of all,
and the response to death must therefore be both individual and collective.

I have argued as well that a collective response to death is especially important for a people who in their national experience has for most of its existence
lived on the edge of extinction. As a group whose history is punctuated by exile and persecution, whose own demise has been predicted repeatedly, the Jews
have been particularly sensitive to death. For all its vaunted history of survival,
the Jewish people has been subject to attack and exile, persecution and genocide for so long that surviving these onslaughts has become a core element of
its identity. Ample references echo this idea in Jewish tradition, perhaps the
most famous being the line repeated annually at the Passover Seder that "in
each generation, they rise up against us to finish us off." A people so anxious
about its survival has, not surprisingly, created a series of customs and traditions that seek to overcome the returning sting of death. Its customs reflect an
ethos that "behind all the vicissitudes of life we preserve our existence intact." [2]

Indeed, we have seen that many of the customs and practices associated with what happens when a Jew dies emerge in the aftermath of some collective Jewish experience of insecurity when collective life was threatened.[3] As it has in its national life found the imperative to survive to be the best defense against the anxiety of extinction, so in the case of its individual members the Jewish people has created a series of practices and rituals meant to counteract the anxiety of Jewish precariousness, to repair morale, to reestablish order, and to ensure the continuity of life, and collective life in particular.[4]

In spite of the Psalmist's declaration that "man is like a breath; his days are like a passing shadow" (Psalms 144:4), a sentiment repeated in liturgy, especially around the High Holy Days, the Jewish period of reflection and atonement, when death actually arrives, much of what Jews do seeks to counteract that impression, showing that while *a* life may be lost, *all* life is not, and even that particular life whose passing is mourned is not completely over. A Jew has died, but the Jews come together, grieve for the loss, support the bereaved, and remind one another that they and the rest of the Jews have survived. "The snare is broken, and we have escaped." Not alone have we escaped, but with the help of others. Moreover, Jews do not passively endure death and its aftermath but have evolved customs and traditions that imply that they can transcend and dominate both.

Many of the Jewish practices that follow upon death and are discussed in this book aim to make Jews recognize that life is not quite so precarious as even the most sudden and unexpected death may make it seem. As such, they draw a clear distinction between physiological death, which must be swiftly acknowledged and dealt with, and the spiritual as well as social life, which becomes reordered but nevertheless continues. For the one who has died, the body has withered, but the soul has escaped and "is bound up in the eternal bond of life," in the classic expression of the liturgy. For those who are bereaved, the wound may have seemed life-threatening, but they, too, have escaped, sustained by the eternal bond of social life. And as the soul is eternal, so too (and in some ways more importantly) is the collective life of the Jewish people. Death has shocked the system, but in the end it has not won the day. In the Psalmist's words, which Jews have traditionally viewed as providing the purest language of their liturgy and the poetic truth of their existence, "The Lord has chastened me sore, but he has not given me over unto death" (Psalms 118:18). This is the same sentiment expressed in the familiar assertion of the poet John Donne: "Death, be not proud, though some have called thee mighty and dreadful, for thou art not so; for those whom thou think'st thou dost overthrow, die not."[5]

From the moment Jews perceive that, as the prophet Jeremiah put it, "death has come up into our windows, and has entered into our palaces" (9:20), they launch a series of activities and rites that try to take control of what may seem to be beyond human control. In much of this effort, as I have tried to show, they engage in behavior whose end is to triumph over death's invasion and limit the damage it has wrought, to prove to themselves that life has not been vanquished. Death may have momentarily stolen away what is most prized "as doth a tiger a sleeping deer," but life, the Jews try to ensure, swiftly tames that tiger.[6]

The role of community in all this cannot be minimized. Obviously, for the deceased, who cannot care for themselves, the community is irreplaceable. Yet for the bereaved, the living who surround them are no less important. For both the dead and the living, then, the source of all death-defying vitality is Jewish collective life, as expressed and sustained by rite and tradition. Neither can the death-defying vitality be retained for any length of time by the individual alone. Repair must take place in the presence of and always with the help of others.[7] Only thus does the Jew manage to face down mortality and the perception of life's impermanence. Hence, whereas the moment of death and bereavement may come to solitary individuals, what follows when a Jew dies occurs in the company of the living. The result, as we have seen, is a remarkable ascent from the feeling of ultimate solitariness and desolation that death engenders to a transcendent, energized solidarity with the living that is the essence of human existence.

As I have tried as well to show, Jews do not simply want to bury the dead and forget them. The dead are given their due, treated with utmost respect, and eased into an otherworldly order, but much more time and effort is expended in demonstrating that there is a continuing community of the living and the dead. Kaddish, *yahrzeit* commemoration, *Yizkor,* and a variety of other practices extend the ties between the living and those they mourn. Furthermore, in this continuing relationship, the dead are able to exert influence over the religious and social life of the living. In what may be one of the great ironies of life, a Jew's death often brings about in the community of the bereaved a Jewish cultural, social, and religious renaissance and communal integration greater than he or she could ever accomplish in life. Out of the concern with the dead come Jewish assembly, study, prayer, and sometimes even a greater fidelity to Jewish goals. In effect, death, suffering, and their commemoration help define a community of concern among those who share in the distress that death arouses and who commemorate the life that it snuffs out. They are bonded together as none other. On the individual level, even those who normally eschew or ignore religion, ritual, tradition, and Jewish custom often find themselves turning toward Judaism and the Jewish community in the face of death and in the desire to deal with it. In collective life, Jewish behavior is intensified by the encounter with and effort to overcome death.

The continuing community of the living and those who mourn them is, of course, evidence of another basic social fact: Jews do not mourn alone. Even when they seek to withdraw in their grief, the customs and practices of Jewish tradition force them into the company of those who are not mourners. As we have seen, there is no absolute withdrawal or retreat from society. Even the privacy of the home is breached as the group besieges the bereaved and takes over almost every aspect of their existence, nurturing them physically and emotionally back to life. In a sense, what the group does for the mourner is an extension of what it wishes it could do for the one being mourned.

The group does not do this out of purely altruistic motives. At least one aim of these rites and traditions is to keep the web of Jewish community from deteriorating. That is why the capacity to turn back the effects of death cannot be generated by a purely personal effort on the part of the individual, and it is why the community is willing to cooperate. Through these customs and traditions the Jewish community expresses and reinforces the sentiments most essential to the moral and social integration of society. And it does so precisely on the occasion of the most severe emotional strain, a fact that effectively boosts individuals' respect for and attachment to Jewish community life.

Nor, as we have seen, can Jews remain endlessly consumed by their mourning or become eternally dependent upon others to care for them. They must know when to stop. In many ways, the community not only helps them mourn but also is there to help them mark each stage and at last the end of mourning. It is the community that engages in "an immense co-operation, which stretches out not only into space but into time as well."[8] It tells the bereaved when the funeral is over, when to rise from the intensive mourning of shivah, when to put an end to Kaddish, and how to recall the dead at *Yizkor*. In effect, through these practices, Judaism seems to promise that there is a fundamental order of life that even death cannot undo, and those who follow and reflect on its traditions will uncover that order.

The Jewish perspective on death is, however, a parallax view. One attitude, reflecting many of the common perspectives of so-called primitive societies, perceives death as a result of sinister, pernicious, injurious external forces— evil spirits, demons, sorcerers, curses, the angel of death, and the like.[9] It further treats the living as having to placate these forces and explains many of these efforts in mystical terms, almost in the language of sympathetic magic. It is characterized by incantations, prayers, ablutions, ritual garb, and even the eating and drinking of special foods.

The other outlook, more characteristic of the postprimitive world, perceives death simply as the inevitable finale of earthly existence: "For dust thou art and to dust shalt thou return" (Genesis 3 : 19). Yet it treats this as a challenge for the living, who need to be supported and find meaning in the breach that death has engendered in life. It recognizes human needs and weaknesses, the power of human relationship and the need for collective survival. Salvation and transcendence over death are not to be found in a permanent withdrawal from life and society even when grief seems overwhelming. The view is parallactic as well in the sense that it acknowledges death as the annihilation of life yet also asserts it as ultimately ineffectual to that end. The eternality of the soul, the continuity of relationships, and even the preparations for resurrection "in the end of days" all reject the dominion of death.

Jewish custom and tradition disclose that whereas Jews have endeavored no less than others to find answers to the question of death's ultimate meaning or to the more personal one of *why* death has made its particular appointment with them, in practice they are more immediately concerned with answering the question that follows hard upon death: What do we do now? Yet in their answers to this question, they also tell us how, in their view, "final meaning is life-power and power over death," which together with its supporting rituals and traditions "saves man from a surrender to death and destruction" by sustaining the idea that there is some meaning and order to existence.[10] And thus at the end of the long, complex encounter with death, the Jew who has taken all the steps laid out by tradition and custom may emerge neither beaten nor depressed but instead "with confidence and with a feeling of an increased energy."[11]

When Jews accompany a corpse to its burial and repeat the Psalmist's time-honored assertion that, "even though I walk through the valley of the shadow of death, I will fear no evil; for you are with me" (Psalms 23 : 4), it may be God to whom the verse refers as accompanying the dead. But in a parallel social meaning, the verse surely also refers to the community of consolers who accompany the mourners, allay their anxieties, and contribute to the confidence of those who have come face-to-face with death. While one of the most revered odes of Scripture repeats God's promise that "I shall put to death, and I shall bring to life; I have wounded, but I can heal" (Deuteronomy 32 : 39), in practice it is no less the community that ratifies death and restores life, recognizes the wounds of bereavement but also acts to heal them.

Even those individuals who prefer not to be swept up in this flurry of community concern and ritual, who would rather skip the public mourning process and bounce back immediately into their old routines, or who want to

grieve alone find themselves forced, even if they turn only slightly toward Judaic traditions, to participate in this gradual yet inexorable return to life that
the community of the living directs and sustains. For Jews, time alone does not
heal; life with people does.

Now the traditionally faithful, who believe that in their attitudes toward
and behavior following death they are obeying God's wishes, may draw
strength more vigorously from all this ritual activity than those who act out of
other motives. Yet even those whose beliefs in God or the realm of the spiritual are far from robust cannot but experience the sustaining force of the collective experiences that are so inextricably bonded to those Jewish traditions
and customs that take over when a Jew dies. Even those in whom the pulse of
Judaism beats very softly, whose Jewish identity is weak, and whose religious
sensibilities are normally muted often find that when they follow even a few
of the time-honored customs of mourning, the Jew in them echoes and re-
echoes in death's wake until it becomes amplified far beyond what it was at the
outset.

If the triumph over death is so much a part of what happens when Jews die,
what are we to make of the theological occupation with otherworldly punishments that so much of Jewish folk belief asserts as following death? After all,
according to venerable Jewish dogma, the dead for whom no Kaddish is recited and in whose memory the congregation has not been summoned for
prayer remain in torment. Does that not suggest the possibility that, at least for
the dead, death may triumph over life? Yet here, too, I believe, we can discover
in the deep structure of this belief a Jewish triumph over death and an effort
to gain control over what seems beyond control.

To see this, one needs first to recall a common element of Jewish theology
and liturgy that has evolved out of the events and narratives of Jewish history.
In this history, Jewish calamity and collective suffering, as elaborated in Scripture and liturgy, are almost always presented as the effect for which the ultimate cause is Jewish wrongdoing and sin. For this transgressive behavior, God
effects retribution. What is key, however, is that the Jewish people by their
own actions have provoked him. *Mipnay chatoenu galinu me'artzenu* (because of
our transgressions have we been exiled from our homeland) is the oft-repeated
paradigmatic refrain of Jewish prayer. Indeed, true believers may come to
terms even with those misadventures and disasters that seem to defy explanation by "discovering" the sins that brought them about.[12] This Jewish theology of punishment for wrongdoing accomplishes something exquisitely clever.
Whereas those who do not hold fast to such beliefs might be forced to see the
vicissitudes of their national destiny as either the product of forces beyond

their control or the result of a chaotic universe that completely ignores them, those who remain convinced that their own misdeeds or transgressions have caused their misery paradoxically thereby empower themselves. In effect, they affirm that there is order and meaning in the universe, and that if they but mend their ways, learn from their mistakes, or do penance they can ameliorate their situation. Punishment may be the result of their sins, but that also means that repair is in their hands.

Applying this same Jewish attitude to the ultimate calamity of death accomplishes much of the same purpose. The believer who is convinced that death carries with it punishment for the sins of a lifetime must look for a remedy. Those who are about to die may repent. "Repent even on the day before you die," the rabbis teach, "and you may attain full redemption." That is, after all, the point of the *vidui* (confessional) recited in the moments prior to one's death. "Penitence and good deeds," the Mishnah informs us, "are like a shutter and shield against the horror."[13] Charity saves one from death. The possibilities are legion.

Once they have breathed their last, however, it would seem that the dead are by themselves, powerless to effect their own rescue or repair—that is the essence of death: utter and complete powerlessness. The community from which the dead have come, however, is *not* equally powerless. It can and does have remedies, and these call upon the living to act on behalf of their dead. Hence, the living do not simply prepare the bodies of the dead for burial— though they surely must do that. They can also prepare them for resurrection, and they can act continuously to stave off the punishments that come with death. To look upon the dead as being subject to these otherworldly punishments and to assert that the living can reach into the beyond, counteract, and even halt these punishments—via Kaddish, via summoning the congregation to prayers, via Sabbath observances, via memorialization and other acts of Jewish significance—is effectively to empower the living profoundly and concomitantly to enfeeble death.

The belief in the penalties and punishments that follow upon death thus serves not simply to warn the living to live a good life in this world so as to avoid the retribution of the next; nor is it simply to urge upon mankind a life of ongoing penance in preparation for the end (as the rabbis would have us believe).[14] It also serves to set the stage for giving the living a profound and far-reaching power over the helplessness that is death. Death may seem to doom the dead, but fear not, for the living can rescue them from the fires of hell. The dead have "lost the ability to be in contact and to influence what goes on" in this world by themselves, and so the living come to their rescue in this as well by acting on their behalf, by being the contact for the dead in this world and maintaining their influence among the living.[15] That is the deeper meaning of "being a Kaddish." And as we have seen, in the anagrammatic logic of kabbalistic mysticism, those who mourn the impoverished dead can even turn them into the spiritually well-to-do.

Of course, for death to be conquered not only do the living have to provide for the continuing welfare of the dead, but in the calculus of human mutuality—if in fact, as the old saying goes, death does not end a relationship—the dead in turn must be able to act on behalf of the living. Because this exchange goes on between the living and the dead, between the corporeal and the incorporeal, it resonates with the echoes of worship. Now it is not unexpected that we should find ancestor worship, among the earliest and most universal sorts of worship, as a kind of *hypnoia* or underthought of this worship.[16] While perhaps difficult to discern in many of the customs and practices described in these pages, some of those primitive inclinations nevertheless are implicit in the spiritual reciprocity and moral equivalence that Judaism fosters between the dead and the living. When the dead serve as advocates and protectors for those among the living who serve their memory, they become extraordinarily close to being objects of veneration, which is why, as noted earlier, the sages were uncomfortable with Jews making too many visits to the graveyard. Yet, the fact that even today for many mourners bereavement inaugurates their first genuinely religious experience suggests that these inclinations are still resident in human emotions.

Those concerned with the spiritual or psychological may choose to explore the nature of the religious experience that attachments to the dead foster among the living; the social anthropologist necessarily focuses more on its precipitating conditions, as I have tried to do in these pages. We have seen how the propinquity of the dead body can arouse these feelings, how acts like tearing a garment in a display of grief or lighting a candle in memory do so, how the recitation of certain words in the company of others who respond with consolation does it. Yet what all these customs and practices of grief ultimately aim to accomplish is to master the encounter with death that would otherwise leave the living overwhelmed or force them into a kind of emotional death, or, as the Scripture puts it, to "go down alive into Sheol" (Numbers 16:30).

While there are many moments in the course of Jewish bereavement and the events that follow it that one could point to as occasions in which the dead make themselves felt, perhaps none is more striking (and universal) than their capacity to hallow time and place. We have seen how Jewish funerals, mourning periods, *yahrzeit,* and *Yizkor* take on the character of sacred time. As sacred time makes the past present, so these moments make the dead present, in the process creating particular family and community holy days. The parallels with formal Jewish holy days are striking. Both carve out some moment that is consecrated, that is set apart from the normal flow of time. Just as Jews light candles on sacred days, so likewise do they light them to commemorate their personal dead. As festivals return again and again, so, too, the commemorations of the dead. As the festival recalls some primordial event of importance in the life of the group that celebrates and thereby regenerates it, so the commemorations of the dead recall the loss of a life that was special to those who remember and regenerate that relationship. In a sense, commemorations of the dead are paradigms of holy days, no less than ancestor worship is a model for divine worship.

Similarly, although the presence of the dead makes a place ritually impure, it also paradoxically can endow a place with sanctity. This is not surprising, since, for much of the last two thousand years, Jews have "maintained a highly complex and ambivalent attitude toward their traditions of sacred space."[17] Nevertheless, there can be no doubt that even the most mundane and forgettable spot becomes wholly transformed either when death occurs there or when the dead are placed in it. Indeed, the relationship is quite direct: the greater or more recent the presence of death, the more numerous or important the dead, the greater the sanctity (and dangers of ritual impurity) of the place. That is what makes graveyards much more than simply sites of disposed bodies.

While the interpreters of tradition provide a number of explanations for the Jewish custom that requires mourners who at the conclusion of a funeral to remove their shoes in the graveyard as they depart the place of burial, this act also undeniably echoes Jewish behavior on hallowed ground. This is a practice that God taught Moses when he warned him to "take off your shoes from your feet, for the place on which you stand is holy ground" (Exodus 3:5). The burial of one's own dead in a place in effect turns that place into one's family's hallowed ground on which those who mourn must remove their shoes. Likewise, in the shivah house (where mourners also walk without shoes), the room in which the one being mourned died is now considered a place particularly worthy for the prayers. Death numinously transforms these places so that they are no longer profane and are set apart from the rest of the world (either temporarily, as in the case of the shivah room, or permanently, as in the case of the place of burial). These places then serve, as we have seen, as special portals for petitions to heaven, places where the bond connecting mourners, the dead, and God are ritually reenacted and affirmed. To be sure, recognition by the living of the significance of the time and the place is no less essential for the consecration. One person's hallowed time and space may be for another wholly profane. We all have our personal holy places and times.

We have also seen that, when a Jew dies, the survivors are given an opportunity to articulate thoughts that in the quotidian sweep of their mundane existence they rarely try to explore. They reflect on the meaning of life and death. Whether at the funeral or as they try to find or offer consolation, those who confront death are given the opportunity to ponder some of the most essential concerns of human consciousness. For all of its pain, death creates the conditions under which persons are willing to entertain thoughts about mortality, their life plan, their attitude toward resurrection and paradise, and, of course, how they and the dead are linked in the web of human affiliations. In eulogies and in their efforts to mourn, the living find themselves plunged into creative efforts to be metaphorical, poetic, or literary.

This is no small matter. If such introspection, philosophizing, and creativity are in fact among the most human of activities, endeavors by which our species can distinguish itself from all other forms of life, one might suggest that death allows those whom it has brushed past and left alive to experience and express what is so particular about our humanity. This, perhaps, is yet another way in which, still today, those who survive death may understand the truth of that verse repeated at the funeral: "The snare is broken, and we have escaped." We are not dead or deadened; we are human beings, still alive.

In this sense, the aftermath of death is a new life, not just for the dead, as preachers and mystics assert, but also for the living. Even as it seems at first to tear at the fabric of society and life, death enables people who are touched by it to realize how connected they are to life and to others among the living, and how even dying cannot breach the bonds between the living and the dead. It gives them a sense of renewed power and confidence in their humanity. Out of the initial feelings of weakness and loss, anguish and anxiety that seize the newly bereaved, there emerge in the end sentiments of encouragement, growth, comfort, and certainty. Terror gives way to calm, dread to courage, death to life. In life there is death, but in death, as it seems, there is also life. Perhaps that is what the sages had in mind when, in an otherwise cryptic passage, the Talmud quotes them as asking, "What shall man do that he may live?" and then offering the answer: "He should bring himself to death."[18]

One last point. While each individual must work out how to assimilate the lessons of the Jewish encounter with death, the practices discussed in these pages aim to provide a favorable environment for doing so. Nevertheless, there are surely Jews for whom all these rites and customs are ruins of a Judaism they have long since abandoned and to which they refuse to return. In a world where for many religion is no longer a matter of fate but purely one of choice, these Jews reject a prefabricated set of answers and choose to do something else. Additionally, there are those for whom this Jewish way of confronting death cannot work because they find themselves in circumstances that the tradition appears to be unable to accommodate. For example, those who are not Jews but mourn them (or vice versa)—this is increasingly common in interfaith families—may discover that however much they are ready to embrace the traditions I have described and analyzed here, those traditions do not return that embrace.

Then, too, there are those for whom there is no body to dispose of, those whose bodies are missing or destroyed. While many of the rites of mourning and many of the efforts to come to terms with the loss still take place, the unfinished and partial character of what happens following such a death is reflected as well in the way that life and the living respond ever after. A year may not be enough to put such a death to rest, as many survivors of the Shoah demonstrate.

And what of those who want to make use of some, but not all, of what the tradition offers—the most common option of modern religion? Is there room for the eclecticism of contemporary pluralism? What happens to the people who choose cremation for their dead—anathema to Jewish tradition, especially after Auschwitz, but certainly in line with some Eastern religions that more and more Jews have found meaningful—yet who wish to combine this with some of the traditional rituals of Jewish bereavement? Or those who wish to have an open coffin and some sort of embalming, an Irish wake, along with a Jewish funeral and shivah. Can they be accommodated? The present-day world, in which boundaries are easily crossed and cultural traditions combined, where increasingly there is a convergence of many religions upon a vaguely defined consensus on teaching and practice, where the particularist and the universalist meet, where a fundamental break with traditional symbolization is at work, presents the greatest challenge to Jewish traditions and customs whose outlook and purpose may not always fit neatly into such unions. If Jewish survival is an undercurrent of what happens when a Jew dies, those for whom this survival has been replaced by assimilation may not be able to take on much of what I have described here.

In fact, some may argue—not altogether beyond reason—that the picture I have drawn here of what happens when a Jew dies is already yellow with age, disintegrating at the margins. Its value is therefore at best academic and historical. This may be what once happened when a Jew died, but soon it will not be the case. As a sociologist, I am certainly not ready to deny that possibility. Yet as a Jew who has recently been bereaved and for whom this book has been part of the process of reordering my life, I can only say that, for now, there are still some Jews for whom much of what I have described does work in the way I have presented it. Whether that will continue to be the case, or whether what I have presented will more and more become the deviant case, only time will tell.

In their consideration of a variety of biblical chronicles of death, the rabbis of the Talmud come at last to the account that holds a central role in the emergent Jewish tradition: the death of the patriarch Jacob, also known as Israel.[19] In an apparently radical challenge to the biblical narrative that describes Jacob's death, Rabbi Yochanan asserts: "Our father Jacob did not die." The other rabbis are dumfounded by this statement and remind Yochanan that the Genesis story describes the eulogies for Jacob, the preparation of his body for burial, and the large funeral procession from Egypt that returned him to the Cave of Machpelah and the land of his fathers, the land that took his name and the name of his people. And it concludes that Jacob's children and the entire community mourned his passing.

But in one of those typical talmudic arguments that reweaves the tapestry of texts that make up Scripture, Rabbi Yochanan finds his proof in another text, the consoling revelation to the prophet Jeremiah that in a "time of trouble for Jacob, he shall be saved" (Jeremiah 30:10). In that prophecy God continues: "Fear not my servant Jacob, neither be dismayed Israel, for I will save you from afar, and your seed from the land of their captivity" (Jeremiah 46:27). That, says Yochanan, is proof that Jacob did not die. Then he concludes that, as long as Jacob's descendants are saved, Jacob lives. If the Children of Israel live, Israel lives. As long as we are connected to those who have gone before us, we are not dead, not as a people and not as individuals. As long as there are those who recall our lives, we live. This is, of course, the ultimate Jewish concern when death arrives: "The snare is broken, and we have escaped."

Notes

INTRODUCTION

1. On the American denial of death, see Peter L. Berger and Richard Lieban, "Kulturelle Wertstruktur und Bestattungspraktiken in den Vereinigten Staaten," *Kölner Zeitschrift für Soziologie und Sozialpsychologie* 2 (1960).

2. I borrow these words from R. A. Kalish, *Death, Grief and Caring Relationships*, 2nd ed. (Monterey, Calif.: Brooks Cole, 1985), 181.

3. Arnold Toynbee has gone so far as to argue that "death is 'un-American,'" in *Man's Concern with Death* (New York: McGraw-Hill, 1969), 131.

4. Philippe Ariès, *The Hour of Our Death*, trans. H. Weaver (New York: Knopf, 1982), 582.

5. See Geoffrey Gorer, *Death, Grief, and Mourning* (New York: Doubleday, 1965).

6. See the *Random House Webster's Unabridged Dictionary*, 2nd ed. *Cryopreservation* entered our vocabulary in the next decade.

7. See Erik H. Erikson, ed., *The Challenge of Youth* (New York: Anchor, 1965), 49.

8. Laurence Wylie, "Youth in France and the United States," in Erikson, *The Challenge of Youth*, 294. Kaspar Naegele, "Youth and Society: Some Observations," in Erikson, *The Challenge of Youth*, 65.

9. C. G. Jung, "The Soul and Death," in *The Meaning of Death*, ed. H. Feifel (New York: McGraw-Hill, 1959), 10.

10. The phrase is Jung's from "The Soul and Death," 6.

11. Melvin J. Glazer, "The London, Ontario Hevra Kaddisha: A Critical Reflection on the Nature of the Experience to Those Who Perform It" (thesis for the Doctor of Ministry degree, Princeton Theological Seminary, 1995), 61.

12. Howard Congdon, *The Pursuit of Death* (Nashville: Abington, 1977), 180.

236 NOTES TO PAGES 3–12

13. John Donne, "Elegie on Mistris Boulstred," in *John Donne,* ed. John Hayward (London: Penguin 1950), 160.

14. Deborah Lipstadt, "The Lord Was His," in *Jewish Reflections on Death,* ed. Jack Riemer (New York: Schocken, 1974), 48.

15. Lyn Lofland, *The Modern Face of Death* (Beverly Hills, Calif.: Sage, 1978), 35.

16. See Charlotte Aull Davies, *Reflexive Ethnography: A Guide to Researching Selves and Others* (New York: Routledge, 1999); and Jay Ruby, ed., *A Crack in the Mirror: Reflexive Perspectives in Anthropology* (Philadelphia: University of Pennsylvania Press, 1982).

17. James G. Frazer, *The Fear of the Dead in Primitive Religion,* pt. III (London: Ayer, 1933; reprint, 1977), v.

18. Jane Littlewood, "The Denial of Death and Rites of Passage in Contemporary Societies," in *The Sociology of Death,* ed. David Clark (Oxford: Blackwell, 1993), 78.

19. Clifford Geertz, *Islam Observed* (Chicago: University of Chicago Press, 1971), 17.

20. See Paul Rabinow, "Representations Are Social Facts," in *Writing Culture,* ed. James Clifford and George E. Marcus (Berkeley and Los Angeles: University of California Press, 1986).

21. See James Clifford, *The Predicament of Culture* (Cambridge, Mass.: Harvard University Press, 1988), 137.

22. See Henry Abramovitch, "Anthropology of Death," in *International Encyclopedia of Social and Behavioral Sciences* (Oxford: Elsevier, 2001).

23. Geertz, *Islam Observed,* 22.

24. Ibid., 4.

25. Sephardic Jews are those who trace their origins to Jewry of the Iberian Peninsula, a Jewry that spread to North Africa and much of the Middle East. Ashkenazic Jewry has its origins in Europe, beginning in the Germanic lands and radiating outward to most of the rest of Europe, excluding those areas such as Bulgaria, the Netherlands, and of course Spain and Portugal, where Sephardic Jews became dominant.

26. See, for example, Shmuel Shepkaru, "From Death to Afterlife: Martyrdom and Its Recompense," *AJS Review: The Journal of the Association for Jewish Studies* 24 (1999): 1–44, who argues that even the Ashkenazic Jewish notion of martyrdom and subsequent heavenly reward, which emerged around the time of the Crusades, and which the Jews translated into their own idiom of *Qiddush ha Shem* and *olam ha-ba,* may have been absorbed from the ideas of martyrdom and heavenly reward that the Crusaders were also promised. The result, he says, was a conception that was "uniquely Ashkenazic, yet not exclusively Jewish" (43).

27. Geertz, *Islam Observed,* 3.

28. Ibid.

29. Philip Rieff, *Fellow Teachers* (New York: Harper and Row, 1973), 10.

30. Robert Hertz, "A Contribution to the Study of the Collective Representation of Death," in *Death and the Right Hand* (Glencoe, Ill.: Free Press, 1960); and Sigmund Freud, "Thoughts for the Times on War and Death," in *Collected Papers,* vol. 4 (New York: Basic Books, 1959 [1915]), 288–317.

31. Freud, "Thoughts for the Times on War and Death," 304.

32. Ibid., 315.

33. Ibid., 317.

GOSESS AND PETIRA

1. Babylonian Talmud *Succah* 53a.
2. *Sefer Hasidim* § 234. See also Chaim Goldberg, *Mourning in Halachah,* trans. S. Fox-Ashrei (Brooklyn: Mesorah, 1991), 44.
3. Yechiel Tukacinski, *Gesher HaChayim* (Jerusalem, 1947), 2:2,1.
4. For a full text of all the variants of these confessions, see Goldberg, *Mourning in Halachah,* 442–44.
5. *Yoreh De'ah* §338.
6. Tukacinski, *Gesher HaChayim,* 2:2,7.
7. Freud, "Thoughts for the Times on War and Death," 309–10.
8. Ibid., 308.
9. Aaron Berechia, *Ma'avar Yabbok, Siftei Ra'ananot 9* (Mantua 1626). See also Goldberg, *Mourning in Halachah,* 52 n. 70; 88.
10. See H. Abramovitch, "Death," in *Contemporary Jewish Religious Thought,* ed. A. A. Cohen and P. Mendes-Flohr (New York: Scribner's, 1987), 131–35; Ariès, *The Hour of Our Death;* E. Badone, *The Appointed Hour* (Berkeley and Los Angeles: University of California Press, 1989).
11. Ariès, *The Hour of Our Death,* 587.
12. H. Abramovitch, "Good Death and Bad Death: Therapeutic Implications of Cultural Conceptions of Death and Bereavement," in *Traumatic and Non-traumatic Loss and Bereavement,* ed. E. Witztum, R. Malkinson, and S. Rubin (New York: Psychosocial Press, 2000), 260.
13. Indeed, in some Jewish folk belief, Tuesdays are in general propitious days for undertaking anything new.
14. See Shepkaru, "From Death to Afterlife," 22–23; and Babylonian Talmud *Berachot* 61b as well as Jerusalem Talmud *Berachot* 9, 14.
15. On the consequences of the absence of such conditions—when there is no corpse or there are no mourners—see Abramovitch, "Good Death and Bad Death."
16. "It is good to die for our country," as the Zionist hero Josef Trumpeldor is said to have declared as he fell in the famous Battle of Tel Hai.
17. See Genesis 25:8 and Nahmanides on that verse.
18. See Genesis 50:23 and Rashi and Onkelos on that verse.
19. *Avot* 5:21
20. Sigmund Freud, "Mourning and Melancholia," in *Collected Papers,* vol. 4 (New York: Basic Books, 1969 [1917]), 153.
21. Ibid., 154, 155.

ONEN

1. Sherwin Nuland, "Foreword," in *Jewish Insights into Death and Mourning,* ed. J. Riemer (New York: Schocken, 1995), xvi.
2. On "liminality," the state of being betwixt and between, no longer what one once was and not yet what one shall ultimately become, see Arnold van Gennep, *The Rites of Passage,* trans. Monika Vizedom and Gabrielle Caffee (Chicago: University of Chicago Press, 1960). See also Victor Turner, *Dramas, Fields, and Metaphors* (Ithaca, N.Y.: Cornell University Press, 1974).

3. Moshe Zvi Naeh, *Nachamu Ami* (Jerusalem, 1993), 9:2, 20. Chaim Goldberg *P'nai Boruch* (Jerusalem, 1986), 20. The person incarcerated in prison—that is, one who is already "dead to the community"—does not qualify as an *onen*, though he or she will have to observe the other rules of those who mourn. *Yoreh De'ah* 741:4, Naeh, *Nachamu Ami*, 22.

4. See Naeh, *Nachamu Ami*, 20–22, who cites a series of Judeo-legal sources for this.

5. Thus, those whose dead for whatever reasons remained unburied overnight, while technically *onenim* even on the next day, were so only in line with a lesser rabbinic edict (*d'rabanan*) and not according to the strict dictates of God's law (*d'oreita*). See Babylonian Talmud *Zevachim* 99b; Goldberg, *P'nai Boruch*, 19.

6. Freud, "Mourning and Melancholia," 154.

7. *Shulchan Aruch* 61.

8. See A. F. Shand, *The Foundations of Character*, 2nd ed. (London: Macmillan, 1920), chap. 10, who writes: "Sorrow appears to have one principal impulse—the cry for help or assistance" (314–15).

9. Harold Schulweis, "Coronary Connections," in Riemer, *Jewish Reflections on Death*, 29. See also Mark Zborowski and Elizabeth Herzog, *Life Is with People* (New York: Schocken, 1962).

10. There are some secondary consequences of this notification. As Lynn Despelder and A. L. Strickland note, "the process of death notification also helps to set apart the bereaved during the period of mourning." *The Last Dance*, 3rd ed. (Mountain View, Calif.: Mayfield Press, 1992), 201.

TAHARA

1. Robert Hertz, "A Contribution to the Study of the Collective Representation of Death," 29–30.

2. Laurie Zoloth-Dorfman, "Doubled in the Darkest Mirror" (paper presented at the meetings of the American Association of Religion, 1998), 2.

3. Simcha Raphael, "Chaim, Death, Grief, and Renewal: Love across Jewish Barricades," *New Menorah*, autumn 1998, 8.

4. See Henry Abramovitch, "The Jerusalem Funeral as a Microcosm of the 'Mismeeting' between Religious and Secular Israelis," in *Tradition, Innovation, Conflict*, ed. Zvi Sobel and Benjamin Beit-Hallahmi (Albany: State University of New York Press, 1991), ch. 3.

5. Rashi, the great biblical commentator, writes, "The kindness one does for the dead is the truest kindness for there can be no expectation of a requite" (Genesis 47:8).

6. Fees are paid for the materials used, as well as for those who administer the Chevra. Commonly these are funneled through funeral parlors that have arranged with particular Chevras to use their services. In Israel, where the Chevras largely have a monopoly, the fees (often channeled through the national social security) are paid directly to the central administration of the Chevra.

7. Sylvie-Ann Goldberg, *Crossing the Jabbok*, trans. Carol Cosman (Berkeley and Los Angeles: University of California Press, 1996), 100.

8. Ibid., 101.

9. Arnold Toynbee says this in his own way: "A human being has a dignity in virtue of his being human; that his dignity survives his death; and that therefore his dead body must not simply be treated as garbage and be thrown away like the carcase [sic] of a dead non-human creature, or like a human being's worn-out boots or clothes." "Traditional Attitudes towards Death," in Toynbee et al., Man's Concern with Death (New York: McGraw-Hill, 1969), 60.

10. Lawrence Hoffman, The Art of Public Prayer (Washington, D.C.: Pastoral Press, 1988), 107.

11. Emile Durkheim, The Elementary Forms of the Religious Life, trans. J. W. Swain (New York: Free Press, 1965), 14–15.

12. Those suicides who try to dispose of their own remains in their acts of life-taking are nevertheless given some sort of funeral.

13. Hertz, "A Contribution to the Study of the Collective Representation of Death," 70.

14. Ibid., 33.

15. Tashbez 749, cited in Aaron Levine, Sefer Zichron Meir, vol. 1 (Toronto: Zichron Meir Publications, 1985), 283.

16. Ariès, The Hour of Our Death, 153.

17. Thomas Lynch, The Undertaking (New York: Norton, 1997), 156.

18. Ibid., 183.

19. Hertz, "A Contribution to the Study of the Collective Representation of Death," 37.

20. Lynch, The Undertaking, 22.

21. Leon Wieseltier, Kaddish (New York: Knopf, 1998), 152.

22. Hertz, "A Contribution to the Study of the Collective Representation of Death," 33.

23. Ibid.

24. Ariès, The Hour of Our Death, 586.

25. See Mircea Eliade, The Sacred and the Profane, trans. W. R. Trask (New York: Harper and Row, 1959), 196, who sees this in all primitive rites of death.

26. This is why any postmortem "destruction" of the body, including autopsy, is prohibited by Jewish law.

27. While secular undertakers who prepare a body for burial (or viewing) do not share these beliefs, demands for respect to the dead (signs reminding them to show such respect are prominent in many of the back rooms where the bodies are prepared) are undoubtedly attitudinal vestiges that come from the domain of religious belief. As Mircea Eliade once noted, "the majority of the 'irreligious' still behave religiously, even though they are not aware of the fact." See Eliade, The Sacred and the Profane, 204.

28. Goldberg, Crossing the Jabbok, 8. Beliefs in resurrection are by no means unique to Judaism. They likely stem from human beings' perception that they are part of nature, and as nature dies and then regenerates itself, so surely must the dead body. After all, if a tree can lose its leaves in the fall and come back to life in the spring, why not people as well? To be sure, the body of literature that deals with Jewish concerns with the apocalyptic and that includes consideration of paradise and resurrection was composed from about the second century B.C.E. to 150 C.E. by writers who often assumed identities of personages from earlier epochs to lend credibility to their ideas—the faithful would of course argue that these are indeed earlier scriptural sources. In fact, the

origins of Jewish ideas of resurrection are surrounded by mystery. Some, like Maimonides, the medieval Jewish philosopher, argued that belief in resurrection is a basic Jewish principle of faith and anyone who denies it is a heretic who loses his portion in the world to come. Others point to the fact that "personal relationships existed between Jewish and Christian seminarians in the same cities of Syria during the early Christian centuries," when these ideas were being explored, and that accounts for the "parallel visions in the Jewish and Christian apocalyptic" ideas of paradise and resurrection (Frank Manuel and Fritzie Manuel, "History of Paradise," *Daedalus* 101 (winter, 1972): 99–100).

Some scholars argue that the idea of resurrection, not expressly mentioned in Scripture, did not become part of Jewish thinking until the second century B.C.E., introduced through exposure to Zoroastrianism and affirmed by the Pharisees who after the destruction of the Second Temple in 70 C.E. managed to make this a part of orthodox faith. Indeed, according to the Jewish philosopher Philo (20 B.C.E. to 50 C.E.), Jews believed that death would be the end of their existence. (See Shepkaru, "From Death to Afterlife," 8, 11.) Flavius Josephus writes that Jews of his time believed that the "soul perishes with the body" (*Antiquities of the Jews* [New York: Bigelow, Brown and Co., 1923], XVIII, I, 16), although elsewhere he noted that the Pharisees thought all souls survive death (*Ant.* XVIII, I, 3). See also Toynbee et al., *Man's Concern with Death* (New York: McGraw-Hill, 1969), 78; and Ninian Smart, "Death in the Judeo-Christian Tradition," in Toynbee et al, *Man's Concern with Death,* 117. For the most important talmudic discussion of all this, the main source remains Babylonian Talmud *Sanhedrin* 90a–112b.

29. See Babylonian Talmud *Sanhedrin* chapter 11, in which these questions are discussed, including the irreverent one of Cleopatra as to whether the dead will be resurrected naked or clothed.

30. Wieseltier, *Kaddish,* 162.

31. Hertz, "A Contribution to the Study of the Collective Representation of Death," 34. The idea of malignant spirits of course has a psychological element along with its more primitive demonistic one.

32. Raphael, "Chaim, Death, Grief, and Renewal," 7.

33. Goldberg, *Crossing the Jabbok,* 111, citing *Ma'avar Jabbbok Siftei Ra'ananut* 3:9.

34. The reason for washing, although subsequently explained by a variety of textual sources (see later discussion), probably may be ultimately traced to a Mishnah in the Babylonian Talmudic Tractate *Shabbat* (151a), which lists among the requirements for preparing a corpse "anointing and washing (or rinsing)." Offering the reasoning behind this, the Code of Jewish Law sees this as done to remove the filth from the dead so that people will not be revolted when moving them (see *Beer HaGola* on *Yoreh De'ah* 352, 4).

35. See Rookie Billet, "We Will Get Better," in Riemer, *Jewish Insights into Death and Mourning,* 286.

36. Mary Douglas, *Purity and Danger* (New York: Praeger, 1966), 62–63.

37. Aaron ben Moses Berachia, *Ma'aver Yabbok* (Mantua, 1626): "The laws of washing." See also Levine, *Sefer Zichron Meir,* 305.

38. Douglas, *Purity and Danger,* 11.

39. Ibid., 2.

40. Midrash Ecclesiastes 5:16, cited in Levine, *Sefer Zichron Meir,* 283.

41. Levine, *Sefer Zichron Meir,* 283.

42. Mircea Eliade, *Patterns in Comparative Religion* (New York: Sheed and Ward, 1958), 194.

43. Mircea Eliade, *The Sacred and the Profane,* trans. W. R. Trask (New York: Harper and Row, 1959), 78; italics in the original.

44. See also Eliade, *Cosmos and History: The Myth of the Eternal Return,* trans. W. R. Trask (New York: Harper and Row, 1959), 59: "Baptism is equivalent to ritual death . . . followed by new birth."

45. In the Sephardic pronunciation of modern Hebrew this would be *mayt.*

46. Tukacinski, *Gesher HaChayim.*

47. Douglas, *Purity and Danger,* 22.

48. Ibid., 169.

49. Cf. ibid., 177.

50. Ibid., 169.

51. Theodor H. Gaster, *Customs and Folkways of Jewish Life* (New York: William Sloan, 1955), 139-40.

52. Ibid., 140.

53. Raphael, "Chaim, Death, Grief, and Renewal," 7.

54. See Y. Ta-Shma, *Minhag Ashkenaz Ha'Kadmon* (Jerusalem, 1992), 36.

55. See, for example, Shabbetai ben Meir HaCohen, *Responsa Yoreh De'ah,* 250; Rabbenu Asher, *Responsa,* sec.13, no. 10:3; and Levine, *Sefer Zichron Meir,* 291 n. 10, who cites other such sources.

56. Moses Schick, *Bet Lechem Yehuda,* 352:4.

57. William Graham Sumner, *Folkways* (Boston: Ginn and Co., 1906), 105.

58. Babylonian Talmud *Shabbos* 151b.

59. Cf. Gaster, *Customs and Folkways of Jewish Life,* 160-62.

60. Hertz, "A Contribution to the Study of the Collective Representation of Death," 27.

61. To make any collection of water suitable for a *mikveh,* according to Jewish law, the rabbis stipulated that only water that has not already been drawn—not been in a vessel or any other receptacle—may be used. Thus rain or melting snow, for example, often collected through a system of descending, vertical pipes, turns a tank of water into a *mikveh.* After a minimum of approximately 190 gallons of undrawn water are gathered, additional drawn water may be added.

Although the *mikveh* is today used for all sorts of dead, at the outset, according to almost all rabbinic sources, it was reserved only for important or revered individuals. In time, however, others wanted their loved ones to receive no less treatment. Given the time-honored Jewish principle that there should be few, if any, distinctions of social status among the dead, this desire was easily assimilated into custom in traditional Jewish circles and remains part of today's *tahara* in many Chevras, especially in traditionalist Jewish communities. See Levine, *Sefer Zichron Meir,* 308 n. 85.

62. In fact, some of the rabbinic sources that explain the origins of this custom suggest that it was reserved primarily for those who in their lifetimes were scrupulous about immersing themselves in the *mikveh* to purify themselves following a seminal emission, a common "defilement" among men. See Tukacinski, *Gesher Ha-Chayim* 100, 5.

63. See Kenneth Burke, *A Grammar of Motives* (Berkeley: University of California Press, 1969), 35, who discusses what he calls "the paradox of purity," which is in a sense the paradox of the absolute. There can be no absolute purity of the dead.

64. Goldberg, *Crossing the Jabbok,* 114.

65. For the many Jewish sources for this, see Levine, *Sefer Zichron Meir,* 323 n. 45.

66. Rabbi David Ibn Zimra (RADBAZ) on Maimonides *Hilchot Avelut* 1:1. See also Jerusalem Talmud *Ketubot* 1:1.

67. Jews are not unique in eschewing knots in the garments of the dead. Gaster, *Customs and Folkways of Jewish Life,* 166, cites a parallel practice among German folkways.

68. The meaning of this name is a matter of some dispute. Some have argued that its root is the same as the Hebrew word for breasts (*Shaddaim*), and thus carries the allusion to the life nourishment that comes from them. Some argue that the term *El Shaddai,* used often in Genesis, refers to the God of the hills (shaped like breasts) that were the sources of life for a people whose livelihood came from those hills. See Menashe Harel, *This Is Jerusalem* (Los Angeles: Ridgefield, 1981), 20–27.

69. Eliade, *Cosmos and History,* 90.

70. Ibid., 92.

71. *Sefer Hasidim* 231.

72. See also Job 34:15.

73. The expression comes from the Elder Pliny HN, ii, 145. *Ma'avar Yabbok* (*Siftei Zedek* 34).

74. Berachia, *Ma'aver Yabbok,* n. 16. See also Levine, *Sefer Zichron Meir,* 324 n. 50.

75. See the "Shach," Shabbetai ben Meir HaCohen, *Responsa Darchei Chesed* 362:101. Cf. Levine, *Sefer Zichron Meir,* 324 n. 47.

76. Abraham Heschel, "Death as Homecoming," in *Jewish Reflections on Death,* ed. Jack Riemer (New York: Schocken, 1974), 70.

77. Midrash Genesis Rabbah 19:8. To be sure, for generations Jews were buried in caves, their bones later gathered up and placed in stone ossuaries. Moreover, as already noted, in Israel people were buried in their shrouds and without coffins for the most part (the exceptions being those whose bodies had been mutilated and soldiers—whose bodies *might* be mutilated). Hence, it is probably correct to assume that the custom of burial in wood caskets came into fashion via some sort of local cultural customs—either to be in line with general practice or to distinguish Jews from others—and then a prooftext was found to support this custom.

78. Berachia, cited in Leon Wieseltier, *Kaddish* (New York: Knopf, 1998), 317.

79. Levine, *Sefer Zichron Meir,* 411 n. 56c, cites a variety of sources for this.

80. Cf. Ecclesiastes Rabbah 5:14, which suggests that when a child is born it clenches its hands as if to say, "The world is mine," but when one dies, his hands are open as if to say, "I take nothing from this world."

81. Babylonian Talmud *Moed Katan* 27a–b.

LEVEIYA

1. Bronislaw Malinowski, *Magic, Science and Religion* (New York: Anchor, 1954), 29.

2. Toynbee et al., *Man's Concern with Death,* 271.

3. Babylonian Talmud *Moed Katan* 25b.

4. Robert Fulton, ed., *Death and Identity* (New York: Wiley, 1965), 342.

5. Hertz, "A Contribution to the Study of the Collective Representation of Death," 77.

6. Ibid., 78.

7. That there is a common impulse to follow a beloved who has died is amply illustrated in the literature on bereavement. See Howard Becker, "The Sorrow of Bereavement," in *Death: Interpretations,* ed. Hendrik M. Ruitenbeek (New York: Dell, 1969), 195–216, esp. 204.

8. *Beraitha* to *Peah* 1:1.

9. *Shulchan Aruch* 361:1. See also *Beraitha Ketubot* 17a.

10. Lynch, *The Undertaking,* 117.

11. Goldberg, *Crossing the Jabbok,* 134.

12. Arnold Van Gennep, *The Rites of Passage,* 147. See also Jane Littlewood, "The Denial of Death and Rites of Passage in Contemporary Societies," in *The Sociology of Death,* ed. David Clark (Oxford: Blackwell, 1993), 75.

13. Malinowski, *Magic, Science and Religion,* 48.

14. Cf. Victor Turner, *Dramas, Fields and Metaphors: Symbolic Action in Human Society* (Ithaca, N.Y.: Cornell University Press, 1967), 450.

15. Richard Huntington and Peter Metcalf, *Celebrations of Death* (Cambridge: Cambridge University Press, 1979), 39.

16. See Robert Lifton, *The Broken Connection* (New York: Simon and Schuster, 1979), 6.

17. Durkheim, *Elementary Forms of the Religious Life,* 401.

18. Raymond Firth, *Elements of Social Organization* (London: Henry E. Walter Ltd, 1951), 64. See also David G. Mandelbaum, "Social Uses of Funeral Rites," in *The Meaning of Death,* ed. Herman Feifel (New York: McGraw-Hill, 1959), 189.

19. Malinowski, *Magic, Science, and Religion,* 50.

20. Mandelbaum, "Social Uses of Funeral Rites," 209.

21. Where burial is at a particularly distant location—abroad, for example—or where the body is disposed of by cremation, this may still be considered part of the funeral's aftermath, although with important distinctions (to be discussed later) from those cases where burial is nearby and immediate. Likewise, sometimes a memorial service is held after the body has been disposed of in one way or another.

22. Hertz, "A Contribution to the Study of the Collective Representation of Death," 46.

23. Clifford Geertz, *The Interpretation of Cultures* (New York: Basic Books, 1973), 162.

24. Among other groups, the consolers will actually be invited not just to view the corpse but also to say something or otherwise communicate their feelings to it.

25. Levine, *Sefer Zichron Meir,* vol. 1, 396 n. 29b.

26. Georg Simmel, *The Sociology of Georg Simmel,* ed. and trans. Kurt H. Wolff (New York: Free Press, 1950), 52, 53.

27. Maurice Lamm, *The Jewish Way in Death and Mourning* (New York: Jonathan David, 1969), 28.

28. Ibid., 38; Gaster, *Customs and Folkways of Jewish Life,* 162.

29. Gaster, *Customs and Folkways of Jewish Life,* 162 n. 36.

30. Wieseltier, *Kaddish,* 65.

31. I owe this insight to Henry Abramovitch.

32. See Wieseltier, *Kaddish,* 65. See also Chaim Binyamin Goldberg, *Mourning in Halachah* (New York: Mesorah, 1991), 116, who notes the many prohibitions in this regard.

33. The practice common among Hasidim of marking the death of their rebbe or grand rabbi by doing a *keriah* is a means of demonstrating a relationship to him that is akin to a bond of family.

34. Erving Goffman, *Strategic Interaction* (Philadelphia: University of Pennsylvania Press, 1969), 31.

35. The desire of the Jews to distinguish themselves by referencing *keriah* to Jewish sources rather than to ancient pagan or Roman ones is, of course, in keeping with all Jewish religiously based explanations. Beyond these references, there is also, as we shall see, a series of ritual associations that link the tearing with several particularly Jewish expressions.

36. Yaakov Moshe Hillel, *Yismach Moshe,* 2d ed. (Jerusalem: Ahavat Shalom, 1997), 47 ("Should We Sephardim in Mourning Tear Our Outer Coats?"). See also Babylonian Talmud *Moed Katan.*

37. Aharon Shimon, *Nahar Mizrayim* (1868: Ne Amon), 137. See also Levine, *Seder Zichron Meir,* 187 n. 40; Gaster, *Customs and Folkways of Jewish Life,* 162.

38. Mark Zborowski, "Cultural Components in Responses to Pain," *Journal of Social Issues* 8 (1951): 16–30.

39. Levine, *Sefer Zichron Meir,* 343, cites the *Kol Bo* on mourning, p. 98, section 5.

40. Hertz, "A Contribution to the Study of the Collective Representation of Death," 125 n. 95.

41. The suggestion has been made that in the verse in Psalm 23 the words "thy rod and thy staff they comfort me," followed by the words, "thou preparest a table before me" are freighted with the barely hidden symbolism of life: phallic potency and plentiful food. These are meant as subliminal antidotes to the brush with death. See Philip E. Slater, *Microcosm* (New York: Wiley, 1966), 105.

42. Abraham Levinsohn, *Mekorei Minhagim* (Berlin: 1847); see also Levine, *Sefer Zichron Meir,* 397 n. 25c.

43. Sometimes this is called an "ethical will."

44. Y. L. Peretz, "Four Generations—Four Wills," in *Stories from Peretz,* ed. and trans. Sol Liptzin (New York: Hebrew Publishing Company, 1947), 177–82.

45. In a classic Jewish joke that plays to this situation, a particularly unsavory character was about to be buried, and no one could be found to offer a eulogy. At last, one old man from the very few who had assembled for this funeral walked slowly to the podium and, after a long pause announced, "Well, his brother was a bigger bastard."

46. Jean-Paul Sartre, *The Emotions: Outline of a Theory,* trans. B. Frechtman (New York: Wisdom/Philosophical Library, 1948), 49.

47. Ibid., 67. On "flooding out," or losing self-control, see also Erving Goffman, *Encounters* (New York: Bobbs-Merrill, 1961), 55.

48. The choice of women for this came from the common cultural assumption in traditional societies that they were far more emotional.

49. Babylonian Talmud *Moed Katan* 27b.

50. See Samuel R. Lehrman, "Reactions to Untimely Death," in Ruitenbeek, *Death,* 222–24.

51. Slater, *Microcosm,* 16.

52. In keeping with this theme, Jews often dedicate particular sacred volumes— Bibles, prayer books, and the like—to the memory of someone.

53. Lamm, *The Jewish Way in Death and Mourning,* 51.

54. Levine, *Sefer Zichron Meir,* 338 n.

55. *Kol Bo* on mourning, Levine, *Sefer Zichron Meir,* 339 n. 68.

56. Babylonian Talmud *Shabbat* 105b.

57. This, of course, is not unique to Jews. Catherine Berndt, for example, reports that in New Guinea some tribes believe that "the spirit is most actively interested in the living immediately after death, becoming less so as time goes by. During this early period the people with whom it has had the strongest ties of affection or antagonism must be on their guard." "The Ghost-Husband: Society and the Individual in New Guinea Myth," *Journal of American Folklore* 79, no. 311 (1966): 348.

58. Hertz, "A Contribution to the Study of the Collective Representation of Death," 37.

59. The reasons for this custom are steeped in Kabbalah and involve protecting a father's offspring from the demonic jealousies of his unborn children, the products of his seminal emissions. These demon counterparts seek to abduct, curse, or otherwise harm those who found life—and they would find no better place to accomplish their nefarious aims than at the open grave of the one from whose loins they sprung.

60. According to Jewish law, those who, seeing a dead person taken for burial, do not join the procession have violated the prohibition of "ridiculing the helpless" (*lo'eg la'rash*). See Goldberg, *Mourning in Halachah,* 127.

61. Eliade, *The Sacred and the Profane,* 10.

62. See Levine, *Sefer Zichron Meir,* 416 n. 65. If a great religious figure is the one borne, the body is not placed on the shoulders and instead is carried with hands lowered as if to show that the pallbearers are not certain that they are worthy. See Joseph Caro, *Kesef Mishna Hilchot Evel,* 4:2.

63. See Numbers 7:9.

64. Gaster, *Customs and Folkways of Jewish Life,* 143.

65. According to Eduardo Mayone Dias (Department of Spanish and Portuguese, UCLA), the "secret Jews of Portugal" (crypto-Jews) have a similar custom in which they recite the following: "May God save you now that you passed away. You were alive as we were. We will be like you. To heaven where you now are, pray to the Lord for us. In this valley of tears, we will pray to the Lord for you."

66. This custom (particularly popular in Jerusalem) is parallel to the tolling of bells in some Christian funerals: "Ask not for whom the bell tolls, it tolls for thee."

67. Erik Erikson, *Young Man Luther* (New York: Norton, 1958), 111. See also Freud, "Mourning and Melancholia," 154–55.

68. Ariès, *The Hour of Our Death,* 138–39.

69. Malinowski, *Magic, Science and Religion,* 87.

70. The fact that in many places this custom has fallen into disuse, or that the line is spoken without the breaking of the pottery, reveals how muted these feelings have become in the contemporary age that seeks to avoid dwelling on matters of death.

71. Marian Henriquez Neudel, "Saying Kaddish: The Making of a 'Regular,'" in *Jewish Insights on Death and Mourning*, ed. Jack Riemer (New York: Schocken, 1995), 181.

72. There is a similar practice of having the poor collect alms among the guests at wedding feasts. Here, too, the tendency to "forget" the collective at a "personal" occasion is reversed by the beggars. As Emanuel Feldman ("Reconciling Opposites: Uncommon Connections in the Halakha of Mourning," *Tradition* 27, no. 3 [1993]) notes: "Feasting and lamenting, *hag* [celebration] and *evel* [mourning] share much" (14). See also *Amos* 8 : 10 and Jerusalem Talmud *Ketubot* 1 : 1.

73. To begin with, in its stopping and starting, this procession is not unique to Jews. In Germany and Portugal, for example, the practice of making regular stops on the funeral route, ostensibly to "shake off evil spirits that might still be hovering about the deceased," was not uncommon, while among the Tigré of Ethiopia the death march is made in seven short stages. See Gaster, *Customs and Folkways of Jewish Life*, 172.

74. Eliade, *The Sacred and the Profane*, 211.

75. Gaster, *Customs and Folkways of Jewish Life*, 144. See also Isaac Lofretz, *Sefer Matamim* (Warsaw, 1889).

76. I owe this information to Steven Siporin, who cites the source in his "Continuity and Innovation in the Jewish Festivals in Venice, Italy" (Ph.D. diss., Indiana University, 1982), 143–48, as well as to a communication from Dario Calimani, who notes as well that this procession sometimes served as a kind of dramatized obituary notice.

77. See, for example, Samuel Heilman, *Defenders of the Faith* (Berkeley and Los Angeles: University of California Press, 1999), 291–99. See also Gaster, *Customs and Folkways of Jewish Life*, 144.

78. Goldberg, *Mourning in Halachah*, 129, citing the *Ma'avar Jabbok Siftei Rannanot* 21.

79. See Levine, *Sefer Zichron Meir*, 416 n. 66. There were even those who urged, when bodies were carried on animal-drawn carts, that the animals doing the pulling be only those considered "kosher" (i.e., pure) by Jewish law.

80. Isaac Oshpal, *Darchei Chesed* (New York, 1975), 59. See also Levine, *Sefer Zichron Meir*, 416 n. 66.

81. On many occasions this prayer is skipped—the eve of the Sabbath or holy days, the first day of the Jewish month, and a host of other "special" days—when such words of supplication are seen as unnecessarily time-consuming or too demanding, drawing attention away from occasions when life is ascendant. In other words, it is omitted on days when life makes its demands for time and when enhanced Jewish activity should not be diminished by the *Tzidduk HaDin.*

82. While belief in demons may seem to come from other times and places, George Frazer argues that the belief in the existence of ghosts is one manifestation of humans' belief in the immortality of the human soul, which has led "race after race, generation after generation, to sacrifice the real wants of the living to the imaginary wants of the dead." Frazer, *Man, God, and Immortality: Thoughts on Human Progress* (Cambridge: Trinity College Press, 1968), 320.

83. See "angel and demon," *Encyclopædia Britannica Online.* <http://www.eb .com:180/bol/topic?eu = 117210&sctn = 12> [accessed December 7 1999].

84. John Donne, "Elegie on Mistris Boulstred," in *John Donne*, ed. John Hayward (London: Penguin, 1950), 161.

85. These "demons," which primitives saw as inhabiting the spiritual world, moderns see as inhabiting the world of the human spirit.

86. Sigmund Freud, *Civilization and Its Discontents* (New York: Norton, 1961). Linwood Fredericksen argues that, "by viewing angels and demons functionally, rather than in terms of their natures, modern man may discover that he has a greater kinship than he has generally realized with men of previous or different cultures in his attempt to gain an advantageous rapport with the transcendent, social, and psychological realms that he faces in everyday life." (see "angel and demon," *Encyclopædia Britannica Online*).

87. Mircea Eliade, *Cosmos and History: The Myth of the Eternal Return*, trans. W. R. Trask (New York: Harper and Row, 1959), 44.

88. This is the custom described more or less by Tukacinski, *Gesher HaChayim,* the standard contemporary manual of traditional customs. Other variations on this custom add statements about how each piece of silver or coin will be donated to charity on behalf of the dead man, the merit of which will protect his soul. Still others recite paeans and petitions to God to protect the soul, always ending with the words "And may his soul rest in eternal life." See Levine, *Zefer Zichron Meir,* 421–27.

89. Hertz, A Contribution to the Study of the Collective Representation of Death, 33–34. See also Gaster, Customs and Folkways of Jewish Life, 168–69.

90. To those who see this transparent ritual as psychologically primitive, one might say that the extravagant expenditure that some mourners make for a luxurious casket or an elaborate funeral may be driven by some of the same basic motives.

91. See Freud, "Mourning and Melancholia," 161.

92. See Paul Radin, *The Trickster* (New York: Schocken, 1971), xxiii.

93. Numerous rabbinic sources stress the importance of this. See Levine, *Sefer Zichron Meir,* 290 n. 7.

94. Traditionally this, too, should be done by members of the community. In some jurisdictions, local state laws and gravedigger union agreements require professionals to do the actual lowering, which increasingly is accomplished by an automated system of pulleys and belts.

95. This belief is, of course, held by many peoples, including those we have sometimes called "primitive." Thus, for example, the Papuans "believe that the spirits of the dead not only exist but possess superhuman powers and exercise great influence over the affairs of life on earth." Frazer, *The Fear of the Dead in Primitive Religion*, pt. I (London, 1936), 5.

96. To be sure, those who believe that cremation has its place might offer the reference by Abraham, who refers to himself as "I who am but dust and ashes" (Genesis 18:27).

97. John Hinton, *Dying* (Baltimore: Penguin, 1967), 24.

98. I thank Martin Jaffee for pointing out this custom and Reuven Fink for helping me to make sense of it.

99. This extended Kaddish is also recited at a *siyum,* the celebration of completion, when Jews mark their having reviewed a tractate of Talmud or some other major section of sacred Jewish texts. This, no less than the completion of a life, is seen as a time for affirming God's majesty.

100. The idea that burial could be a prelude to resurrection is, of course, an ancient one. For example, the fact that in Paleolithic burials the skeleton has often been found lying on its side in a crouched position has been interpreted by some prehistorians as

evidence of belief in rebirth because the posture of the corpse imitated the position of the child in the womb (see "Death rite," *Encyclopedia Britannica*). For some of the basic talmudic discussions of this see, Babylonian Talmud *Sanhedrin* 90a–112b.

101. Joseph Dov Soloveitchik, "The Halakhah of the First Day," in Riemer, *Jewish Insights into Death and Mourning*, 79.

102. Babylonian Talmud *Sanhedrin* 19a.

103. Gaster, *Customs and Folkways of Jewish Life*, 175.

104. Berechia, *Siftai Renanot*, 20; Psalms 72:16.

105. Abner Weiss, *Death and Bereavement: A Halakhic Guide* (New York: KTAV, 1991), 88.

106. Babylonian Talmud *Eruvin* 54a.

107. I thank Rabbi Moshe Miller for this reference.

108. I owe these explanations to Nathan Katz, professor and chair, Department of Religious Studies, Florida International University. See also Wieseltier, *Kaddish*, 560.

109. Even among those who embrace tradition, this custom is not always practiced, for there are those who argue that there can be no consolation at the cemetery or even in the first, and most difficult, three days of mourning.

110. Malinowski, *Magic, Science and Religion*, 52.

SHIVAH

1. Van Gennep, *The Rites of Passage*, 147.

2. Sigmund Freud, *The Problem of Anxiety*, trans. Henry A. Bunker (New York: Norton, 1936), 157–58.

3. Susan Sered, *Priestess, Mother, Sacred Sister* (New York: Oxford University Press, 1994), 130.

4. Freud, "Mourning and Melancholia," in *Collected Papers*, vol. 4, trans. J. Strachey (New York: Norton, 1959), 154.

5. Ibid., 155.

6. Aaron ben Jacob HaCohen in the fourteenth century; see Wieseltier, *Kaddish*, 486.

7. Bradley Shavit Artson, "The Shivah Minyan," in Riemer, *Jewish Insights into Death and Mourning*, 160.

8. The last term is one given by Ashkenazic Jewry; Sephardim and Israelis often refer to it as "*Yom Hashanah*," the day of the year (although in a popular contemporary Sephardic booklet containing special prayers for this observance—published by Saleh Mansour in Jerusalem—the occasion is also called *yahrzeit*).

9. See Robert Lifton, *The Broken Connection* (New York: Simon and Schuster, 1979), 17.

10. Where the dead are not buried but are disposed of in other ways, the onset of mourning commonly comes upon return from the ceremony of disposal or when the bereaved learn of their loss (at least within a year of it).

11. Midrash Rabbah Vayikra.

12. See Babylonian Talmud *Moed Katan* 21a—25b.

13. Joyce Slochower, "The Therapeutic Function of Shiva," in Riemer, *Jewish Insights into Death and Mourning*, 146.

14. Eviatar Zerubavel, *The Seven Day Circle* (Chicago: University of Chicago Press, 1989), 7.

15. Berachia, *Sfat Emet*, ch. 19. To be sure, Joseph's seven days of mourning came *before* his father died; this, however, was enough to hint at what his descendants should do afterward. Cf. *Amos* 8:10 and Babylonian Talmud *Moed Katan* 20A.

16. J. Riemer, Introduction, in Riemer, *Jewish Insights into Death and Mourning*, 14.

17. Feldman, "Reconciling Opposites," 14.

18. Malinowski, *Magic, Science and Religion*, 53.

19. Ibid.

20. Ibid., 51.

21. Wieseltier, *Kaddish*, 210, citing *Sefer HaRokeach;* and Levine, *Sefer Zichron Meir,* 449 n. 139, who quotes a variety of rabbinic responsa. It is well known, moreover, that in Jewish tradition the laving of the hands is a substitute for and symbolic echo of complete ritual immersion and purification in a *mikveh,* particularly where such immersion is not practicable.

22. Gaster, *Customs and Folkways of Jewish Life*, 175.

23. Levine, *Sefer Zichron Meir*, 450 n. 145; *Ma'avar Jabbok* 43:9.

24. *Yoreh De'ah*, sect. 393.

25. The mourners' not attending to their personal appearance is, of course, not unique to Jews. See, for example, T. O. Beidelman, "Utani: Some Kaguru Notions of Death, Sexuality, and Affinity," *Southwestern Journal of Anthropology* 22 (1966): 354–80, esp. 363. The prohibition is actually on leather shoes; thus some mourners who do not want to go around in their socks may wear slippers or shoes made from materials other than leather. But all these foot coverings are viewed as signs of spiritual sequestration.

26. Geoffrey Gorer, *Death, Grief, and Mourning* (New York: Doubleday, 1965), xxxiii. This is, of course, a variation on Arnold van Gennep's tripartite rites of passage: separation, transition, and incorporation. See *The Rites of Passage*.

27. Some have argued that because contemporary society has been successful in treating disease and putting off the scourge of premature expiration, death has increasingly become associated with old age and is less something that the young experience. See, for example, Robert Blauner, "Death and Social Structure," *Psychology* 29 (1966): 278–94.

28. I owe this recollection to Irene Riegner.

29. See Hillel, *Yismach Moshe*, "Is It Permissible for the Mourner during Shivah to Stand at the Pulpit as Prayer Leader?" who writes: "for the mourner in *shivah* does not have his wits about him, and he is most troubled by the thoughts of his mourning, and he cannot orient his thoughts well enough to lead others in their obligations [to pray]" (80). Then, of course, as well, there is the expectation that at least at the outset of *shivah* the mourner will largely remain silent—and how can the silent, any more than the dead, praise God? (92).

30. Isserles 384:3; Tukacinski, *Gesher HaChayim*, 20:3,3.

31. I thank Henry Abramovitch for this point. See also C. M. Parkes and R. S. Weiss, *Recovery from Bereavement* (New York: Basic Books, 1983).

32. Jerusalem Talmud *Moed Katan* 3:5. See also Goldberg, *Mourning in Halakah*, 179 n. 8.

33. Babylonian Talmud *Moed Katan* 27b.

34. Gaster (*Customs and Folkways of Jewish Life,* 176) traces these to customs of the ancient Greeks and Romans whose impact on ancient Jewry is well established. Both of these peoples saw the egg as a symbol of eternal life.

35. *Kad Ha'Kemach;* see also Wieseltier, *Kaddish,* 314.

36. Freud, "Thoughts for the Times on War and Death," 306.

37. Ibid., 307.

38. Indeed, at least one rabbinic source allows those who freshly mourn to fast, although few others can be found to support this custom. Cf. Shlomo ben Virga Ha-Ropheh, *Sheveit Yehuda,* ch. 378.

39. *Shulchan Aruch Orach Chaim* 167:18.

40. Gaster, *Customs and Folkways of Jewish Life,* 177.

41. Not only do visitors *bring* nourishment to the mourners, but according to some interpreters of tradition, no visitor may *take* anything away from the house in which shivah is being observed. See Hillel, *Yismach Moshe,* 31, who cites Rabbi Akiva Eger as a source.

42. Thanks to Henry Abramovitch for this idea.

43. See also Berechia, *Ma'avor Ya'abok* Sefat Emet 15. The Talmud also suggests that the Hebrew word *ner* means both "candle" and "soul" (Babylonian Talmud *Shabbat* 30 a,b).

44. *Zohar Balak.* Similarly, the *Zohar* commenting on *Vayechi* describes the connection between the lit candle and paradise. Jewish mystical literature is replete with references to candles placed in the caves where such figures as Moses and Aaron, as well as the forefathers Abraham, Isaac, and Jacob, went to their final rest and to how these lights served as the conduits to the heavenly Garden of Eden. See Naeh, *Nachamu Ami,* 51 n. 1. See also Steven Oppenheimer, "The Yahrzeit Light," *Journal of Halacha and Contemporary Society,* no. 37 (1999): 101–16.

45. Lamm, *The Jewish Way in Death and Mourning,* 102; Berechia, *Sefat Emet,* 15.

46. *Yoreh De'ah* 376:1.

47. Babylonian Talmud *Berachot.* This is also found to be true in Scripture. See Ezekiel 24:17, Job 2:1, and Psalms 115:17.

48. Racine, *Andromède* III, 3.

49. Slochower, "The Therapeutic Function of Shiva," 147.

50. Sigmund Freud, "The Theme of the Three Caskets," in *Collected Papers,* vol. 4 (New York: Basic Books, 1959), 253.

51. See Bernard Lipnick, "Who's the Host? Who's the Guest?" in Riemer, *Jewish Insights into Death and Mourning,* 151–52.

52. In fact, for Jewish mourners who find themselves distant from the tradition, the imperative to act according to the norms of contemporary culture and its demands of sociability may be so great that they cannot take advantage of the license to break the common rules of social interaction that shivah allows.

53. I thank Henry Abramovitch for this insight.

54. Babylonian Talmud *Shabbat* 66b.

55. Hananel ben Hushi'el (d. 1055), a North African scholar and commentator who wrote a commentary to the Talmud, which served as bridge between Babylonian/North African scholars and traditions and those of Europe and Palestine.

56. Wieseltier, *Kaddish,* 29.

57. Babylonian Talmud *Shabbat* 127a.

58. Babylonian Talmud *Kiddushin* 30b; Babylonian Talmud *Ketubot* 111b; Babylonian Talmud *Sanhedrin* 89a.

59. See, for example, a reference to Rabbi Sheshet, who referred to Torah study as "my soul's joy" (Babylonian Talmud *Pesachim* 68b).

60. Babylonian Talmud *Ta'anit* 7a.

61. Babylonian Talmud *Moed Katan* 15a. The reference to Ezekiel (24:17) concerns God's command to the prophet when his wife had died.

62. The fact that some commentators suggested that Job was not a Jew did not appear to trouble those who used this verse as support for a Jewish prohibition on Torah study.

63. The Code of Jewish Law, *Yoreh De'ah* 384:4.

64. The reasons for this practice are steeped in mysticism and numerology. There are seventeen Mishnahs in this chapter. Seventeen is the same as the numerical value for the Hebrew word טוב (*tov*, good). Moreover, not only does every Mishnah end with the phrase "purest of all," but the last one in the chapter ends with "pure, both inside and outside," a reference, according to some, to the body and soul of the deceased.

65. Wieseltier, *Kaddish*, 43, 116, quoting talmudic and liturgical sources.

66. *Shulchan Aruch* 393:3; this custom is also supported by Rabbi Moses Isserles, meaning that both Sephardic and Ashkenazic traditions endorse the practice.

67. The so-called private practices, including the ban on sexual relations, bathing, and Torah study, are, however, to be maintained.

68. Naeh, *Nachamu Ami,* 17:7, p. 45.

69. Babylonian Talmud *Sanhedrin* 19a.

70. Gaster, *Customs and Folkways of Jewish Life,* 174.

71. Becker, "The Sorrow of Bereavement," 206.

72. I am indebted to Professor Zev Goldberg for this reference.

73. Defining an "ex-Jew" as, among other things, "a rootless cosmopolitan," Philip Rieff explains that "an ex-Jew is someone who, having stopped going to synagogue, declines to go to church." This is the Jew of secularized civil society. See Rieff, *Fellow Teachers* (New York: Harper and Row, 1973), 77–78 n. 46.

74. Melanie Klein, "Mourning and Its Relation to Manic-Depressive States," in *Contributions to Psycho-Analysis, 1921–1945* (New York: Hillary, 1940), 61. See also Abramovitch, "The Jerusalem Funeral," for a discussion of where this does not always work.

75. Gorer, *Death, Grief, and Mourning,* 62. Gorer argues that such working-through "dissipates this anger in a symbolic and, to a great extent, unconscious fashion," so that it does not "turn in on itself and result in the self-reproach and self-punishment which are the most marked symptoms of melancholia" (133).

76. *Shulchan Aruch* 395:1.

77. Those who do not pray in the shivah house but do so in the synagogue wait until all the worshipers have left the sanctuary. See Naeh, *Nachamu Ami,* 24:1, p. 76.

78. Naeh, *Nachamu Ami,* 21:14, 71. Actually, in Hebrew these words much more closely parallel the consolation greeting that until then has been used to address mourners.

79. Judah Hasid, *Book of Glory,* quoted in Rabbi Elazar Rokeach (1160–1238) of Worms *Sefer Harokeach.* See also Wieseltier, *Kaddish,* 210.

80. Freud, "The Theme of the Three Caskets," 254.

SHLOSHIM AND KADDISH

1. Huntington and Metcalf, *Celebrations of Death*, 93.

2. See *Yoreh De'ah* 390:4.

3. Indeed, the Talmud itself suggested that one add to the name of the dead the expression "may their memory be a blessing" (Babylonian Talmud *Ta'anit* 28a).

4. Freud, "Mourning and Melancholia."

5. Lifton, *The Broken Connection*, 109.

6. Deuteronomy 21:13. Maimonides *Hilchot Avelut* [The Laws of Mourning] 6:1.

7. See, for example, the Ravad (Rabbi Abraham ben David of Posquieres, Provence).

8. To be sure, a number of rabbis suggested that throughout the year of mourning one should remain unsettled and therefore abandon one's regular seat even on Sabbath. See Rama, Shach, and Radbaz, among others.

9. Babylonian Talmud *Moed Katan* 23a.

10. See Goldberg, *Mourning in Halachah*, who cites the *Aruch HaShulchan*, Maimonides, *Gesher HaChaim*, and a variety of other sources (338 n. 13).

11. See Goldberg, *Mourning in Halachah*, 247, who quotes Rabbi Moses Isserles (Rama 391:2). See also Tukacinski, *Gesher HaChayim*, I, 21:8a.

12. Goldberg, *Mourning in Halachah*, 339 n. 16; see also Tukacinski, *Gesher HaChayim*, I, 21:8a.

13. Marcel Mauss, *The Gift*, trans. Ian Cunnison (New York: Norton, 1967).

14. See *Yore De'ah* 391:2. In Jewish law and custom, assemblages of many people (ten or more) for a sociable occasion necessarily implies "pleasure." This perhaps is the codal expression of the norm that ethnographers Elizabeth Herzog and Mark Zborowski articulated as follows: "for the Jews, life is with people." See Zborowski and Herzog, *Life Is with People* (New York: Schocken, 1962).

15. A common "excuse" was to make the mourner part of the enabling personnel of the occasion.

16. See Goldberg, *Mourning in Halachah*, 254; Tukacinski, *Gesher HaChayim*, I, 21:8g.

17. Much has been written about the Kaddish, and I cannot and will not repeat it here. A particularly comprehensive treatment can be found in Leon Wieseltier, *Kaddish*, already cited heavily in these pages.

18. See S. N. Eisenstadt, *The Israeli Society* (Jerusalem: Magnes Press, 1967) [in Hebrew]; see also Zborowski and Herzog, *Life Is with People*.

19. Clifford Geertz, "Religion as a Cultural System," in *The Interpretation of Cultures* (New York: Basic Books, 1973), 104.

20. Geertz, "Ethos, World View, and the Analysis of Sacred Symbols," in *The Interpretation of Cultures*, 127.

21. Should he be in the synagogue and according to the Ashkenazic tradition.

22. Wieseltier (*Kaddish*, 418–19) quotes a commentator he identifies only as "Ovadiah," who writes: "In my humble opinion, it seems to me that, since not every individual is ready and competent to lead the service in its entirety, . . . the ancient sages established something that would be the same for everybody—the kaddish at the end of the service which is easy and everybody knows. Thus, an individual who has acquired knowledge should lead the afternoon and evening and morning services, for the

more he prays and the more he multiplies the saying of kaddish, the better for the souls of the dead; and an individual who does not possess the strength or the knowledge to say all the prayers will say the kaddish, so that nothing will be lacking." In fact, so ubiquitous is this prayer that it is often transliterated so that even the illiterate in the Hebrew *alef-bet* can read it in the indigenous tongue.

23. Adin Steinsaltz, public lecture in Russia 1994.

24. Babylonian Talmud *Berachot* 3a.

25. Wieseltier, *Kaddish,* 54.

26. See Maimonides, *Seder Tefilot HaShanah,* in the section *Ahava* of *Mishna Torah.* See also Tukacinski, *Gesher HaChayim,* 30b.

27. The challenge thrown down to the Romans called for extra protection from heaven.

28. Menachem Schmelzer, "Kaddish" (paper presented at the Meetings of the Association for Jewish Studies, Boston, December 21, 1998), citing the thirteenth-century work *Sefer Machkim* by Rabbi Nathan bar Judah.

29. Cf. Wieseltier, *Kaddish,* 46.

30. Schmelzer, "Kaddish," 6.

31. Wieseltier, *Kaddish,* 29, 53.

32. Babylonian Talmud *Soferim* 19:12.

33. For additional sources, see Tukacinski, *Gesher HaChayim,* 30:3.

34. The *Machzor Vitry* is a eleventh-century French liturgical source and commentary composed by Simcha ben Samuel of Vitry (Marne, France), an outstanding disciple of the exegete and rabbi Rashi, and whose son married Rashi's daughter. The *machzor* drew heavily from Rashi's own liturgy and rulings, documenting practices from the eleventh century, later editions of which include practices up to the fourteenth. Others ascribe this story to an earlier source, the Midrash Tanchuma (circa eighth century B.C.E.) and cite the rabbi as being Yochanan ben Zakkai, famous head of the Palestinian talmudic academy. For additional sources, see Tukacinski, *Gesher HaChayim,* 30:3,2. See also Wieseltier, *Kaddish,* 41.

35. Wieseltier, *Kaddish,* 127.

36. Freud, "The Theme of the Three Caskets," 254.

37. See David ben Josef Abudraham, *The Order and Meaning of the Weekday Shacharit [morning service]* (Jerusalem, 1959), 69.

38. See Tosafot in Babylonian Talmud *Berachot* 3a. The Tosafists were disciples and students of Rashi.

39. Wieseltier, *Kaddish,* 81.

40. Goldberg, *Crossing the Jabbok,* 39.

41. This is a foreshortened version of the longer blessing that the immediately bereaved recites: "Blessed art thou O Lord our God the true judge." The Hebrew phrase that closes this blessing, *"dayan ha emet,"* may also be translated as "the judge of truth."

42. Soloveitchik, "The Halakhah of the First Day," 80.

43. Tukacinski, *Gesher HaChayim,* 30:8,6.

44. Naeh, *Nachamu Ami,* 89 n. 14. See also Tukacinski, *Gesher HaChayim,* 30:8,12.

45. Tukacinski, *Gesher HaChayim,* 30:8,12.

46. See Goldberg, *Mourning in Halachah,* 366 n. 69a.

47. Although this line was censored in the fourteenth century in prayer books of the Ashkenazic tradition out of fear of reprisals from the Church, it has made its

reappearance in many recently reissued versions. See, for example, *Art Scroll Mesorah Publications*.

48. Freud, "Thoughts for the Times on War and Death," 309–10.

49. Soloveitchik, "The Halakhah of the First Day," 83.

50. These words are Wieseltier's (*Kaddish*, 420), who recited Kaddish for his father around the same time as I recited it for mine, and around the same time as I reached this truth that is so much of the orphan's growing kaddish understanding. See also his comments: "What kind of a father was your father? In rising to say the kaddish, you have given an answer: he was the kind of father who taught his son to do *this*" (386–87).

THE TWELVE MONTHS AND YAHRZEIT

1. Hertz, "A Contribution to the Study of the Collective Representation of Death," 48.

2. Shamai Kanter, "A Year of Grieving, A Year of Growing," in Riemer, *Jewish Insights into Death and Mourning*, 175.

3. Babylonian Talmud *Berachot* 47a.

4. Babylonian Talmud *Shabbat* 152b. The expression "bones gathered up," appearing often in ancient accounts of Jewish death, refers to the practice of allowing corpses to decompose, often in family burial caves, for a year's time. Then the remaining bones, stripped of the flesh, were gathered up and placed in a family charnel pile or a small ossuary in which all the remains of the family's dead were kept (see the next chapter). See Steven Fine, "A Note on Ossuary Burial and the Resurrection of the Dead in First-Century Jerusalem," *Journal of Jewish Studies* 51, no. 1 (2000): 69–76.

5. The not uncommon experience of the death of infant siblings was considered to be far more ambiguous—indeed, those who died before reaching thirty days of life were not even formally mourned according to the dictates of Jewish law and custom. The rabbis clearly felt that forcing full-fledged mourning so frequently might socially and psychologically debase the experience. Moreover, the ubiquitousness of childhood death in premodern times, coupled with the common consideration of children as not fully part of the social fabric until they reached majority, also led to a tacit social diminution of childhood deaths—though, one suspects, not necessarily of the grief associated with them.

6. Babylonian Talmud *Kiddushin* 31b. See also Goldberg, *Mourning in Halachah*, 284 n. 11.

7. See, for example, Harold M. Schulweis, "I Am Older Now: A Yahrzeit Candle Lit at Home," in Riemer, *Jewish Insights into Death and Mourning*, 198–99.

8. In certain cases, the mourning of students or disciples for a great teacher, whom the Jewish rabbinic tradition treated like a parent, was by this same token also extended for a year—although the mourning was far more symbolic and less often characterized by concrete practices.

9. *Kol Bo Al Aveilus*, 373 n. 29.

10. Naeh, *Nachamu Ami*, 28:11. See also Goldberg, *Mourning in Halachah*, 359 n. 36.

11. Leon Wieseltier, quoted in Jonathan Mark, "The Last Kaddish," *New York Jewish Week*, August 6, 1999, 8.

12. Freud, "Thoughts for the Times on War and Death," 310.

13. Alan Leicht in Mark, "The Last Kaddish."

14. Yaakov Moshe Hillel, *Yismach Moshe,* 2d ed. (Jerusalem: Ahavat Shalom, 1997), 10:1; Goldberg, *Mourning in Halachah,* 352–53 nn. 3, 4, offers the entire range of opinions and sources, the most famous being Isserles, *Yoreh De'ah,* 366:4.

15. *Ecclesiastes* 7:20 and *Kallah Rabati* 3. There is a reference to such sinning in the Zohar, which asserts that each dying person sees a vision of Adam and is moved to cry out "Because of you I must die," to which Adam replies that, while it is true that he once committed a sin for which he was severely punished, he alone is not responsible for what each of his children suffers. Then, as if to make his case, he adds, "But you, how many sins have you committed," in answer to which a list of the dying man's misdeeds is reviewed, ending with the line "There is no death without sin."

16. Wieseltier, *Kaddish,* 421.

17. See Moshe Feinstein, *Iggrot Moshe Yoreh Deah,* 4, 6. See also Berechia, *Siftai Emet,* 22. Mazliach Maimon, *Yalkut Ha Kaddish* (Beersheba, 1995), explains that it is "because of the masses," and their understandings about what is being implied in an extended Kaddish recitation, that the mourner must stop early (15:B).

18. Marian Henriquez Neudel, "Saying Kaddish: The Making of a 'Regular,' " in Riemer, *Jewish Insights into Death and Mourning,* 180.

19. Wieseltier in Mark, "The Last Kaddish."

20. Wieseltier, *Kaddish,* 455.

21. For daughters who choose this approach for the entire year of mourning, this is not always a ritually meaningful change.

22. Goldberg, *Mourning in Halachah,* 379–80.

23. Wieseltier (*Kaddish,* 465–66), quoting (and translating) the rulings of Joseph Hahn Nordlingen, rabbi of Frankfurt in 1630. See also Berechia, *Siftai Renanot,* 29.

24. See Berechia, *Siftai Renanot,* 29: "And all the *mitzvahs* and good deeds that Jews do leads them to Eden and all fresh interpretations of the Torah are destined to be intellectually enlarged in the world to come."

25. Berechia, *Siftai Renanot,* 31.

26. See Goldberg, *Mourning in Halachah,* 379 n. 35.

27. Ariès, *The Hour of Our Death,* 95.

28. *Zohar Acharai Mot.*

29. The Hebrew month is lunar, and hence twelve months make up slightly less than a solar year.

30. Midrash Proverbs 31:10 See also Riemer, *Jewish Insights into Death and Mourning,* 283–84.

31. Babylonian Talmud *Moed Katan* 21b.

32. Cf. Freud, "Mourning and Melancholia," 153.

33. Mandelbaum, "Social Uses of Funeral Rites," 342–43.

34. Hertz, "A Contribution to the Study of the Collective Representation of Death," 78.

35. Freud, "Mourning and Melancholia," 166.

36. This is a Yiddish word for "anniversary" that has become the accepted term for an anniversary of death (even among many Sephardic Jews for whom Yiddish is not indigenous and who also refer in Hebrew to the day as "*Yom Hashanah*" or in Spanish as "*Annos*").

37. The earliest mention of this is in Tractate *Nedarim*. See also Gabriel Zinner, *Nitei Gavriel*, vol. 2 (Brooklyn, N.Y.: Moriah, 1995), 72:1–6; Hillel 9:11.

38. Tukacinski, *Gesher HaChayim*, 32:A.

39. Zinner, *Nitei Gavriel*, 72:1. To be sure, in the atmosphere of religious revivalism characteristic in some of the precincts of Orthodoxy, there are some who have begun practicing this custom again.

40. Recall the collection of charity at the time of the funeral.

41. The concept of *tikkun*, variously translated as "repair" or "restoration," has its origins in Kabbalah and the belief that human, this-worldly life is a kind of undoing of the divine spark that requires vigilant spiritual repair. After death, *tikkun* is necessary to enable the soul, which is nothing more than a spark, to be restored to the original divine light. This was a theme that eighteenth-century Hasidism, which shaped many of the contemporary customs surrounding Jewish death, embraced as its own. Many early Hasidim described life as *yerida l'tzorech aliya*, a (this-worldly) descent that needed to precede the (otherworldly) ascent. See, for example, Mendel Piekarz, *Ideological Trends of Hasidism in Poland* (Jerusalem: Bialik, 1990), esp. 37–50.

The many practices of *tikkun* are described in a variety of sources. Among the most comprehensive listing is to be found in Zinner, *Nitei Gavriel*, 70:A.

42. Although some referred to this as an "unveiling," that term and the practice of revealing a monument inscription from beneath a veil are not really Jewish customs. Rather, Judaism speaks of *hakamat mazteva* (erecting a monument).

43. This custom has been traced from the community of Worms. See Zinner, *Nitei Gavriel*, 75:1 n. 1.

44. Ibid.

45. See *Sefer Alui Neshamot*, ed. Saleh J. Mansour (Jerusalem, 1961).

46. See Seth D. Kunin, *God's Place in the World: Sacred Space and Sacred Place in Judaism* (New York: Cassell, 1998), 34. This is the case not only for the individual but also for the group. Hence, exile from the Jewish homeland, a kind of symbolic death, is defined as "descent," while rebirth and return are defined as "ascent" to the holy land.

47. Tukacinski, *Gesher HaChayim*, 2:27, 1. See also Babylonian Talmud *Shabbat* 152b.

48. See David Assaf, *The Kaddish* (Haifa, 1966), 239.

49. Adin Steinsaltz, *Yahrzeit* (New York: Bikur Cholim of Staten Island, n.d.), n.p. See also Zinner, *Nitei Gavriel*, 71:1.

50. See Zinner, *Nitei Gavriel*, 71 n. 8.

51. Tukacinski, *Gesher HaChayim*, 1:32, 8.

52. Eliade, *The Sacred and the Profane*, 68; italics in the original.

53. Ibid., 107.

BEIT OLAM AND YIZKOR

1. Ariès, *The Hour of Our Death*, 476.

2. Shepkaru, "From Death to Afterlife," 1–44, sums up the matter as follows: while the Talmud (Babylonian Talmud *Sanhedrin* 91b) asserts that "the resurrection is deducible from the Torah," in fact the Sadducees and Pharisees by no means agreed on the matter of resurrection and embraced the innovative phrase and idea of "*olam ha-ba*," the world (or eternity) to come. This term, which has come to be understood popularly as paradise or in some cases as the world after resurrection, was in its earliest

expression taken simply to represent "a new order in the terrestrial realm that would be attained by the believer" (11). *Beit olam* resonated with the concept of *olam ha-ba*. In a sense, the graveyard was the terrestrial nexus to the world to come; it was "*beit olam (ha-bah),*" an eternal resting place for those who somehow still live.

3. Gaster, *Customs and Folkways of Jewish Life,* 178–79, derives this from Job 30:23, Ecclesiastes 12:5, and Isaiah 32:18.

4. See Mary Douglas, *Purity and Danger* (New York: Routledge, 1993), and also Lamm, *The Jewish Way in Death and Mourning,* 188.

5. Jerusalem Talmud *Shekalim* 1:1 2:5. As noted in the previous chapter, this talmudic decree notwithstanding, the timing of the monument's erection has traditionally been subject to variation by custom.

6. Kunin, *God's Place in the World,* 30.

7. Jerusalem Talmud *Shekalim* 2:7, 47a.

8. See Simon Rubin, "Loss and Bereavement: An Overview," in *Loss and Bereavement in Jewish Society in Israel,* ed. Ruth Malkinson, Simon Rubin, and Eliezer Witztum (Tel Aviv: Ministry of Defense, 1993), 25.

9. This is seen often these days at the graves of important rabbis, especially among the Hasidim and among followers of Sephardic miracle rabbis. See, for example, Zvi Sobel, *A Small Place in Galilee: Religion and Social Conflict in an Israeli Village* (New York: Holmes and Meier, 1994); and Yoram Bilu and Eyal Ben-Ari, eds., *Grasping Land: Space and Place in Contemporary Israeli Discourse and Experience* (Albany: State University of New York Press, 1997).

10. See, for example, a description of the pilgrimage to the grave of Rabbi Shimon bar Yochai in Heilman, *Defenders of the Faith,* 117–39.

11. These are but a few of the many such grave sites that have become places of prayer and pilgrimage for Jews.

12. See Arthur Green, "The *Zaddiq* as *Axis Mundi* in Later Judaism," *Journal of the American Academy of Religion* 45 (1977): 3.

13. Eliade, *The Sacred and the Profane,* 43.

14. There is obviously a parallel here with the way Jews created other scared spaces. Hence the Holy Temple in Jerusalem was the sanctum sanctorum, but synagogues elsewhere (places where a quorum of Jews assembled for worship) were *mikdash me'at* (a smaller temple).

15. The image of a gate is a common symbol in cemeteries and on ossuaries and funerary urns.

16. See, for example, Deuteronomy 12:20. "Take heed to yourself that you be not snared by following them [the other nations around you], after they are destroyed from before you; and that you inquire not about their gods, saying, How did these nations serve their gods? that I may also do likewise." See also the commentary of the thirteenth-century French rabbi Chizkiya *Chizkuni* on Deuteronomy 16:22.

17. See Goldberg, *Crossing the Jabbok,* 26–27, who dates the establishment of Jewish cemeteries to sometime in the mid-fourteenth to early fifteenth centuries.

18. Moses Sofer, *Sefer HaDrashos,* cited in Goldberg, *Mourning in Halachah,* 384 n. 10.

19. Indeed, the interest of some in collecting and analyzing these texts attests to the capacity that these monuments have to "change the subject" from death to a narrative about life. See James Frazer, *Folklore in the Old Testament* (London: Macmillan, 1918), 283–91.

20. Even in the Jewish state, those whose identity is embraced after death by some other overarching status may be buried in a graveyard that reflects that. Hence the fallen soldiers are often laid in military cemeteries and national leaders put in national shrines.

21. *Yoreh De'ah* §144.

22. See Mansour, *Sefer Alui Neshamot,* for this line from Ecclesiastes 7:1. See also Freud, "Thoughts for the Times on War and Death," 310.

23. *Shulchan Aruch* 340:15, 344:20.

24. Wieseltier, quoting from the verses of Ephraim of Regensburg, a twelfth-century poet writing about the Second Crusade, *Kaddish,* 352.

25. Tukacinski, *Gesher HaChayim,* 1:29, 7. The veiled anti-Christian reference is also unmistakable here.

26. Ibid.

27. Ibid., 1:29, 9; and 32, 8.

28. The ambivalence that some felt in this kind of intimate contact with the dead may be seen in the assertion by some codifiers that it is forbidden to "lean" on the monument. Cf. David ben Shmuel HaLevi, *Taz* (1657), §§1.

29. Talmud Babylonian Talmud *Sotah* 34b; *Taanit* 16a.

30. Mansour, *Sefer Alui Neshamot,* 112.

31. See the introduction to Moses Alter, *Yismach Moshe,* on the Prophets. See also Goldberg, 42:20 n. 41.

32. Code of Jewish Law, *Orach Chayim* 559:10. See also Babylonian Talmud *Berachot* 5a. For Freud's iteration of this principle, see "Thoughts for the Times on War and Death," 309–10.

33. Menachem Mendel Schneerson, *Sichos in English* 20 Teves Kislev, 5755 "Yartzheit of Rambam" (Brooklyn).

34. Henry Abramovitch, personal communication.

35. *Orach Chaim* 224:8.

36. Lamm, *The Jewish Way in Death and Mourning,* 195.

37. See Mauss, *The Gift.*

38. Gaster, *Customs and Folkways of Jewish Life,* 180.

39. See Shalom Shachne Cherniak, *Mishmeret Yisrael* (Warsaw, 1928), 5: §32. Cf. Tukacinski, *Gesher HaChayim,* 29:16, who disputes this rule. A number of commentators explore the question by distinguishing between one who never visited at all and then came for the first time and one who once visited and then stopped doing so. They also qualify the failure to visit, differentiating between failures that were avoidable and those that were not. As with the living, so, too, with the dead the vicissitudes of a relationship are complicated. Therefore, one needed to be careful about prohibiting graveside visits.

40. Gaster, *Customs and Folkways of Jewish Life,* 182–85.

41. Ibid., 186.

42. Ibid., 185.

43. Freud, "Thoughts for the Times on War and Death," 308.

44. Gaster, *Customs and Folkways of Jewish Life,* 192.

45. Ibid., 193; italics in original.

46. Although the term *resurrection* has been commonly used as a translation, the original Hebrew retains a far more ambiguous character.

47. Gaster, *Customs and Folkways of Jewish Life,* 192.

FINAL THOUGHTS

1. *Avot* 1:14.

2. Freud, "Thoughts for the Times on War and Death," 307.

3. The period following the Crusades is most prominent here (see the discussion of Kaddish) but is by no means unique. The period of the Roman persecution at the start of the common era or the periods when pogrom and genocide were active likewise yielded many customs associated with death and its commemoration. And the Shoah and several of the life-threatening wars against modern Israel have begun to make their own contributions in this regard, as the previous chapter demonstrates.

4. "Death represents a threat to the existence of the society and that is why every society has laws of mourning whose objective is not simply to offer support to the bereaved but as well to set the general order and organization of mourning." Eliezer Witztum and Ruth Malkinson, "Bereavement and Commemoration in Israel: The Dual Face of the National Myth," in *Loss and Bereavement in Jewish Society in Israel*, ed. Ruth Malkinson, Simon Rubin, and Eliezer Witztum (Tel Aviv: Ministry of Defense, 1993), 237.

5. John Donne, *Holy Sonnets* X, in *The Elegies, and the Songs and Sonnets* (Oxford: Clarendon Press, 1965), 170.

6. This phrase comes from the Sanskrit epic *The Mahabharata of Krishna-Dwaipayana Vyasa*, translated into English prose from the original Sanskrit text, by K. M. Ganguli, 11 vols. (Calcutta: Bharata Press, 1884–96).

7. See Robert Bellah, "Religious Evolution," *American Sociological Review* 29 (1964): 358–74, who argues this is a quality of primitive and archaic religions.

8. Durkheim, *Elementary Forms of the Religious Life*, 29.

9. See Joseph Campbell, *The Power of Myth* (London: Doubleday, 1988). For the Jewish version, see Babylonian Talmud *Baba Bathra* 70b.

10. Lifton, *The Broken Connection*, 21; Malinowski, *Magic, Science and Religion*, 51.

11. Durkheim, *Elementary Forms of the Religious Life*, 240.

12. This is not always easy and often requires extraordinary theological twists. Thus, for example, the ravages of the Shoah—so perplexing to many—have been explained by Rabbi Joel Teitlebaum, the previous grand rabbi of the Satmar Hasidic sect, as divine punishment for the heresies of secular Zionism. "Believe not what is," wrote Augustine in his explanation of the faith of the devout, "but believe what is absurd."

13. *Avot* 4:11.

14. Babylonian Talmud *Shabbat* 153a.

15. Bruno Bettleheim, *The Uses of Enchantment* (New York: Vintage, 1977), 180.

16. The term comes from Hellenic culture and refers to the idea that the literal sense of something is not its most profound meaning.

17. Green, "The *Zaddiq* as *Axis Mundi* in Later Judaism," 329. The places Jews consider holiest—the inner sanctum of the Temple in Jerusalem, for example—are also the places that can cause death if improperly entered.

18. Babylonian Talmud *Tamid* 32a.

19. Babylonian Talmud *Taanit* 5b.

Glossary

aleinu: short term for the final prayer with which each service ends and with which Jews praise God and distinguish themselves and him from all others

aron: casket

Beit Haleveiyot: funeral home

Beit Olam: "home everlasting"; a term for a graveyard; also sometimes called *Beit Ha Chayim* ("house of the living")

challot: loaves of bread with which Sabbath or holiday meal is begun

chesed shel emet: true loving-kindness; a term for how the living treat the dead

chiyuv: "one who is obligated" to lead the prayers or to mourn

cohen: Jewish member of a priestly class or tribe

doresh al hamaytim: ancestor worship

el moleh rachamim: "God full of mercy"—opening words of the Jewish song of the dead

ephod: a long apron, part of Jewish shrouds

gosses: one whose death is imminent

haftarah: readings from Scripture that follow weekly Torah reading

haredi: the ultra-Orthodox (singular); literally, one who trembles before God

haredim: the ultra-Orthodox (plural); literally, those who tremble before God

kalus rosh: attitude of levity

kappara: redemption from punishment of one's immortal soul

kavin: measures of volume; nine are equal to between seven or eight gallons; the measure used for washing a corpse

kelicha: a device made of two wooden rungs connected by eighteen metal rungs and used to carry a corpse

keriah: ritual rending of a garment at time of bereavement

kiddush hashem: death that sanctified God's name

kittel: white robe used as a ceremonial garment for men and as a burial shroud for both sexes; worn during worship on High Holy Days, by bridegroom during the wedding, and by the leader of the Passover seder

kutonet: a white tunic, part of Jewish shrouds

lashon kodesh: holy tongue

leviyas hamayt: accompanying the dead

ma'amadot: standstills at a funeral

matzevah: burial monument

mayt: the dead one

meilitz yosher: advocate at the Court on High

mikveh: ritual bath

mincha: afternoon prayer

mitron: hood once worn by mourners

mitznefet: a white linen semicircular cap, part of Jewish shrouds

mitzvah: any of the collection of 613 commandments or precepts in the Bible or of the additional ones of rabbinic origin, relating to the religious and moral conduct of Jews; also any good or praiseworthy deed

nefesh: soul; sometimes refers to burial monument

neshamah: soul

niftar: the dead person; one who has been released from this life

ohel: tent; also mausoleum

olam ha-ba: the world to come; paradise

onen: singular of *onenim*

onenim: the bereaved before burial

parochet: mantle used to cover the ark holding the Torah scrolls

petira: death

Seder: a ceremonial dinner that commemorates the Exodus from Egypt and includes the reading of the Haggadah; held on the first night of Passover

seudat havra'ah: meal of recovery

shivah: seven-day period of mourning

shliach tzibbur: prayer leader; literally, "messenger of the congregation"

shloshim: thirty-day period of mourning

shmira: guardianship (usually over a corpse)

Shoah: the Holocaust, from the Hebrew word meaning "desolation"

shomer: guardian

shul: the synagogue

Simchat mere'ut: exchange of visits and meals between friends

slichot: penitential prayers

sovev: linen winding-sheet for the dead

tahara: purification; ceremony for preparing dead for burial

tallit: prayer shawl

tallit katan: small fringed four-cornered garment to be worn as part of a Jew's clothing

techiyat ha'metim: bringing the dead to life; resurrection

tefillin: phylacteries; leather boxes containing Scripture that an adult man wears on his head and arm during his daily prayers

tikkun: restoration and repair

vidui: confessional

yahrzeit: yearly anniversary of death

yarmulke: skullcap

yehi zichro baruch: "may his memory be a blessing"

yichud: first union of newlyweds

yud-beit chodesh: twelve-month period (of mourning)

zaddik: one who is righteous; a person of outstanding virtue and piety; also the leader of a Hasidic group

Index

Text: Bembo and Rotis Semi Sans Light
Display: Rotis Semi Sans Light
Design: Barbara Jellow
Composition: G & S Typesetters
Printing and binding: Haddon Craftsmen